Hillary Clinton in the News

Hillary Clinton in the News

Gender and Authenticity in American Politics

SHAWN J. PARRY-GILES

UNIVERSITY OF ILLINOIS PRESS

Urbana, Chicago, and Springfield

© 2014 by the Board of Trustees
of the University of Illinois
All rights reserved
Manufactured in the United States of America
1 2 3 4 5 C P 5 4 3 2 1

♾ This book is printed on acid-free paper.

Library of Congress Cataloging-in-Publication Data
Parry-Giles, Shawn J., 1960-
Hillary Clinton in the news : gender and authenticity in American
politics / Shawn J. Parry-Giles.
pages   cm
Includes bibliographical references and index.
ISBN 978-0-252-03821-1 (hardback)
ISBN 978-0-252-07978-8 (paper)
ISBN 978-0-252-09604-4 (ebook)
1. Clinton, Hillary Rodham—Press coverage. 2. Clinton, Hillary
Rodham—Relations with journalists. 3. Clinton, Hillary
Rodham—Public opinion. 4. Press and politics—United States.
5. Stateswomen—Press coverage—United States. 6. United
States—Politics and government—1989-
I. Title.
E887.C55P37   2014
973.929092—dc23 [B]   2013031713

This book is dedicated to the strong women in my family, past and present, including my grandmothers, mother, aunts, sister-in-law, nieces, and mothers-in-law.

Contents

Acknowledgments

I began collecting television news broadcasts of Hillary Clinton in 1996. I am indebted to many people who contributed to the project over the past seventeen years. I received faculty-support awards from both Monmouth College and the University of Maryland, including GRB and RASA grant awards and course releases from UM's Graduate School. I am grateful to three department chairs who offered support for these grant applications, including William Wallace, Edward Fink, and Elizabeth Toth.

I also am beholden to the archivists with the following libraries and historical societies who offered support in completing the historical work for this project: American Antiquarian Society, Filson Historical Society, Franklin D. Roosevelt Presidential Library, Gerald R. Ford Presidential Library, Herbert Hoover Presidential Library, Houghton Library of Harvard College Library, Jimmy Carter Presidential Library, Library of Congress, Lyndon B. Johnson Presidential Library, Massachusetts Historical Society, National First Ladies Library, and especially Vanderbilt Television News Archive.

I also want to extend my appreciation to the staff of the University of Illinois Press for providing a smooth publication process of utmost professionalism. I owe particular gratitude to acquisitions editor Daniel Nasset for his strong support of this project.

In addition, I want to express appreciation to Hillary Clinton's 2008 presidential campaign staff for giving me access to the Clinton press bus during the New Hampshire primary. I also want to thank POTUS XM for providing press credentials that made traveling on Clinton's press bus possible. Such access afforded me the opportunity to take the photograph that appears on the front cover of this book. And I want to express special appreciation to Kathy Kendall for letting me tag along with her as she navigated the New Hampshire primaries.

I also received research support from several students, including Vonetta B. Martin, Kate McFarland, Naomi Mersky, Aryan Rodriquez, Kate Shaw, and Rachel Smith. I am particularly indebted to five UM Ph.D. students—Megan Fitzmaurice, Katie Kuhn, Jessica Lu, Jade Olson, and Yvonne Slosarski—for their close editing work once the manuscript was completed. Megan and Katie also took on the herculean task of creating a most impressive index. I also owe a debt of gratitude to Sheila Bodell for bringing the index to completion. I too am most appreciative of Maria E. denBoer's very close reading of the manuscript in the final stages of editing.

In addition, I want to express gratitude to former and existing graduate students who helped me conceptualize the project in important ways through conversations about their research in media studies, feminism, visuality, nationalism, race studies, and rhetoric and public address: Tim Barney, Jason Black, Diane Blair, Lisa Burns, Lisa Corrigan, Abbe Depretis, Terri Donofrio, Megan Fitzmaurice, Elizabeth Gardner, Lisa Gring-Pemble, Kim Hannah, Lauren Harris, Lindsay Hayes, Diane Hemmings, Amy Heyse, James Kimble, Katie Kuhn, Na Young Lee, Tiffany Lewis, Jessica Lu, Jade Olson, Alyssa Samek, L. Ayu Saraswati, Artesha Taylor Sharma, Yvonne Slosarski, Belinda Stillion Southard, Stephen Underhill, and Ric Winston.

The project has also been shaped by the important feedback I received from numerous individuals through journal and book chapter reviews, panel discussions, colloquium and convention presentations, and co-authorship opportunities. I wish to acknowledge their important contributions to the project: Karrin Anderson, Diane Blair, Carl Burgchardt, Karlyn Kohrs Campbell, Diana Carlin, James Chesebro, Paul Chilton, Celeste Condit, Stacy Cordery, James Curran, Bonnie Dow, Cara Finnegan, Rod Hart, Diane Hope, David Kaufer, Sahar Khamis, Beata Beigman Klebanov, Michal Krzyzanowski, Ron Lee, Martin Medhurst, Kathryn Olson, Lester Olson, Bartholomew Sparrow, Molly Meijer Wertheimer, and Ruth Wodak. In particular, I am most appreciative of the sage guidance and vision of Vanessa Beasley and Mary Varvus in helping me revise and strengthen the project in immeasurable ways.

I also am indebted to many colleagues, former professors, and friends from the University of New Mexico, Indiana University, Monmouth College, the University of Maryland, and elsewhere who have helped shape my scholarly thinking for more than two decades: Linda Aldoory, James Andrews, Nate Atkinson, Vanessa Beasley, Thomas Benson, Bonnie Thornton Dill, James Darsey, Leroy Dorsey, Robert Gaines, Michael Gurevitch, Farhat Haq, Lisa Hogan, Mike Hogan, Susan Holmes, Sue Huseman, Dick Jensen, David Kaufer, Kathleen Kendall, Seung-Kyung Kim, James Klumpp, Brooke Liu, John Lucaites, Kristy Maddux, Martin Medhurst, Cheryl Meeker, Claire Moses, Trevor Parry-Giles, Deborah Rosenfelt, Jody Roy, David Sawyer, Jan Schuetz, Shawn Spano, Mari Boor Tonn, Elizabeth Toth, Glen Williams, Andrew Wolvin, and David Zarefsky. I particularly wish to express gratitude to James Andrews, Vanessa Beasley, Mike Hogan, Dick Jensen, David Kaufer, and Mary Vavrus for being model teacher-scholars and friends—demonstrating a strong commitment to the study of rhetoric (and media) while maintaining their sense of humor, humility, and humanity.

This book is dedicated to the women members of my family who have served as exceptional role models in my life and those who represent the next generation of strong women to carry on the family tradition. I am always mindful of the challenges they accepted and the obstacles they endured, instilling in their grandchildren, children, and nieces and nephews a strong work ethic and moral foundation and a dogged determination to persevere in the face of hardship.

The men in my life also deserve considerable gratitude. I could not have stronger character exemplars than my father and my brother. My two sons—Sam and Eli—have brought more joy to my life than I ever could imagine. And Trevor has lived through the entire project, from conception to completion, showing support, patience, and sage advice throughout. I am mindful and forever thankful for having such strong family support.

* * *

Certain themes in this book (chapter 1 and chapter 3) are reflected in "The 'Image Bite,' Political Language, and the Public/Private Divide: NBC News Coverage of Hillary Clinton From Scorned Wife to Senate Candidate," co-authored by David S. Kaufer, Shawn J. Parry-Giles, and Beata Beigman Klebanov and published in the *Journal of Language and Politics* 11 (2012): 336–56 with kind permission by John Benjamins Publishing Company, Amsterdam/Philadelphia, www.benjamins.com.

Portions of the introduction originally appeared in "John F. Kerry: Speech before the U.S. Senate Committee on Foreign Relations" (1971), authored by Shawn J. Parry-Giles, *Voices of Democracy* [online journal] 2 (2007): 99–125, published through a joint venture between the University of Maryland's Center for Political Communication and Civic Leadership and Pennsylvania State University's Center for Democratic Deliberation.

Portions of the introduction originally appeared in "The Rise of the Rhetorical First Lady: Politics, Gender Ideology, and Women's Voice, 1789–2002," co-authored by Shawn J. Parry-Giles and Diane M. Blair, *Rhetoric & Public Affairs* 5 (2002): 565–99 and published by Michigan State University Press.

Certain themes of this book (introduction, chapter 3, and the conclusion) are reflected in "Political Authenticity, Television News, and Hillary Rodham Clinton," authored by Shawn J. Parry-Giles, edited by Roderick P. Hart and Bartholomew Sparrow, and published in *Politics, Discourse and American Society: New Agendas*, 2001, 211–27 with kind permission by Rowman & Littlefield Publishers.

Certain themes of this book (introduction, chapter 1, and chapter 3) are reflected in "Mediating Hillary Rodham Clinton: Television News Practices and Image-Making in the Postmodern Age," authored by Shawn J. Parry-Giles and published in *Critical Studies in Media Communication* 17 (2000): 205–26 with kind permission by Taylor & Francis, www.tandfonline.com.

Introduction

Hillary Clinton in the News:
The Historical Context

During a June 1, 2007, *Today* show interview, *Washington Post* journalist Carl Bernstein declared that presidential candidate Hillary Clinton was "inauthentic"—the central claim of his book, *A Woman in Charge*.[1] Such authenticity difficulties have dogged the former first lady-turned-senator-turned presidential candidate from the moment she entered the national spotlight. When Clinton was running for the U.S. Senate from New York, Maureen Dowd of *The New York Times* similarly charged: "We have lost all hope of getting any shred of authenticity from either Bill or Hillary—unless it's the authenticity of the deluded."[2]

Although a central critique of Hillary Clinton throughout her national political career, anxieties over the authenticity of U.S. political leaders have represented a national preoccupation since the nation's founding.[3] The intensifying force of photography in the nineteenth century, and radio, television, and the Internet in the twentieth century, exacerbated questions about realism, particularly for U.S. politics. In his 1961 book, *The Image*, Daniel J. Boorstin argued that "what we believe to be real" serves as one of the more pressing political questions for many Americans.[4] David Greenberg went so far as to identify an authenticity "crisis" associated with the "rise of the image" and the marketing of political candidates like any common household product, eroding the genuine feel of "democratic politics."[5] Americans have consequently grown fearful over an inability to discern what is real from that which is fake,[6] particularly in the wake of politically tumultuous events such as the Vietnam War, Watergate, Iran-Contra, the Clinton impeachment, and the Bush administration's war on terrorism. These presidential abuses of power and deceit attracted intense media scrutiny and accustomed the American people to political scandal.

One does not need to dig deeply to recognize the news media's authenticity preoccupation. Writing for *Newsweek* magazine prior to the 2000 presidential campaign, Howard Fineman addressed the authenticity dilemma in contemporary politics, charging that "No plain politician . . . can give America what it seems to want in the post-Clinton era: an authentic leader who isn't merely the sum of the polls he takes."[7] During the 2004 campaign, David Brooks, a syndicated columnist for *The New York Times*, juxtaposed John Kerry's authentic image in the 1960s with what Brooks labeled as his inauthentic image during the 2004 president election. "'Authenticity' was such a big concept" in the 1960s, Brooks claimed, making it not at all surprising that the 2004 Democratic Convention "dwelt obsessively on the period in his life when Kerry was authentic," diverting attention away from "the last 20 years of [his] rising inauthenticity."[8] And in an article entitled "Turning Up the Authenticity," written in the run-up to the 2008 presidential election, Ron Fournier of the *Washington Post* questioned, "Can you fake authenticity?" In answering his own question, Fournier replied: "Probably not, but it might be worth a try if you're running for president at a time when voters think leaders lack integrity."[9]

The U.S. news media's preoccupation with matters of authenticity and political image making is the subject of this book, especially as authenticity questions permeated the television news coverage of Hillary Clinton. This study in particular explores the news media's representations of Clinton as one of "the most loved and hated presidential wives in American history,"[10] spanning the period from Bill Clinton's 1992 presidential campaign through Hillary Clinton's own 2008 presidential bid. Throughout, Clinton's various public roles attracted the attention of news organizations, particularly her actions as a surrogate campaigner, legislative activist, financial investor, international emissary, scorned wife, and political candidate. Although Hillary Clinton represented the subject of the camera's gaze, this project interrogates first and foremost contemporary television news practices in the United States from a feminist perspective,[11] examining the evolutionary news narratives and visual framing devices used to cover one very public political woman over the span of sixteen years. This coverage is situated within the historical and gendered spaces of the American nation-state.

U.S. Nationalism, Character Assessment, and the Gendering of American Politics

Scholarship on nationalism and its connection to theories of character and authenticity, gendered politics, and news function as the primary critical lenses used to examine the television news coverage of Hillary Clinton. A central assumption of nationalism scholarship is that nations are primarily rhetorical constructions—what Benedict Anderson calls "imagined communities."[12] The critical task in understanding the imagined community is in examining how nations are rhetorically conceived and, in turn, how these rhetorical representations circulate and evolve over time.[13] Fundamental to nationalism rhetoric is the persistent struggle over matters of "national identity," which, in turn, produces insight into the sustenance of "national character" and the character dynamics of a nation's citizens.[14] Conceptions of character reflect what Vanessa B. Beasley calls a "double-edged sword," where nationalism rhetoric simultaneously promotes a "shared identity" yet also "encourage[s] exclusion, intolerance, and even inhumanity."[15]

From the nation's genesis, the ideal character traits of U.S. citizens have remained a cultural concern for political leaders eager to instill the most "moral and intellectual virtues" in its citizenry.[16] Questions of authenticity have been foundational to these character concerns. In addressing the period of George Washington's presidency, Barry Schwartz argues that "the authenticity of [one's] character constituted the foundational virtue through which all . . . other virtues were made credible."[17]

Examining the character ideals of the nation-state at various points in U.S. history offers considerable insight into the ideological assumptions about citizenship, gender, race, sexuality, and class that continue to resonate today. These ideological disputes ultimately play out in a variety of mediated texts and contexts, from political culture to popular culture, from high art to low art—saturating the American people with messages about national identity and individual character.[18] Biographies have represented an important means of issuing character judgments throughout Western civilization. And throughout U.S. history, journalists have served as some of the nation's most popular biographers, parsing out character judgments that reverberate ideologically.[19]

JOURNALISTS AS BIOGRAPHERS AND CHARACTER JUDGES

Since antiquity, life writing in the West functioned as a means by which to identify noble and faulty character models for republican nations, fashioned after the heralded *Plutarch's Lives* of ancient Rome.[20] Questions of character also preoccupied U.S. political leaders and the reading public most visibly during the founding era. David Waldstreicher observes that in the aftermath of the American Revolution, "both nation and state had a reputation, a character, to establish."[21] Early biographical writings, focused on elite political leaders, served as one important way of espousing ideals of national and individual character. American biographers consequently assumed the mantle of character appraisers from the nation's founding forward.[22]

Biographies served didactic ends by elucidating a variety of public and private virtues. Some championed the republican ideals of the new nation by turning the spotlight on the public lives of valiant military and political leaders. President Washington, for one, epitomized the embodiment of selfless ideals like benevolence, patriotism, and sympathy.[23] Others, reflecting the life-writing practices of James Boswell's eighteenth-century biography of Samuel Johnson, turned to the private reaches of one's life to uncover the backstage actions and private virtues of public figures. By glimpsing into the private lives of public notables, Boswell and those who mimicked his biographical style boasted of an ability to issue authentic judgments about a subject's honesty, kindliness, and humility—virtues perceived to be rooted in the human soul.[24] Still other life writings developed out of a unique American context involving campaign biographies of political leaders. The earliest political biographies championed party politics and the men, from David Crockett to William Henry Harrison, who participated in partisan practices from the 1820s onward. Expressions of rugged individualism, self-madeness, and exalted achievements were most privileged in these partisan tales.[25] Regardless of the biographical focus, life writings heralded character ideals and flaws as a means of socializing the American people for citizenship.[26]

The burgeoning news and literary markets in the early nineteenth century acted as increasingly important platforms for publishing character sketches of American leaders. In writing about American lives for newspapers, magazines, and book publishers, biographers carefully studied political figures like Andrew Jackson and Abraham Lincoln.[27] In the process, U.S. journalist-biographers acted as champions and guardians of American character ideals, attending to the virtues, vices, and "flaws" of their subjects by the mid-nineteenth century.[28] These biographical practices would persist and flourish, as journalists seamlessly moved back and forth from the world of news to the world of life writing, functioning as some of the most prolific biographical writers and character assessors throughout the nation's history.[29]

A recent example shows the fusion of journalism, biography writing, and character assessment, involving *New York Times* journalist Jodi Kantor and her

2012 book, *The Obamas*. During an interview with David Brooks, Kantor described how she had written a series for the *Times* entitled "The Long Run," which was a response to the "restrictive" nature of campaigns awarding minimal "access" to candidates. The focus of the series was to "learn" more about the "biographies" of political candidates by "delv[ing] deeply into their pasts and characters." Her book, Kantor explained, represented "an outgrowth of those stories." Kantor demonstrated how easily she moved from writing shorter newspaper pieces to penning full-length biographies, with character functioning as a key ingredient for both. The association of the "soul" with life writing was most visibly revealed when Brooks contemplated "the soul of people under the brutality of politics, the glare of publicity, and the falseness of universal love."[30] That Brooks would raise this issue in talking to a biographer showed the longstanding tradition of character assessments in life writing and political practice.

One primary point of contention, then as now, centered on just how far journalistic and biographical reporting should intrude into the private reaches of a person's life, exposing not only the virtues worthy of cultural emulation but also the foibles found in any magnification of a life. On one side of the fault line was the growing belief expressed by the *United States Democratic Review* in 1851 that the truth should be exposed, challenging the popular panegyric style of life writing. "The unworthy deeds of any distinguished individual should not be passed over in silence," the author insisted. In ignoring one's "faults . . . a good reputation" may be "easily acquired," yet the "truth, is not only lost . . . falsehood is propagated."[31] Not all would agree with the practice of exposing one's faults and failures, especially in exposés of the living. An 1889 *New-York Tribune* writer complained of the disrespectful practice of publishing "allusions of an unpleasant character to still living persons."[32] Although controversial from its inception, the biographical focus on the sordid gossip of public figures sold newspapers from the early nineteenth century forward and attracted a reading public enticed by stories crossing the lines of public decorum and decency.[33]

Differences of course existed in the ways in which women were documented in published life accounts compared to their male counterparts. Recounting women's lives became a common means by which to promulgate religion and morality, strengthening the gender ideals of an era. Many nineteenth-century biographies exalted women who lived a life of Christianity and charity. Yet there was also a growing U.S. fascination with the queens of England. Biographies about these uniquely political women would portend the danger of feminine "political power."[34] One sample violation of feminine protocol was addressed in Sidney Lee's biography of Queen Victoria, where he contended in 1903 that he was not "offended" by Queen Elizabeth's "mode of rule," but by "her lack of feminine modesty."[35] The unease over women's intrusion into political spaces was further evidenced in the rising popularity of political campaign biographies of the nineteenth century, where wives and family members of U.S. political candidates were often left out of a candidate's life story altogether.[36]

Spatial assumptions circulating in life writings helped ideologically guard against women's access and entry into particular public spaces, with socially sanctioned and contested consequences for violating gender rules.[37] The Victorian era was well known for reinforcing the separation of male-public and female-private spheres, where middle- and upper-class Anglo-white women in particular were charged with "creating in material terms a sanctuary [home] from the masculine, public world."[38] These spatial codes of behavior served a "disciplining" role for persons within the nation-state.[39] For white women of means living under the influence of the Victorian age, entrance into the public spaces, which included the act of voting, violated the expectation that they could function appropriately as the "angel in the house."[40] Reinforcing these norms of decorum, women writers extended their Christian mission from the home to the nation-state by promulgating character models worthy of emulation. As Mary G. Chandler argued in her 1856 book, *The Elements of Character*, "there is one thing . . . which God is ever seeking to aid us in building up, and which he permits us to hold absolute control; and this is Character."[41] The negative depictions of women who violated gendered character rules helped discourage spatial transgressions. Public women were often viewed in one of two sexualized ways. Some were depicted in "de-feminized" terms—as lesbians or unsexed spinsters. Others were portrayed as hyper-sexualized public women (i.e., prostitutes)— "publicly accessible" to men.[42] The behaviors of women were disciplined, in part, by the representations of gender norms embedded in the discourse of the nation-state.[43] In the process of limiting women's "spatial mobility," Glenda Law contends, gender rules interfered with women's "acquisition of spatial knowledge/power" and thus their "broader social roles."[44]

These gendered spatial restrictions were clearly visible in the historical performances of first ladies. Yet, first ladies and the wives of other political candidates would simultaneously become some of the first "political" women to violate the gender protocol of the nation's most public and political spaces.

FIRST LADIES AS POLITICAL WOMEN IN THE GENDERED NATION

Without question, the earliest first ladies recognized the contested nature of the first lady role and the unwelcomed restrictions placed on their public and political actions. Social mores of the era can be culled from their own private writings and the press coverage about them. Martha Washington noted, for example, that there were certain "bounds set" for which she "could not depart" in relation to her "publick" role, making her "feel like a state prisoner."[45] Abigail Adams also knew she could not talk too openly about politics, telling her nephew that even as she wrote to him with a sense of "freedom," she also recognized the political quagmire she faced, necessitating personal "discretion" in political disclosures.[46] Louisa Adams—Abigail's daughter-in-law turned first lady—wrote of how her actions could easily become the subject of political gossip. She complained bitterly on January 20, 1820, that "the most trifling occurrences are turned into political machinery—even my countenance was watched at the Senate."[47] Newspaper accounts of Sarah Polk also cordoned off the appropriate boundaries for first lady comportment. She was celebrated "as the pride and support of the Democratic party" because of her "lady-like reserve and abstinence from all overt political action."[48] Lucretia Garfield came to understand the political protocol for first ladies, regretting her innocent misstep of entering Washington, D.C.'s City Hall to see Alexander Hamilton's portrait. After greeting several political officials there, she was portrayed as "having called on the Mayor at City Hall," entering, thus, a decidedly male political preserve. The mortification she felt was on full display in her diary, where she lamented: "I wonder if I shall ever learn that I have a position to guard."[49]

Like the British queens, first ladies (and other political wives of Washington, D.C.) represented some of the nation's first women to enter the more public and political spaces of contestation. Even as the actions of women were often restricted in the early decades of the republic, the nation's capital, with its political focus, offered privileged white women of Washington, D.C., more public freedoms. Describing early life among the political elite in the capital city, Catherine Allgor speaks of a more promiscuous setting,[50] as white women entered "public places that in other cities remained the sole province of men." White women accordingly "ate, drank, and slept politics . . . as spectators in public and as interlocutors on the inside."[51] Louisa Adams made this point most clearly when she talked of first ladies and political wives sitting in the galleries listening to speeches delivered before Congress and the Supreme Court.[52]

Setting precedents within the first century of the nation's genesis, first ladies were visibly altruistic in their public service, venturing outside of the private sphere and gaining leadership experiences through their philanthropy.[53] Martha Washington tended wounded soldiers in camp sites while Mary Lincoln visited them in hospitals as part of her service to the Sanitary Commission.[54] Edith Wilson supported the American Red Cross during World War I; she served as the honorary president for Washington, D.C.'s chapter of the Woman's Volunteer Aid.[55]

The first ladies from 1920 onward also modeled acts of benevolent volunteering through their public appearances and messages. They engaged in volunteer activities involving the Girl Scouts, beautification, health, and education—actions that fell outside the parameters of governmental activity. Yet, these activities still revealed the public contributions of women to the nation-state and their local communities. In the process, certain contemporary first ladies transformed themselves into public activists, particularly for the concerns of women and children. As Anastatia Sims explains, "new ideas about government's responsibility for the physical and moral welfare of its citizens" enabled "women to step out of the domestic circle and into the public arena."[56]

Most first ladies worked to cultivate the ideal woman-citizen through benevolent acts of volunteerism. Others, however, assumed more politicized stances on social welfare issues, involving themselves in legislative battles that attracted followers and hecklers. Ellen Wilson became publicly engaged in Washington, D.C.'s National Civic Federation Sanitary Housing Company, working to improve the sanitary conditions for African Americans living in the nation's capital. In an unprecedented move for a first lady, the first Mrs. Wilson lobbied for and attached her name to the Slum Clearance Bill—popularly known as "Mrs. Wilson's Bill."[57] Expanding congressional activities further, Eleanor Roosevelt's unconventional behavior as first lady raised eyebrows and provoked public consternation among certain political elite. Her support of a Public Works furniture factory at Arthurdale prompted criticism from Congress that the first lady was spending taxpayer money on a "West Virginia commune." Roosevelt also sparked the ire of congressional representatives when she attended the hearings of the House Un-American Activities Committee in support of the American Youth Congress. According to Senate associate historian Donald Ritchie, critics suggested that Roosevelt should realize that she was not simply an individual who could associate with anyone she wished. Roosevelt testified before Congress in 1940 and 1942 on behalf of migrant labor populations, calling for legislation to improve the living and working conditions of migrant workers.[58]

Lady Bird Johnson and Rosalynn Carter likewise involved themselves in congressional activities that revealed the contested legacy of the first lady position. Johnson chaired the controversial Committee for a More Beautiful Capital and helped achieve passage of the Highway Beautification Act of 1965, attracting immense opposition from oil companies and roadside businesses. Johnson's activism resulted in the production of billboards that read "Impeach the First Lady"[59] and news stories that expressed disapproval for her creation of "a new . . . American constitutional government: . . . the unofficial, unpaid 'traveling saleslady' for the President."[60] Carter was the next first lady to testify in front of Congress as the honorary chair of the Mental Health Commission in 1977, resulting in the Mental Health System Act of 1980.[61]

Certain first ladies were outspoken on significant political issues of great controversy. Eleanor Roosevelt, for example, supported civil rights advancements in more public ways than her presidential husband.[62] Both Betty Ford and Rosalynn Carter—one a Republican and the other a Democrat—were bold advocates of the Equal Rights Amendment (ERA)—a signature issue of second-wave feminism. Ford often appeared in public with a button that boasted: "ratify ERA in 1975"—the year before the 1976 presidential election.[63] Carter too evidenced unwavering support for the ERA during a 1979 interview with *U.S. News and World Report*: "I'm not going to give up on it. We are forming a task force in the White House to help educate people about what the ERA is so that they can talk to their legislators."[64] For both Ford and Carter, their support for the ERA remained steadfast even as their husbands faced public scrutiny as presidential candidates. By the end of feminism's second wave, precedent-setting first ladies took on controversial political issues that challenged more traditional profiles of the position.

The demarcations between the male-public sphere and the female-private sphere were thus clearly disrupted by presidential wives; the spaces that they occupied were uniquely political and very public, expanding their sphere of authority.[65] The White House, located in the nation's capital, was foremost a national political site even as it functioned as the first family's home.[66] The activities of first ladies, whether inside or outside the White House, have long been construed in political terms. The women who performed these roles were at once confined by gendered prescriptions yet simultaneously empowered by the uniquely public and political nature of their position, their class status, their whiteness, and their presumed heterosexuality.[67] Over time, an institutional memory formed, which governed, at least in part, each woman's performance of the role.[68] Some first ladies performed the role in more traditional ways that conformed to the institutional expectations of the position and the gender norms of the era while others expanded the political reaches of the position and helped recast the gendered model of first lady comportment. The twentieth-century legacies in particular of Lou Hoover, Eleanor Roosevelt, Lady Bird Johnson, Betty Ford, Rosalynn Carter, and Nancy Reagan would help set the stage for Hillary Clinton's grand entrance.[69]

The spaces that Hillary Clinton and other political women occupy today reflect the inheritance of the nation-state's entrenched patriarchal structures. Yet, these sites also offer liberating opportunities for women who have access to such privileged terrain. J. Ann Tickner argues that "nationalist identities are more ambiguously gendered" than they perhaps once were in U.S. history.[70] And others like Geoff Eley and Ronald Grigor Suny see nationalism as a location not only to "resist the uncontrollable transformations of our time" but also as a space of "'cultural recovery' that could potentially lead . . . to acceptance, even celebration, of difference."[71] The news media, as integral forces in the workings of the nation-state, aid in the creation of "political meaning," at times reifying power that helps "manage public opinion," and at other times destabilizing ideologies steeped in tradition.[72]

The "politics of the image" functions as one important subject area where rhetorics of nationalism play out in American politics,[73] contributing to a fixation on *political authenticity* that is decidedly character based, gendered, and ultimately packaged by the U.S. news media for public consumption.

THE RISE AND FORCE OF POLITICAL AUTHENTICITY

Although questions surrounding authenticity represent a contemporary phenomenon, anxieties over authenticity are historically rooted in Western-based assumptions of truth and human character. Issues of authenticity symbolized significant ethical issues for Plato, who feared that citizens could not distinguish between "the genuine" and the "fake" in courts of law.[74] Elaborate means were established by students attending Aristotle's school to try to ascertain the genuine soul of an individual. Many classical intellectuals consequently turned to the pseudoscientific means of physiognomy to evaluate the external appearance of individuals as a measure of their inner character emanating from the soul.[75]

In a more modern sense, conceptions of authenticity were often grounded in assumptions of morality, truth, individualism, and culture. Prior to the late eighteenth century, few recognized the differences among humans to be morally significant; thereafter, notions of "self-truth and self-wholeness" came to be assumed and valued, with greater interest in intuiting right from wrong.[76] The rise of the unique individual, distinct from all others, helped place greater attention on assessing an individual's true self.[77] In isolating the anxiety between cultural expectations and the growing force of the unique self, Alessandro Ferrara expresses how "all ethics of authenticity try to respond to the modern tension between morality and self-realization."[78]

While some continued to centralize the role of the individual, theorists also moved toward a more social understanding of authenticity that rejected an "essentialism" of the self.[79] Ferrara, building on the theories of Jean-Jacques Rousseau, asserts that "there is no such thing as an authentic identity which does not presuppose a moment of recognition on the part of another."[80] Elaborating on Martin Heidegger's conception of "Da-sein" and authenticity,[81] Taylor Carman suggests that "we are ourselves above all in the eyes of others."[82]

The interplay between the cultural and individual understandings of authenticity became most acute in the social and political turbulence of the 1950s and 1960s—a period that further fused politics with matters of authenticity.[83] Marshall Berman calls "the problem of authenticity" one of "the most politically explosive of human impulses" in contemporary U.S. society, relating it to "the social and political structures men live in [that] are keeping the self stifled, chained down, locked up." The mission, as defined by the New Left, involved an "intense concern with *being oneself*."[84] The search for the authentic individual was at the heart of the New Left movement and represented "a widespread preoccupation" for U.S. politics.[85]

The hunt for authenticity moved from the context of New Left politics to the mainstream political environment as journalists continued to search for what many believed were political "truths" and genuine political images. Reflecting on the intersection between theories of authenticity and more traditional notions of nationalism, Nira Yuval-Davis argues that "authenticity assumes fixed, essential and unitary constructs of culture, identities and groupings."[86] National narratives that erase "the confusion and contradiction" and posit a more mythic Americanness predicated on an image of rightness and ethical superiority help reify a perceived sense of the "real."[87] The anxiety produced by the often scandal-ridden presidencies of the mid- to late 1960s and beyond helped create a political quest for the genuine candidate. And though politics has always been about image making,[88] there appears to be a growing concern with what W. J. T. Mitchell calls a "nostalgia for a lost authenticity understood as responsible representation."[89]

CONCEPTUALIZING POLITICAL AUTHENTICITY

The more contemporary struggle over authenticity is associated with the larger complexities of image making that constitute a key component of U.S. political discourse.[90] For the purposes of this study, I define *political authenticity* as a "symbolic, mediated, interactional, and highly contested process" involving political actors, their opponents, and the news media in assessing public policy positions and the veracity of a political leader's public image "on the grounds of truth and realism."[91] Political authenticity derives from character concerns as candidates (and their surrogates) attempt to authenticate a candidate's image as their political opponents, in turn, attempt to inauthenticate it. The news media ultimately enter the image fray and become self-appointed arbiters of political authenticity within this image-making struggle. This political exercise operates within a public-political sphere, culminating in socially constructed images that masquerade as political reality. This realism is rooted, Margaret Morse contends, in the assumption that news functions as a "privileged discourse, invested with a special relation to the Real."[92] Even though journalists portend an ability to capture the real, any conclusions about realism represent image constructions and audience judgments rather than individual essences. Political authenticity consequently represents a cultural and symbolic phenomenon rather than a search for any individual's true self; any conclusions about political authenticity ultimately operate in the realm of what Jean Baudrillard terms the "hyperreal," where discernments between truth and reality are nearly impossible to differentiate.[93]

Various press assumptions inspire the frenzied news quest to (in)authenticate candidate personas.[94] One supposition is that image messages mask a candidate's true character—a character that is presumably knowable through the assessment of personality traits that express the genuine self.[95] Journalists accordingly assume a responsibility for seemingly unmasking that image in order to capture the presumed genuineness of a candidate's character.[96] These self-appointed roles, rooted in historical news practices, stem from a journalistic posture of insider access and authority that legitimates their presumption as image-making mediators.[97] And while journalists may recognize that they can never uncover the truly *authentic* nature of the individual, they seem particularly determined to showcase the *inauthentic*, accenting their authority as the vanguards of political truth and interrogators of political impersonation.[98] The journalistic criteria for authenticity evaluation commonly exhibit ideological commonplaces of gendered nationalism deeply rooted in U.S. history.

AUTHENTIC WOMANHOOD AND AUTHENTIC MANHOOD

Even as image assessments center on the individual, authenticity judgments take place within the history of gendered expectations and norms. The individual is often evaluated against idyllic notions of authentic womanhood and manhood fostered within the U.S. nation-state—gendered renderings that are influenced by intersecting conceptions of family, race, sexuality, and class.[99] Deviations from the cultural archetypes of femininity and masculinity, which take on characteristics of nature and nurture, can be celebrated for evidence of gender progress. Gender transgressions can also become the object of scorn and derision for those judged as straying too far from gender ideals. These historical constructs can form the basis of cultural anxiety and skepticism over an individual's authenticity, leading to a preoccupation with what some view as a political leader's anomalous behavior that can attract enhanced media scrutiny.

From its genesis, the nation was conceived in familial terms.[100] The British, of course, depicted themselves as the "mother" country to the children of the American colonies. Those presidents who helped forge the political design of the new nation—George Washington, John Adams, Thomas Jefferson, and James Madison—have historically been described as the nation's "founding fathers." Phrases like "sexual union" were also commonplace in public discourse of the early 1800s, which Rogan Kersh maintains "drew parallels to the union of wife and husband."[101] Depicting the nation in familial terms helped ground social and class differences in nature, with women's "subordination . . . to man and child to adult" construed as "a natural fact," Anne McClintock contends.[102] Family-nation conflations contributed to the power dynamics in the home and in the nation-state,[103] with marriage empowering men over women privately and publicly.[104]

As "fatherland" served as the "force behind government,"[105] the nation's "mothers" were expected to fulfill their own unique citizenry roles as well.[106] Even though republicanism marked politics as a male preserve,[107] women's national roles were important in their own right as exemplified by the ideology of "republican motherhood." Mothers of the Revolutionary era and beyond were expected to commit themselves to the promulgation of "civic virtue,"[108] Linda K. Kerber maintains, by refusing "to countenance lovers" uncommitted "to the service of the state" and by dedicating themselves to raising "sons who were educated for . . . responsible citizenship."[109] The republican mother accordingly was imbued with the power to prepare her children for citizenship by instilling moral and religious commitments in the private spaces of the home—virtues that were integral to the ideology of authentic womanhood.

The historical assumptions of authentic manhood and womanhood were most vivid in the rhetoric of Theodore Roosevelt, whose turn-of-the-twentieth-century discourse relied on gendered, familial, and militarized conceptions of U.S. nationalism. Authentic manhood was rooted in more militarized and masculine ideas of citizenship. Governor Roosevelt argued in "The Strenuous Life" speech from April 10, 1899, that "a man's first duty is to his own home, but he is not thereby excused from doing his duty to the State." As president, Roosevelt reinforced traditional gender roles, constructing men as workers and women as mothers; deviations from the norm held out dire consequences for Roosevelt: "When men fear work or fear righteous war, when women fear motherhood, they tremble on the brink of doom; and well it is they should vanish from the earth."[110] Roosevelt's discourse evidenced clear conceptions of authentic manhood and authentic womanhood, steeped in familial and martial terms, and representing the ideological underpinnings of U.S. citizenship.

As with first ladies, volunteerism has represented an important part of women's citizenship overall—efforts consonant with visions of authentic womanhood. Yet, women's venture into the public and political spaces in particular has been the most controversial, particularly when they took to the public podium before audiences of men and women.[111] Certainly, women were active members of nineteenth-century social movements involving abolition, suffrage, temperance, antiprostitution, and antiwar protests.[112] While such activism helped alter the political landscape, certain traditional expectations persisted.[113] In her analysis of post–Civil War conduct literature, Nan Johnson furthers the discussion on women and rhetorical performance, arguing that the ideal woman was portrayed as "graceful . . . calm . . . quiet" and "rhetorically meek." Because women's rhetorical power was invested in the home and purportedly separated from the public and political power of men, a woman who spoke publicly was often depicted as a "shrieker," contradicting the competing image of the "quiet angel" of the home.[114] Women's entrance into such political spaces correspondingly came at a social cost.

Gender expectations and consequences are still visible in more contemporary contexts; women still report a need to temper their "talk" with men, Deborah Cameron claims, in order to lessen the degree of "face threat" in professional encounters.[115] Talking more explicitly about women and politics, Erika Falk observes that women have historically been viewed as "unnatural" political actors and "incompetent leaders," culminating in assumptions that they are less "viable" political contenders.[116] Throughout U.S. history, the movement of women into the nation's public spaces not uncommonly was filled with warnings and roadblocks—legacies that were still visible in women's political participation near the turn of the twenty-first century when Hillary Clinton became a national public figure.

Journalists help police gender boundaries through their reliance on traditional conceptions of authentic womanhood and manhood in their judgments of political authenticity. Of course, *traditional* ideas are not inherently more oppressive for women just as *progressive* ideas are not always more productive.[117] These constructs—tradition and progress—nevertheless served as markers of Hillary Clinton's authenticity. At times she was championed for her progressive gender performances. Yet, she was more routinely critiqued for her violation of tradition, undermining a sense of her authentic womanhood. Because of her high public profile, Hillary Clinton serves as a revealing case study into the news media's gendered judgments of political authenticity, offering great insight into the complex character traits expected of U.S. political women.

Framing Hillary Rodham Clinton

Political images emerge from cultural and ideological negotiations among multiple stakeholders in the political process—political actors, professional image makers, corporate media conglomerates, campaign fundraisers, journalists, political pundits, as well as news consumers and voters. The political leaders themselves obviously hold significant sway over their own image-making activities as news organizations are forced to keep pace with their performances.[118] Regardless of the sources, political images are most commonly communicated to audiences via mediated channels. Certainly, for most of us, we come to "know" Hillary Rodham Clinton through the news media. Because political images are a product of mediation, the news media are awarded important levels of power in the construction, perpetuation, and interrogation of political images.[119]

This book accordingly attends to the role of the news media in the political image-making process, examining television news broadcasts as the texts of analysis. In assessing the ways in which the verbal and visual representations of Hillary Clinton circulated within television news, I utilize *news frames* as a means to analyze Clinton's television coverage. The critical assumptions aligned with early framing theory consider how news is narrated and visualized, with attention also given to the details left out of such stories.[120] As Robert Entman and Susan Herbst explain, the "process of framing" involves the news media's selection processes, "sorting into a coherent narrative some facts or observations and deleting many others."[121] Of particular importance are the discursive choices made by members of the press, particularly word choices, phrasings, and visual representations.[122] As Todd Gitlin and other scholars recognize, "A story is a choice, a way of seeing," which often culminates in a level of consistency over time.[123] While many of these decisions may well have been deliberate choices on the part of journalists, news producers, and corporate news executives, the decisions also reflect the larger ideological commitments of the nation-state surveyed earlier in this chapter. These frames thus consist of what Stuart Hall calls *"mental representations"* that "we carry around in our heads" in relation to individualized "objects, people and events" (e.g., Hillary Clinton). Frames also include a broader "system of representation" that involves "complex relations" among a cluster of "concepts" (e.g., authentic womanhood, feminism, tradition, progress).[124] For this study, I unpack clusters of meanings that animate in the news frames of Hillary Clinton.

Questions of authenticity serve as key criteria of evaluation in framing the political image. Kathleen Hall Jamieson and Paul Waldman contend that a source of agreement among many in the news is the assumption that the "real motives" of political officials are "camouflaged by stated motives,"[125] turning journalists into detectives searching for character truths. Often, "the real" of a political life is understood as most recoverable from the "backstage" of the political process or from the private reaches of that life, necessitating the journalistic intrusion into such "private" spaces.[126] An image competition results, with the news organizations attempting to locate their cameras in cordoned-off spaces as political officials, in turn, try to manage the "backstage" moments in order to maintain control over their own political images.[127]

Over time, a consensus builds across the press as popularized news frames portend an aura of realism. Jamieson and Waldman refer to such patterns as "consensual" frames that persist in "memory."[128] Collective memory frames— frames that circulate over time in relation to ideologies, people, issues—are aided not only by the narratives that the news media relay but also by the visual images that accompany the stories. Barbie Zelizer suggests that "much of our ability to remember depends on [visual] images," which ensures the "staying power" of certain frames preserved in memory.[129] Memory frames become a crucial ingredient of image making that helps constitute political identity in ways that "naturalize" the political images of political officials.[130]

News frames are routinely understood as gendered discourse that reifies "masculinist assumptions" in the news. In order to disrupt a "masculinsation of the news accounts," Stuart Allan calls for a "gender-sensitive analysis of news discourse."[131] While women certainly have become a key target audience for newsmakers, the questions that are of utmost concern for this study are the ways in which the U.S. news media frame women political leaders. Falk identifies what she calls a "woman frame," which connotes that women in politics are typically doing something "unusual."[132] In discerning the differences between the news coverage of men versus women, Mary Douglas Vavrus contends that the "female candidate . . . must be settled in her private, domestic life before she can venture into the public sphere," suggesting that women must first attend to "hearth and home . . . as they are preparing to tend to affairs of state."[133] When women violate notions of authentic womanhood, the consequences can produce a cultural disciplining of feminist tendencies in an attempt to control "transgressive bodies" on the public stage.[134] Disciplinary actions, Michel Foucault explains, can involve a "social 'quarantine'" that functions as a measure of social deterrence and constraint.[135]

Although rhetorical disciplining contributes to the constraints that women face, women are not without agency in the disciplinary process. As Jane Arthurs and Jean Grimshaw argue, women are not "entirely disciplined or constrained by the relations of power operating in society."[136] Hillary Clinton, through her time in the political spotlight, has shown a tremendous amount of political agency, which routinely attracted heightened levels of animosity from political opponents, the news media, disapproving political watchers, and American voters. The "instability" of Hillary Clinton's "television image," Mary Ellen Brown maintains, was due to her "refusal to be silenced,"[137] helping to ramp up the intrigue and contempt directed toward her political choices and messages.

THE EVOLUTIONARY TELEVISION NEWS COVERAGE OF HILLARY CLINTON

While the critical focus of this study centers predominantly on Clinton's tenure as first lady and U.S. Senate candidate from 1992 to 2001, each chapter begins and ends with press coverage of Clinton as a 2008 presidential candidate to show the consistencies and changes of news frames over time. The conclusion also considers the coverage of Clinton as U.S. secretary of state from 2009 to 2013. In portraying the fluidities of the news frames in the telling of Clinton's political story, this longitudinal analysis magnifies the baseline frames that accompanied Clinton in the formation of her news biography. Stock visual imagery of Clinton likewise accompanied her throughout her political journey,[138] revealing the decontextualized practices involving television news visuals and their contributions to the collective memory frames of Hillary Clinton.

The texts of analysis include a selection of more than 1,200 television news broadcasts from the major networks and select cable news organizations, including broadcasts from *ABC World News Tonight*, *CBS Evening News*, CNN, Fox News, MSNBC, *NBC Nightly News*, and segments of network morning programs. While many of the stories lasted for only minutes, other broadcasts represented more in-depth features, including MSNBC's *Time & Again*, ABC's *Nightline*, and special broadcasts from the White House by morning news anchors. I began taping such newscasts in 1996 and continued through 2008, retrieving additional broadcasts from the Vanderbilt Television News Archive (Vanderbilt University). In certain circumstances, transcripts were acquired from Lexis-Nexis or the websites of news organizations. The majority of the evidence cited in the study derived from my own transcriptions of the television news texts, where I recorded not only the language of the news broadcasts but also the visual images and the salient sounds that accompanied the news narratives.[139] All aspects of the news coverage were considered, including statements from journalists, political pundits, partisan proponents and opponents, voters, and Clinton herself.

This book examines news texts surrounding key moments in Clinton's national political career, focusing specifically on the 1992 presidential campaign, the health care debate, the Whitewater investigation, Clinton's international travel as first lady, the Bill Clinton–Monica Lewinsky affair, Clinton's campaign for the U.S. Senate seat from New York, as well as her bid for the presidency. This wide-angle view of Clinton's life in the news offers an important and unique opportunity to trace the evolution of news frames across multiple news organizations, a variety of controversial issues, and unprecedented changing political roles of one woman over the span of nearly two decades. When viewed in aggregate form, the news media served as the first brush of Clinton's political biography, featuring a didactic life story of Clinton that emphasized character attributes and flaws and epitomized women's national character ideals at the turn of the twenty-first century. The baseline news frames that developed out of Clinton's 1992 coverage as a campaign surrogate for her husband helped authenticate Clinton as a politically outspoken and out-front feminist who violated the traditions of authentic womanhood. Future coverage often returned to these baseline frames as a means of imagery juxtaposition and authenticity evaluation as Clinton's national biography unfolded in the media spotlight.

From the moment that Clinton stepped onto the national stage in early 1992, the television news media gave the appearance of twenty-four-hour surveillance of the first lady, maintaining a Clinton watch through the duration of her time in the political limelight. The news frames that culminated out of such surveillance themes ultimately functioned as rhetorics of constraint, which contributed to the disciplining of Hillary Clinton for her gendered spatial violations of political protocol.[140] Whenever Clinton intruded too far into the historically masculine political campaign, the legislative arena, and legal spaces—metaphorically construed as contests of sports and war—her political comportment became most visibly challenged. Particularly controversial was her entrance into the 1992 campaign as "co-president," the houses of Congress as a health care activist, the legal sphere as an allegedly corrupt investor, the 2000 campaign as U.S. Senate candidate, and the 2008 presidential contest as a viable Democratic contender. For these news stories, the negativity of Clinton's news frames became most pronounced, with an emphasis on her personality and likeability problems, her rejection of traditional womanly duties in the home, her status as a political lightning rod, her audacious political ambition, and, ultimately, her inauthentic performances as the nation's first lady, flouting gender tradition and protocol.

During the 1992 campaign and in the aftermath of the health care debate and the Whitewater controversy, a familiar news-framing pattern developed. Following Clinton's very public and empowered role in her husband's campaign and as one charged with reforming health care, Clinton was discursively disciplined for her outspoken and overly visible presence in such spaces of power. The news frames during these periods of backlash marked Clinton's transgressions in overstepping the national boundaries of authentic womanhood and first lady comportment. These periods were followed by frames that punctuated her silencing and sidelining by Clinton presidential staffers as a means by which to protect her husband's political viability and to guard the nation-state from an overbearing first lady.

A common pattern of empowerment followed by retribution and silencing ultimately reflected a cycle of domestic violence involving the rhetorical disciplining of a woman framed as an unruly feminist. Although typically targeting an individual in the private reaches of the home, "domestic" violence in this context transcended the private sphere and played out in the public spaces of the nation-state; Clinton's disciplining was consequently visible for all to see as a first lady rhetorically punished for violating authentic womanhood ideals. The victimhood frame popularized during the Clinton-Lewinsky scandal furthered her disciplining as a scorned woman admonished to the "private" spaces as wife and mother.

Once Clinton was disciplined and sidelined from the politicized spaces and acting instead as a first lady performing the trappings of tradition, news scrutiny more commonly dissipated. As a victim of her husband's deceit or as a more ceremonial first lady conforming to the position's traditions, Clinton enjoyed higher approval ratings. These moments seemingly coincided with a patriarchal realignment of her marriage and the presidency that exhibited the reassertion of male power and control. Yet, as soon as Clinton stepped back into the spaces of political controversy, the news surveillance intensified, the negative baseline frames quickly returned, and the cycle of rhetorical disciplining began anew. Most disturbingly, once Clinton entered the electoral spaces of politics as a candidate, the news frames exuded a rhetoric of sexual violence—a rhetoric of violence inspired by portrayals of an inauthentic political woman acting outside the confines of gender tradition.

Hillary Clinton, however, did not retreat in spite of the cultural disciplining during or after the 2000 Senate campaign. In representing her own candidacy instead of her husband's, Clinton empowered herself to defy the political obstacles placed before her by the news media and political opponents primed with memory frames that were well entrenched after nearly eight years in the national spotlight. Achieving victory and setting new political precedents, Clinton persevered in ways that would portend her viable run for the presidency and her selection as a U.S. secretary of state.[141] Yet, while Clinton's own defiance was awe inspiring and precedent setting, the magnitude of the disciplining and rhetoric of violence that she faced served as a cultural warning for other women who might dare to enter the political arena and violate the protocols of authentic womanhood. Clinton, privileged by her celebrity, political connections, whiteness, economic status, and heterosexuality, possessed the means by which to challenge the political patriarchy.[142] Even for other women of privilege, the didactic lessons gleaned from Clinton's life story functioned as a warning that they too could face similar authenticity scrutiny, public humiliation, and threats of violence should they follow in Clinton's political footsteps.

Chapter 1 represents the first installment of Hillary Clinton's news biography and examines the news coverage of Clinton during the 1992 presidential campaign and her entrance onto the national stage of politics. This chapter recounts the baseline news frames that laid the foundation for judgments of Clinton's authenticity against which future frames would converge and diverge. Clinton's comments about not being Tammy Wynette and not staying home and baking cookies or hosting teas would arguably serve as the most formative media moments for Clinton. These media moments linguistically and visually acted as stock frames that authenticated Clinton as a feminist and inauthenticated her as a woman of tradition. Clinton's political image was framed as a political intruder violating the protocol of presidential campaigning; an anomalous candidate's wife rejecting the trappings of home and domesticity in favor of feminist principles; and a political lightning rod who exuded personality problems that promised to disrupt her husband's presidential bid and undermine the traditions of first lady. The perception that Clinton was too talkative and too centralized in the spaces of electoral politics ultimately challenged the masculinization of the presidency and the gender assumptions of the nation-state. The news media accordingly depicted a more feminized presidential sphere that challenged Bill Clinton's virility and exacerbated a sense of fear over the disruption of presidential gender norms. The chapter ends with a look at the extension of these baseline frames into the 1996 campaign.

Chapter 2 examines Hillary Clinton's leadership during the congressional health care debate and the investigations surrounding Whitewater. The press surveillance of Clinton continued as she left the political spaces of the campaign and entered the deliberative spaces of Capitol Hill and the legal terrain of shady land deals. Portrayed as holding secret meetings over health care and deceptively investing in properties during Whitewater, questions of authenticity permeated the coverage of Clinton from 1993 to 1995 as she lived out the promise of a Clinton co-presidency. The verbal and nonverbal reactions to Clinton's intrusion into the typically male spaces of Congress were most visible as male congressional leaders and journalists exuded senses of discomfort, amusement, and derision with her political presence and her outspoken leadership. The overarching message communicated by the press was that during the health care debate, she once again talked too much and exerted too much control over her husband and his administration. Contrastingly, Clinton's unwillingness to talk enough served as evidence of her illegal wrongdoing during the Whitewater investigations. During both controversies, Clinton was pictured as smiling through the tumult, promulgating a sense of discordance between the seriousness of the allegations and her public comportment. Clinton would consequently be disciplined through a rhetoric of violence for her outspokenness and her spatial violations as she was punished for such political and legal impropriety, corroding, once again, idyllic notions of authentic womanhood. Journalists would track Clinton's eventual retreat to the private spaces of the White House where, many complained, she purposefully eluded the glare of the news camera—messages that reified this period in Clinton's news biography as one of subterfuge and deceit.

Chapter 3 analyzes the coverage of Clinton's international excursions beginning in 1995 and ending with the media frenzy over the Clinton-Lewinsky scandal from 1998 through early 1999. As Clinton entered the international spaces of politics as a U.S. emissary, she was framed increasingly as the silent and more appropriately gendered first lady, visualized in the global spaces yet given minimal voice in primetime news coverage. At the first sign of discord, however, the surveillance and scrutiny would begin again, especially coinciding with her very public and outspoken actions during the 1995 Fourth World Conference on Women in China. The dissipation of controversy over most of Clinton's seventy-eight international trips as first lady suggested that the true spaces of contestation for vocal political women existed within the boundaries of the nation-state.[143] Once positioned outside of the nation's borders, such political talk and international exigencies appeared inconsequential to important political matters. Hillary Clinton would use this time outside the national spotlight to build her resume and political experiences in foreign policy and diplomatic relations that proved invaluable to her future political career.

With the onset of the Clinton-Lewinsky scandal in early 1998, the traditional gender order that was destabilized during the 1992 campaign and the health care debate was ultimately restored through the news framing of Clinton's life story, complete with scandal, sexual intrigue, and secrecy. Hillary Clinton played the scorned woman, ultimately standing by her man in this chapter of her news narrative, where her extensive travel schedule seemingly aided Monica Lewinsky's ability to sexually stalk her unsuspecting husband. Lewinsky accordingly was featured as the national temptress whose sexual promiscuity threatened the presidency and the nation-state. That the news cameras filmed Lewinsky from the perspective of Bill Clinton's male gaze helped naturalize his actions, especially for a president needing to recover his masculinity from an overbearing wife who overstepped the bounds of political and marital power. Bill Clinton seemed to bear the least responsibility for the affair according to such gender logic, where "all the president's women" would shoulder the burden for his sexual misdeeds in the news world.

Ultimately, the visual and verbal framing of the first lady's marital humiliation and temporary political exile served as another means by which to discipline Hillary Clinton. In the process, the traditional roles for women were naturalized through images of a faithful and supportive wife more ideologically consonant with historical notions of authentic womanhood. Clinton's credibility rebounded during this period as she was framed as a ceremonial emissary representing her country, the rescuer of her husband, and a moral compass for the nation. That she seemingly accepted her husband's personal lapses and stood by his side helped save the national union and salvage her marriage. Clinton's high approval ratings and the framing of Clinton in more authentic womanhood terms would be short-lived, however, as the rumors of her impending Senate bid spread even before the impeachment scandal came to an end.

Chapter 4 features the extensive television news coverage of Hillary Clinton as a candidate for the U.S. Senate. In many ways, the news broadcasts reflected the memory frames that circulated throughout her time as first lady, from her image as a political lightning rod who suffered from personality problems to that of a victimized wife. Questions surrounding her political authenticity were central to the news frames from the early murmurs of a possible Clinton Senate run. Clinton was correspondingly depicted as an inauthentic political candidate because of her questionable motives for office, her lack of geographical ties to the state of New York, her lack of political experience, and her shifting views on contentious political topics. These inauthenticity judgments suggested to the press and Clinton's Republican opponents that she lacked an overall fitness and preparedness for elective office.

Most troubling, the metaphors featured in the news frames of her Senate candidacy conflated commonplace notions of sports, violence, and politics with the sexualization of women to create a rhetoric of sexual violence. The language of certain journalists suggested that if Clinton dared enter the contentious spaces of New York politics, she invited any sense of political aggressiveness that followed, reminiscent of the language historically linked to women and rape. Even as her candidacy gained greater credibility and her lead in the polls expanded, journalists continued to predict her inevitable failure. They stressed her uncommon celebrity, furthering the sense of her political fakery and her actions as an audacious political woman overstepping the boundaries of authentic womanhood and political protocol.

As is well known, Clinton was successful in her bid for the U.S. Senate, testifying to her own tenacity and political agency. Yet, Clinton arguably was forced to overcome additional authenticity obstacles that male candidates typically have not had to endure. Clinton's news biography ultimately issued a tale of forewarning to other political women who consider stepping into such masculine political spaces. Certainly, Clinton's first lady successors seemed to heed the "anti-Hillary" warnings by remaining more firmly entrenched within the bounds of authentic womanhood. The conclusion grapples with the implications of the nation's press covering a precedent-setting first lady through news frames steeped in stereotypes, tradition, and gendered preoccupations with political authenticity.[144] It is to the first chapter of Hillary Clinton's national news biography that I now turn.

CHAPTER 1

Hillary Clinton as Campaign Surrogate

U.S. Presidential Campaigns—1992 and 1996

O n January 20, 2007, Hillary Rodham Clinton ended weeks, months, and even years of speculation with the simple words, "I'm In," as she announced her formation of a presidential exploratory committee for the 2008 presidential campaign.[1] The person whom *Washington Post* journalist Carl Bernstein called the "most famous woman in the world"[2] had finally ventured into what MSNBC's Tucker Carlson described as the "longest full-scale, full-blown, talk-about-it-every-day run-up to a national election in American history."[3]

For Hillary Clinton's 2008 presidential campaign, the issue of her political authenticity occupied the attention of many in the press—a preoccupation that had dogged the first lady from 1992 onward. During the 2008 contest, many journalists suggested that Clinton's most authentic self was displayed during two key mediated moments from the 1992 presidential campaign. The first involved her response to allegations of Bill Clinton's alleged extramarital affairs during a January 26, 1992, *60 Minutes* special: "You know, I'm not sitting here, some little woman standing by my man like Tammy Wynette."[4] The second involved her reaction to Democratic primary candidate Jerry Brown's questions about her unethical legal practices when Bill Clinton was governor of Arkansas. The following day, Clinton justified her decision to "fulfill my profession" instead of having "stayed home and baked cookies and had teas."[5]

Revealing the force of these mediated memories some fifteen years after their initial airing, Tucker Carlson and Rosa Brooks of the *Los Angeles Times* engaged in a poignant exchange on January 29, 2007:

CARLSON: When was the last time you heard Hillary Clinton say something really courageous, counterintuitive, something that all the cool kids disagree with . . . ?

BROOKS: About 1992 . . .

CARLSON: The "baking cookies" line?

BROOKS: Yes, the baking cookies line, the Tammy Wynette line . . . That was the real Hillary.[6]

The preoccupation with Clinton's authenticity and the mystery surrounding her true political image was revealed most vividly in the sentiments of MSNBC's Chris Matthews on June 1, 2007, when he referenced Bernstein's argument that Clinton's "biggest problem is that she appears inauthentic." He then wondered aloud: "But if the woman isn't Tammy Wynette, is no cookie baker and nobody's fool, then who is she?"[7]

For many journalists, Hillary Clinton's most authentic moments were aligned with what some called her feminist commitments. Of Clinton's political image in the early stages of her national public life, Paula Zahn of CNN remembered the Clinton of 1992 as the "outspoken feminist who put down the stand-by-your-man crowd." Yet, by the 2008 campaign, many in the news business had come to question her commitment to feminism. Republican strategist Amy Holmes argued on *Paula Zahn Now* in March 2007 that "Hillary [was] trying to soften her image" away from that of a "feminist" to avoid what she argued was her tendency to be "shrill or difficult" as reflected by the "I don't stand by my man" utterance.[8]

These image transformations suggested Clinton's lack of political authenticity in favor of political expediency. In 1992, one cultural anxiety expressed by *CBS Evening News* related to the potential of Hillary Rodham Clinton to feminize the spaces of the presidency by being "out front and outspoken . . . a symbol of the national debate about women and work and power."[9] By the time she stepped into the spaces of the 2008 presidential campaign, however, the concern by some became her exhibition of too much masculinity and not enough feminism. During a CNN broadcast from June 18, 2007, media scholar Susan Douglas of the University of Michigan asserted that "people feel like Hillary has tried too hard to be more like a man," losing what Carol Costello of CNN pondered was "her mantle of political feminism" in favor of "political masculinity."[10] The frames of Clinton's feminism, thus, converged with notions of her political inauthenticity to raise doubts about her true political convictions.

Even as Clinton was portrayed as all empowering in certain stories about her presidential candidacy, other journalists undermined the strength of her political leadership. When Chris Matthews wondered aloud about Bill Clinton's role in a Hillary Clinton White House, he concluded that "some people think Bill Clinton is still the boss."[11] Eugene Robinson of the *Washington Post* dubbed Hillary Clinton a "wonkish mommy" during a MSNBC broadcast from January 22, 2007, undercutting her political clout through a demeaning reference to Clinton's "mommy" status.[12] These constructions of Clinton, of course, worked to undermine her power rhetorically even before a final decision was made by voters over her presidential preparedness.

The press coverage of the 2008 political race thus reflected the news frames and linguistic residuals from the 1992 campaign, where Clinton was depicted as "polarizing," as possessing "likeability" issues, and as a political "lightning rod" regardless of the political role she served.[13] The television news coverage of the 1992 campaign provided the *baseline news frames* that were subsequently used to authenticate and inauthenticate Clinton not only in 1992 but over the next sixteen years of her presence in the national spotlight. If Clinton's behavior seemed to contradict the character traits naturalized in the baseline frames, the press would amplify a Clinton makeover that chipped away at her political authenticity. This chapter therefore sets the stage for the remainder of the book by identifying the baseline news frames used by the television news media in its coverage of Clinton as a campaign surrogate during her husband's 1992 and 1996 presidential bids. These frames tell us much about television news practices as well as the ideological meanings associated with the gendered nation at the turn of the twenty-first century.

Specifically, this chapter shows how Clinton's authenticity was reified through baseline news frames associated with her comments about Tammy Wynette and cookies and teas. The chapter also examines the press frames of Clinton as a political partner, a radical feminist, and a political lightning rod. All of these themes were eventually folded into the linguistic frame known simply as the "Hillary Factor," which stood in stark contrast to more traditional conceptions of authentic womanhood. Most reflective of Clinton's contested yet authentic image involved the perception of her *outspokenness* and her *overexposure* in the spaces of the 1992 Democratic primary. Yet, as the 1992 Democratic National Convention neared, the news media began to detect a Clinton makeover that resulted in the reduced visibility and increased silencing of Hillary Clinton by the Clinton campaign. By the summer of 1992, the baseline frames would serve an inauthenticating role as journalists invoked them to evidence Clinton's changing political image.

The themes associated with Clinton's feminism, still visible during the 1996 presidential campaign, showed the stronghold of cultural stereotypes in personifying political women as embodiments of tradition *or* progress.[14] Most resistant to any reconstitution efforts were the feminist images that depicted Hillary Clinton as aggressive, lacking in grace and warmth, and unlikely to fit the traditional model of stay-at-home moms and doting spouses. The latter frames in particular helped inauthenticate the Clinton marriage and turn it into a partnership for political gain. The overarching press thematics from both campaigns suggested that Clinton's transgressive behavior as a candidate's wife precipitated disciplinary intervention by Bill Clinton's staff, culminating in a more diminished role for Clinton publicly. Without such disciplinary actions, the political logic suggested, Clinton stood to harm her husband's candidacy irreparably.

Hillary Rodham Clinton of 1992—The Baseline News Frames

Hillary Clinton burst onto the 1992 national scene with considerable fanfare and flourish. The U.S. news media would be forced to contend with how best to cover a candidate's wife who unabashedly sought a public and decidedly political role within a presidential campaign. The early coverage of Clinton would become most formative in how she would be framed from that time forward as a political spouse, first lady, Senate candidate, and presidential contender—roles that contradicted the ideological tenets of authentic womanhood.

In the section that follows, three distinct yet overlapping baseline news frames are examined in the coverage of Hillary Clinton: *stock frames*, *residual frames*, and *linguistic frames*. Stock frames represent shorter news snippets extracted from television news broadcasts that become recycled sound bites.[15] With *residual frames,* a statement or an idea continues to be recycled in news broadcasts but the context that generated the idea and often the individual who first issued it are no longer referenced. *Linguistic frames* represent catchphrases invented by the news media that function as linguistic shortcuts, standing in for a host of behaviors and personality characteristics.

STOCK FRAMES

The two most important stock frames from the 1992 campaign integrated visual imagery with Hillary Clinton's statements about Tammy Wynette and cookies and teas. Once Clinton uttered these statements, the press routinely decontextualized the sound bites and then recontextualized and recirculated them throughout 1992 and beyond as authenticating moments for Hillary Clinton—a new personality on the national political stage. These recycled frames—meeting the threshold of "sound bite sabotage"[16]—symbolized Clinton's feminism, which news organizations construed as an affront to traditional women and a threat to her husband's candidacy.

As previously indicated, the first national media moment for Hillary Clinton involved the January 26, 1992, *60 Minutes* interview she conducted with Bill

Clinton at her side. The Clintons appeared on the popular CBS news magazine after allegations surfaced of an extended extramarital affair between the Arkansas governor and a local news reporter—Gennifer Flowers. During the broadcast, both Clintons testified to the strength and endurance of the Clinton marriage in spite of significant marital strain. The sound bite involving Tammy Wynette referenced the country-and-western singer's famous 1968 hit song—"Stand By Your Man." Clinton made the animated statement in response to Steve Kroft's insinuation that the couple stayed together for political purposes—as "some sort of an understanding or arrangement." Once Bill Clinton scoffed at Kroft's insinuation, Hillary then uttered the phrase associated with the more traditional singer ("I'm not sitting here, some little woman standing by my man like Tammy Wynette"). Showing a strong sense of resolve, Clinton followed with another forceful statement, which she punctuated by clinching her fist and thrusting it up and down as she professed: "I honor what he's been through and what we've been through together. And you know, if that's not enough for people, then heck, don't vote for him."[17] Throughout the interview, Hillary also pledged her spousal support in nonverbal fashion by placing her arm on the sofa behind Bill's back, by looking supportively at her husband as he spoke, by affirming his statements with a nod of the head, and by touching his arm in a display of interpersonal affection.

On Election Day in 1992, Jim Wooten of ABC News extended the implications of Clinton's political performance when he referred to the period surrounding the *60 Minutes* interview as "pure melodrama" and a "national soap opera."[18] The importance of the interview to Clinton's political biography was shown in Kroft's memory of the exchange many years later. Kroft boasted that the 1992 interview had "been called one of the great performances of American presidential politics."[19] Apart from Hillary Clinton's debut as an outspoken political wife willing to defend her husband, this moment would also provide the initial hints of a Clinton partnership based more on shared political aspirations than a marriage founded on mutual love and affection.

Nearly two months after the *60 Minutes* interview, a second stock frame also gained media traction during the 1992 Democratic primary. As with the Tammy Wynette utterance, Clinton's cookies and teas comment would become the subject of continual re-airing for years to come. Multiple news cameras caught the statement as Bill and Hillary Clinton campaigned together in Chicago's Busy Bea Coffee Shop the day before the Illinois primary.[20] Reacting to Jerry Brown's allegations of corruption between the governor's office and her own Rose Law Firm, Clinton struck a bold, assertive, and slightly irritated tone. Viewers were situated by the camera within the conversational flow as if part of the group of reporters gathered to witness Clinton's much anticipated response. As Clinton spoke, she was surrounded mostly by white men who were all standing near the lunch counter or gathered around her. Clinton's profile was visible to the camera as if she were speaking to someone in front of her. Clinton had the look of a campaigner; she exuded a commanding presence. During the sound bite, Clinton talked rather than listened and gestured vigorously with one hand as she held a drink in the other. Bill Clinton was among the onlookers, positioned over her shoulder as if a bystander to the exchange. Because Bill Clinton was far enough removed from Hillary's conversational circle, he would eventually be cut out of most of the subsequent re-airings. The presence of the cameras that surrounded Hillary Clinton implied that she and not her husband was the centerpiece of the media spectacle.

Of the cookies and teas expression, *CBS Evening News* journalist Richard Threlkeld subtly critiqued the amount of attention the statement attracted: "How important is a candidate's past political life or whether someone fought in Vietnam or found a way to avoid it. And now as Hillary Clinton is asking, 'must a wife sacrifice her career if it might interfere with her husband's career?' Not the sort of campaign issues the voters were expecting."[21] NBC News, however, put a different spin on the initial declaration. As the camera crew followed Clinton outside of the diner, she elaborated on her initial response—a response that Andrea Mitchell framed as a political gaffe: "Worried campaign aides urged her to soften the message right away." NBC then played Clinton's response that presumed the complexities of choice associated with second-wave feminism: "It could be a full-time mother and homemaker, it could be a full-time career person, to balance the two, to have those decisions at different stages of your life, are very tough ones."[22]

Issuing a juxtaposition of the two stock frames, NBC, through correspondent Lisa Myers, showed the enduring resonance of certain media moments as journalists returned to the same messages in future news stories. Myers initially offered a summarizing statement that celebrated Clinton's role in the *60 Minutes* story yet foreshadowed the dark days ahead for the Clinton campaign because of Hillary's most recent cookies and teas snafu: "Hillary Clinton's strong performance during the Gennifer Flowers episode," Myers concluded, "helped save her husband's candidacy. But now, she may be fast becoming an issue herself."[23] Myers derived a similar conclusion the following month, positing more positively how the *60 Minutes* interview evidenced how Clinton "took charge and helped rescue his candidacy." Yet, the cookies and teas expression also revealed, Myers claimed, how "she also hurts him. Many women are still fuming over th[at] remark."[24] In NBC's coverage, Clinton was credited with rescuing her philandering husband's presidential campaign. Yet she was also sufficiently warned that her more controversial image as an assertive political wife could ultimately doom her husband's candidacy.

Myers's statements also illustrated how both stock frames commonly appeared together in newscasts, becoming central features of Clinton's news biography. These mediated practices were not lost on Hillary Clinton. She noted in her memoir—*Living History*—that some journalists "merged" the passages "into one quote" as if she had "uttered both phrases in the same breath—not fifty-one days apart."[25] The coupling of these two media moments served an authenticating function for Clinton as the news media used them as indices of her true character. From these two unscripted political moments, the news media created sound bites that efficiently and succinctly reinforced the authenticity baseline for Clinton's press biography and made for dramatic television news coverage.[26]

The controversial nature of these statements enhanced their force as authenticity indicators. Scholar John Fiske refers to oppositional statements as a sense of "unedited rawness"—"a thinking with [one's] tongue that, in its rawness, gives a sense of authenticity."[27] Statements like Clinton's Tammy Wynette and cookies and teas comments were often understood as unconscious expressions, devoid of the political image control that sullies political statements. David S. Kaufer and Brian S. Butler elaborate on this notion of authenticity in their discussion of a "sensory space," which is perceived as a "wellspring of a speaker's deepest motives and missions" that only becomes public if the person in question wishes to make the private and thus more authentic public (or if the person speaks in a more unfiltered manner). Kaufer and Butler contend that the idea of the "unified and authentic person deep down is of course a romantic myth." What becomes most important is the use of the myth for "rhetorical purposes."[28] Hillary Clinton's alleged lack of political sensitivity to traditional women in these pressure-packed moments of the campaign implied that her sensory spaces were exposed. What appeared to the press as two unscripted moments revealed to many in the news business the true Hillary Clinton, at least for those few seconds of sound bite drama.

RESIDUAL FRAMES

Other related frames would likewise take hold in the 1992 campaign. One in particular was most attributable to Bill Clinton's own words and the Clinton political partnership ("buy one, get one free"), which popularized the idea of a Clinton co-presidency. In this case, Bill Clinton's words were distilled into the summative frame of a Clinton political team. Even though the sound bite of

Bill Clinton would eventually fade from view, a residual frame remained in the news coverage of the Clintons. Repeating the idea of a Clinton co-presidency in news broadcasts helped naturalize the commonplace of a Clinton political partnership.

Early in the Democratic primary, Bill Clinton uttered the words: "I always say that my slogan might well be, 'buy one, get one free.'"[29] The phrase—"buy one, get one free"—gained more political footing in March 1992 when coupled with Hillary's cookies and teas comment. This period represented an increased focus on "unprecedented scrutiny and criticism of a political wife's thoughts, deeds, and ambitions," according to Jackie Judd of ABC's *Nightline*. By March 26, 1992, Bill Clinton was forced to answer direct questions about a Clinton "co-presidency." In response, Governor Clinton reasserted his role as the couple's political decision maker: "No, she wouldn't be a co-president. We have our differences of opinion and, in the end, I have to decide."[30] By April, the presumption of a Clinton partnership was in full view when Lisa Myers made the following remark to NBC news anchor Tom Brokaw: "Hillary and Bill Clinton are running as a team and the American people will just have to get used to it, Tom."[31] Throughout the coverage of 1992, references to the Clinton partnership persisted as revealed through such phrases as "full partner,"[32] "Power Partner,"[33] "formidable political team,"[34] "personal and political partnership,"[35] and "two Clintons for the price of one."[36] When featuring visual images of the Clintons together on the campaign trail, Hillary Clinton was routinely portrayed as an active campaigner—shaking hands, giving speeches—alongside her husband, the presidential contender.

Imagining the presidency as a "two-person career" is steeped in political practice. As Karlyn Kohrs Campbell explains, a historical examination of the first couple demonstrates that "cooperative efforts" between the president and first lady are necessary if the presidency "is to be pursued successfully."[37] The news media nevertheless raised questions about the propriety of a co-presidency. These residual frames were multipurposed and easily transitory. Noticeably absent, though, was coverage that depicted a Clinton marriage grounded in a loving relationship.

A second residual frame was that of Hillary Clinton as a "radical feminist." The frame's endurance was rooted in its service to the Republican Party's political strategy and its ideological resonance with many of the other news frames from 1992. Cokie Roberts on *ABC World News Tonight* noted in August 1992 that "there is a concerted Republican effort to portray Hillary Clinton as an out of the mainstream radical."[38] This view became even more entrenched in the aftermath of Patrick Buchanan's Republican National Convention speech. ABC featured

Buchanan's response to allegations that Hillary Clinton supported the ability of children to sue their parents in a 1974 opinion piece, reinforcing her radical views, according to Republican leaders. As Buchanan proclaimed: "This, my friends, this is radical feminism."[39] Buchanan would go on to defend his attacks against Clinton on the *CBS Evening News*, emphasizing her level of frankness on controversial issues that implicated the Clinton partnership: "She is out there as an activist. She makes these statements. She's very proud of the positions she's taken, her husband supports those positions, and that in essence allows us, as Republicans, to say this is what Bill Clinton or Clinton and Clinton represent to Americans."[40] The following evening, ABC news anchor Peter Jennings asked President George H. W. Bush—the Republican incumbent in 1992—if Hillary Clinton was a "legitimate target." After first responding, "I don't like going after the wife," Bush then justified the concerted campaign against Hillary: "If you're out there on issues, taking your case to the people on issues, and you have an activist past and you're a very aggressive lawyer sitting at the ABA Association presenting views, that's a little different than if you're not taking positions."[41] The theme of Hillary Clinton as a radical feminist and the presumption of a Clinton partnership were clearly undercurrents in the Tammy Wynette and cookies and teas frames.

Although the news media would still attribute the phrase "radical feminism" to Buchanan in later stories, this phrase too would typically circulate untethered from Buchanan's original expression. Residual frames thus can preserve the syntax from the original utterance but sever the words from their original context. Short phrases like "radical feminist" can easily become distilled frames with widespread currency in the news media's rush to disseminate meaning efficiently and swiftly. Their utility ultimately contributes to their repeated uses, and their repeated uses ultimately enhance their naturalization of the candidate image.

LINGUISTIC FRAMES

Linguistic frames are directly attributable to the U.S. news media rather than political actors and also serve as a short-handed means by which to simplify the meaning-making process.[42] Often, linguistic frames were seamlessly interwoven with stock frames and residual frames throughout the television news coverage of the 1992 presidential campaign, representing a sense of ideological consonance involving Hillary Clinton's contested political image.

In search of an even more efficient means by which to easily reference the totality of the Clinton phenomenon, the U.S. news media created the linguistic frame known simply as the "Hillary Factor." This phrasing was sufficiently abstract to allow for a variety of underlying meanings associated with Clinton's controversial role in her husband's campaign. By May 12, 1992, CBS News was initially talking about the "Hillary Factor"—a theme that derived from a series of print news articles. To get at the "Hillary Factor," CBS featured a radio DJ asking his listeners the following question: "You like her or not like her?" One caller responded, "She's hard as nails," and another said, "She would like to be president."[43]

By the general election, this formative frame took greater hold with a *Time* magazine cover featuring a portrait photograph of Hillary Clinton slightly smiling and staring into the camera. The caption from the September 14, 1992, story read: "The Hillary Factor: Is She Helping or Hurting Her Husband?" In a subsequent broadcast, Mark Phillips of CBS News made the following observation about this growing Hillary Clinton phenomenon: "[W]hile nobody talks about the Barbara factor, there's lots of talk about the Hillary factor." When used, the "Hillary Factor" generally served as an umbrella term for what the press and the Republican opposition dubbed as her negative attributes. Phillips contended that while "Bill Clinton did say early on that voters would get two Clintons for the price of one . . . the second Clinton in the package did sometimes say things that got her into trouble." CBS then turned back to the stock frame of cookies and teas to evidence the trouble Hillary Clinton brought to the campaign. In this one broadcast, CBS integrated three baseline frames—cookies and teas, Clinton partnership, and the "Hillary Factor"—to reveal the downward drag Clinton brought to her husband's candidacy.[44]

NBC Nightly News also utilized the "Hillary Factor" for a retrospective of the Clinton campaign on November 19, 1992. The story featured the Clinton presidential transition team and Hillary Clinton's presence in presidential planning meetings. NBC journalist Bob Kur offered the following observations about the presidential transition: "Other first ladies have been influential behind the scenes but as she drove herself around Little Rock this week, Hillary Clinton seemed ready to be more public about steering things her way." To emphasize the role that she might serve in a Clinton administration, CBS played a sound bite from Clinton trumpeting her own political assets: "You know I've drafted legislation. I've testified about legislation. I understand how the pieces of a budget fit together, things that I can bring to the table in trying to implement an agenda on behalf of children that I think will be beneficial." At the conclusion of the story, Kur tied the "Hillary Factor" back to the notion of a Clinton partnership: "Bill Clinton used to tell campaign crowds that if they voted for him, they'd get Hillary too. If this week is any indication, that's one promise that will be kept."[45]

Clinton as a "lightning rod" would serve as a second linguistic frame from 1992 that symbolized most vividly the threat she posed to the Clinton campaign and the nation at large. Bob McNamara of CBS News made the following remark in May: "Already a household name, Hillary Clinton isn't a candidate but a lightning rod." As McNamara uttered this phrase, video images progressed sequentially from campaign scenes involving the Clintons and the Bushes to stock footage of suburban families. The final scene was marked by pictures and sounds of threat. A nightscape scene of a bridge was aired with vivid lightning flashes brightly lighting the sky. Accompanying sounds of thunder punctuated the aura of danger. Dan Rather closed this story and the entire newscast on a note of impending controversy: "The changing and sometimes conflicting roles of women, part of our world tonight."[46] Journalist Mark Shields used the same reference to the "lightning rod" during a CNN broadcast from August 15 when he suggested that Hillary Clinton "had been under wraps really in the Democratic campaign because of fear that she was sort of a lightning rod for criticism."[47] Wherever she ventured, the metaphor suggested, Clinton attracted attention—the kind of attention that could prove hurtful if not fatal to her husband's campaign.

These baseline frames were formative for a variety of reasons that have everything to do with news practices. First, language frames become part of the news vernacular, functioning as a short-cut for framing an issue or a person that saves time and explanation.[48] Often the linguistic frames like the lightning rod can be transported to new storylines and visual images with ease; they represented a consonant dimension of Clinton's association with radical feminism and her equalized partnership with her political spouse. And, intact, yet highly reductionistic stock frames reliant on sounds bites—Tammy Wynette and cookie and teas—could also be easily reinserted into new narratives. When resurrected, they acted as memory frames that connoted synecdochical and agreed upon themes that were strengthened through "inter-media" repetition.[49]

Second, frames assume ideological force, offering an implicit, and at times explicit, judgment about Hillary Clinton's character or political performance. One would be hard pressed to identify positive attributes associated with most of the baseline frames. Early on, some journalists framed the Tammy Wynette statement as a moment when Hillary Clinton saved her husband's Democratic candidacy. Later on, it came to stand in for her unusual outspokenness and her political partnership with her husband. The notion of the Clinton partnership and the "Hillary Factor" on their own could reflect more neutral depictions. Yet, their association with other negative frames that reified Clinton's feminism, her questionable anomaly as a political spouse, or her role as a political lightning rod quickly contaminated the frames' more benign qualities.

Third, frames serve an accumulative effect. Initially interwoven in a single news story, they reappear; their reappearance reinforces a sense of consubstantiality over newscasts and across news stations. Once recirculated across news organizations, their repetition can serve a snowballing effect as they become a naturalizing and authenticating force in the political image of Hillary Clinton. The themes derived from Clinton, her husband, staffers, opinion leaders, scholars, the Republican Party, and the news media. Regardless of their origin, they become part of a grand news media biography that wrapped the Clinton image into a tidy and simplified image package. As Todd Gitlin charges, news organizations "borrow angles, issues, and questions from each other,"[50] a practice vividly on display in Clinton's baseline frames. The end result is a reification of the political image that, Kathleen Hall Jamieson and Paul Waldman contend, helps "mold public understanding and opinion by deciding what is important and what may be ignored."[51]

In delving deeper into the visual and verbal news frames of Hillary Clinton, it became clearer that the primary source of critique focused most on Clinton's level of political talk and public exposure, even as the news media championed the progress that career women like Clinton personified during what was popularly known as the Year of the Woman.

Hillary Clinton—Embodiment of Political Progress and Political Controversy

While most of the baseline frames emphasized the negative attributes associated with Hillary Clinton, the coverage of this modern-day political wife also recognized her achievements and the overall progress of many career women of her generation. In an April 7, 1992, NBC broadcast, Lisa Myers stressed just how impressive Hillary Clinton actually was: "If Hillary Clinton weren't married to Bill, you probably would have heard of her before now. She is that talented and that driven." Such a persona of empowerment was reinforced by the camera positioned below Clinton and looking up to her as she listened with an intense look of attention to Bill Clinton's campaign speech in New York. Her facial expressions lacked emotion and were devoid of the iconic, Stepford qualities expected of the adoring and smiling political wife. When Myers defined Clinton as a strong campaigner, we see Clinton actively working a rope line during a political event. Offering the ultimate in political compliments, Myers concluded: "In fact, some in Arkansas, friend and foe alike, say the wrong person is on the ticket."[52] This position of empowerment was substantiated by Liz Carpenter—a former staffer for Lady Bird Johnson—who asserted in a November 1992 story for ABC News that women are "raring for Hillary to go" because "[a]fter all, most of the women in this country work. And here's somebody who is one of us and understands our problems."[53] In reflecting the views of the Clinton campaign, political staffer James Carville reinforced the image of Clinton as a role model of gender progress: "Mrs. Clinton is exactly the kind of woman we need in America. She's a strong woman, she is supportive of her husband. She's got her own career and her own ideas."[54]

Clinton's entry onto the national stage coincided with the 1992 Year of the Woman—inspired by the treatment of Anita Hill by U.S. senators during Clarence Thomas's Supreme Court nomination hearings. As the election unfolded, Democratic and Republican women in particular came together to support the candidacy of more women for public office. The Year of the Woman theme was also championed across news stations;[55] undoubtedly, Clinton's persona fit a demographic bloc of voters (and news audience members) who seemingly found inspiration in such political performances and campaign themes. Speaking more generally, Lisa Myers of NBC News spoke to the activist sentiment, declaring: "This year for the first time in history, it seems to be a bit of a political disadvantage to be a man."[56]

Even though many in the news media scrutinized Hillary Clinton's contributions to the Clinton campaign, news organizations also suggested a level of unfairness in the treatment of Clinton. Noting the double standard that Clinton was facing in the 1992 campaign, NBC's Andrea Mitchell concluded her August 7, 1992, broadcast with a note of irony: "Politicians in both parties like to say that this is the Year of the Woman. But that doesn't necessarily apply to the politician's wife."[57] Mark Phillips of *CBS Evening News* critiqued the prevalent sexism of politics when he asserted on September 9 that the controversy surrounding Clinton "is really about a lot more than one woman's views or one woman's career. It's about politics lagging behind real life." Phillips's statement was corroborated by Barbara Lippert of *Adweek Magazine* who argued: "The reality is that most women are working and do have to work, and yet, we seem so threatened to see a woman who's doing it."[58] Journalists thus stepped carefully when trying to balance coverage that at once celebrated women's advancements in the public sphere of work and politics with a visible effort to champion the stay-at-home moms who likewise consumed the news.

The news media also quickly acknowledged that women were not a homogeneous voting bloc. Instead, the coverage suggested that women's views and lifestyles could be easily distilled into two opposing and contentious camps composed of progressive career women (personifying feminism) and more traditional stay-at-home moms (personifying authentic womanhood). The Tammy Wynette and cookies and teas baseline frames helped harden the division, featuring hot button issues that pitted women against one another—a common trope in the news framing of women. Bob McNamara from the *CBS Evening News* used the cookies and teas footage to exhibit the contention that Hillary Clinton had "become a symbol of the national debate about women and work and power." To demonstrate the gender dispute, CBS interviewed women about their views on Clinton. One woman, identified as a Democrat, sat with her child on the couch and issued the following indictment: "I was ready to like her. Not now . . . after what she said . . . She obviously doesn't have respect for what I do." According to this woman, even though the women's movement was allegedly about "choice," she deduced from Clinton's cookies and teas statement that if you select "homemaker," you have selected the "wrong choice."[59] During the national convention, ABC aired both the Tammy Wynette and cookies and teas clips as a means of accentuating the animosity that women expressed toward Clinton's public statements. Cokie Roberts noted that while the Wynette reference "made some women angry," it did not make them nearly "as angry as Mrs. Clinton's defense of her law practice in Arkansas," which was emphasized with the re-airing of the cookies and teas footage. Roberts concluded: "The furious response from women all over the country sent the candidate's wife into a far more traditional role."[60]

Barbara Bush ultimately became the face of tradition and authentic womanhood in the news dramas of the 1992 campaign—frames that were also negatively tinged. Advertising her recent news column entitled "Why I'm Standing by Hillary Clinton," Rita Grimsley Johnson argued in a CBS broadcast from May 1992 that "Barbara Bush is . . . a dying breed of women who never have worked. That's right out of the 1950s. That's Mrs. Cleaver."[61] Nearly four months later, CBS would reinforce another gender theme, concluding that "The wives represent as much of a generational and philosophical choice as the husbands."[62] Reflecting the commonplace of the storied "cat fight" that predominated the feminist-antifeminist debate over the ERA during the 1970s and 1980s, media scholar Susan J. Douglas speaks of the "spectacle" featuring "two women, often opposites, locked in a death grip" with no winner declared.[63] In 1992, Hillary Clinton and Barbara Bush were key performers in the news media's political spectacle.

Thus, while the Year of the Woman theme attracted coverage that was praiseworthy of women's progress, this celebratory treatment was tinted with stereotypical images of women vying against one another. Much of the coverage emphasized a level of critique that focused predominantly on two pressing issues for Hillary Clinton's public persona—her overabundance of talk and her propensity to upstage her husband in the public spaces of the campaign. Any deviation from such perceptions of outspoken strength and public visibility embedded in the baseline frames would eventually provoke charges of a campaign makeover that directly challenged Clinton's political authenticity.

OUTSPOKEN AND OVEREXPOSED

For the news media, Hillary Clinton's outspokenness and overexposure in the political partnership were clearly in evidence on Super Tuesday when she spoke in advance of the victorious Democratic nominee. NBC's Lisa Myers reinforced this theme in a March 16, 1992, broadcast where she pondered: "At times, some could be confused about which Clinton is on the ballot. When he won big on Super Tuesday, guess who led off in primetime?" NBC then showed Hillary Clinton delivering an emotive statement of encouragement: "We believe passionately in this country and we cannot stand by for one more year and watch what is happening to it." Clinton's centrality in the campaign led Myers to suggest that the candidate's wife "is practically a running mate." The problematic nature of Clinton's level of outspokenness and spatial centrality was implied visually as well. NBC displayed visual images of Hillary Clinton delivering speeches while the candidate was reduced to the status of onlooker positioned behind or to the side of his wife. These images circulated in the background as NBC recounted the ethical allegations involving Clinton's law firm and the Arkansas governor's office. While reporting on the Clintons' ethical and legal challenges, NBC featured a law professor from the University of Arkansas, Little Rock, speaking to the "problems of appearance." The appearance issues were easily transferred from the couple's ethical dilemmas to the contemporary political scene as Hillary Clinton *appeared* as a political equal, grabbing the political spotlight and sidelining her husband in the process—a matter of outspokenness and spatial impropriety.[64]

NBC would continue its attention to Super Tuesday as Hillary and Bill Clinton collectively basked in their hard-won primary victories. The following week, Andrea Mitchell narrated a story where she expressed a level of annoyance as the caption—"The Clintons"—appeared on the screen: "Election night on Super Tuesday. The networks are all waiting for the winning candidate. But first his wife appears, not just to introduce him but to give her own speech." Mitchell identified most explicitly the issue as one of space in terms of the Clinton partnership: "Hillary Rodham Clinton has been *front and center*, a full partner since she first met Bill Clinton in law school." Mitchell furthered the theme of visibility when she noted that "it is not yet clear how voters, especially women, will react to Hillary Clinton's high campaign profile." Foreshadowing the impending problems, Mitchell suggested the level of risk and danger involved with Clinton's campaign visibility: "The Clinton campaign is embarking on a high wire act, trying to attract voters that can relate to Hillary Clinton without alienating all the rest."[65]

Certainly, NBC was not alone in identifying Clinton's preponderance for outspokenness and overexposure—characteristics typically at odds with conceptions of authentic womanhood. During a March 27, 1992, *CBS Evening News* broadcast, news anchor Connie Chung introduced a story by Giselle Fernandez with the following introductory comment: "It's not Mrs. Clinton's style to stay in the background." While punctuating her propensity to be front and center, Fernandez coupled these spatial irregularities with her talkative tendencies: "Yes, there have been other outspoken women but she is perhaps the first to unabashedly walk alone, even at the risk of upstaging her husband." As in other broadcasts, the visual images that accompanied the storyline featured a Hillary Clinton in campaign mode, shaking hands on a rope line and signing autographs as if she were the political star of importance. The theme that Hillary Clinton acted more like a candidate than a political wife was reinforced by Fernandez, who reported that "Hillary Clinton maintains her own grueling campaign schedule. She walks in the small town parades but she's just not for appearances. She talks politics, policy, strategy, with the force of a candidate herself." Clinton's unusual talkativeness and spatial exposure again appeared to set her apart from past candidate wives to the point that "put Bill Clinton in the unprecedented role of 'standing by his woman'" on ethical matters linked to her Arkansas legal career. Reinforcing the backlash to Hillary Clinton's campaign speech from Super Tuesday, Fernandez commented: "Some Democrats were stunned Super Tuesday by that speech, quote 'wife' sounded like [an] unofficial running mate." Paul Costello—Rosalynn Carter's aide—responded directly to Clinton's use of "we" during her Super Tuesday speech: "The president of the United States is not a 'we,' it's an 'I.'" These comments suggested for Fernandez why Republicans felt Barbara Bush represented a more acceptable first lady model—"strong, but traditional."[66]

As the campaign progressed, Hillary Clinton's level of talk seemed to inspire even further indignation, which positioned her as a clear anomaly without historical precedent. Drawing on the cookies and teas stock frame to visually evidence Clinton's extraordinary outspokenness, Andrea Mitchell of NBC News asserted that "even in an age when other candidate's wives have full-time careers, this political wife is something different."[67] In an April 1992 story, Lisa Myers accented the problematic dimensions of Hillary's talkativeness, explaining that she was forced "to apologize this weekend for her swipe at George Bush, suggesting in an interview with *Vanity Fair* that he had his own extramarital affair." When airing the apology, NBC portrayed Clinton admitting: "Yes, it was a mistake. People were asking me questions at the time, and I responded but nobody knows better than I the pain that can be caused by even discussing rumors." Myers accentuated the extent of Clinton's anomalous and aggressive actions with one striking comment: "If her husband becomes president, Hillary as first lady could make Eleanor Roosevelt seem timid." Clinton walked alone in this new role, Myers suggested, as some depicted her as an "overly ambitious, aggressive political animal."[68] These negative sentiments seemingly defied images of first lady decorum and authentic womanhood. According to Andrea Mitchell, Bill Clinton was ultimately forced to address his wife's political outspokenness: "Today, [Bill Clinton] denied reports that his wife had vetoed Nebraska Senator Bob Kerrey" as a possible vice presidential choice. Bill Clinton appeared most incensed by such charges associated with Hillary's alleged political talk: "It was an outrageous misrepresentation of anything anybody ever said. Hillary never said anything like that."[69] While conveying Hillary's level of public outspokenness in more negative terms, any attempts to alter such campaign comportment quickly attracted the suspicion of many within the news business. The allegation by some in the press was that the Clinton campaign sought to hoodwink the American people with a Hillary Clinton makeover.

CLINTON'S CAMPAIGN MAKEOVER

Concerns over an image transformation for the press seemingly exposed an inauthentic Clinton attempting to slide surreptitiously into more traditional gender roles during the general election.[70] When introducing a story captioned "Campaign Makeover," NBC anchor Tom Brokaw offered the following assessment that reinforced Clinton's outspokenness and overexposure: "The political image makers are hard at it this year. They worried that Hillary Clinton was coming off as too bright, too outspoken, too upfront. So, they asked her to warm it up a bit." In evidencing the makeover, Andrea Mitchell charged that Clinton had "a new softer hair do. A new best friend—Tipper Gore," who the "campaign thinks . . . makes Hillary seem less threatening to conservative audiences." Mitchell juxtaposed the Clinton from the primary period with the Clinton of the general election, recalling from memory Clinton's visibility on Super Tuesday: "When the wives are introduced these days, it's to take a bow and step back. Not to give a victory speech on primetime television as Hillary did on Super Tuesday." The accompanying images of the new Hillary portrayed her as the silent and adoring spouse gazing approvingly at her candidate husband or hanging out at a Bingo game with Tipper Gore. In assessing the public's response to the makeover, Mitchell declared: "The crowds seem to like the new Hillary." The evidence of approval was visualized with a sign that read, "Hillary is a babe." Yet, in suggesting an alleged forgery in terms of Hillary Clinton's new look, Mitchell compared the old to the new: "To others, the old image persists"—a statement fortified by a female Iowa voter who called Clinton "a liberal career woman, not a homemaker like Tipper."[71]

After Bill Clinton's victory in November 1992, the coverage of the presidential transition period underlined the stark differences between the more liberal, progressive Clinton of the Democratic primary versus the more traditional Clinton of the general election. In a retrospective of the campaign, CBS's Mark Phillips posited that Clinton's controversial presence in the campaign ultimately led to major changes in her "role, comments, and even her look." Phillips issued the following observation as video was featured of Clinton writing on the blackboard and then holding her husband's umbrella as he gave a speech in the rain: "There she was this week in a far more traditional posture, holding her husband's umbrella."[72] In these images, Clinton was now positioned quietly behind her husband in a more supportive spousal role rather than serving as an outspoken and out front political partner. Lynn Sherr of ABC also reinforced the changing image of Hillary Clinton in November 1992, using her reduced level of talk and public visibility as markers of the transformed Hillary: "She softened her image and proved she too could gaze adoringly at her husband."[73] Clinton's campaign makeover was thus framed by images of tradition often expressed through a rhetoric of softness and warmth; images of feminism, conversely, were more routinely captured through a rhetoric of hardness and iciness.

LANGUAGE OF TRADITION/LANGUAGE OF PROGRESS

When taking an aerial snapshot of the 1992 campaign coverage, Hillary Clinton's high levels of talk/visibility were equated with anomalous behavior atypical for a candidate's wife; her low levels of talk/visibility, in contrast, represented traditional feminine behavior more equated with authentic womanhood. The subtle juxtaposition of a political wife who was hard and cold versus a woman who was soft and warm distinguished most vividly the linguistically preferred cultural archetype. As Robin Tolmach Lakoff contends, culture represents the "construction of shared meaning"; those who control the language possess the "ability and the right to make meaning for everyone."[74] This coverage says much about the gendered nation and women's political authenticity from the last decade of the twentieth century and beyond.

Both the frames of progress and tradition though were imbued with negative connotations in their authentication of Clinton and Bush. The negative images of progress were visible in the depictions of Hillary Clinton as "professional, outspoken, some say threatening." This threat was most starkly symbolized by those who characterized Clinton as "hell in a headband," referring to her tendency to wear headbands during the primary period. Contrastingly, Barbara Bush, as the embodiment of authentic womanhood, was often portrayed as emerging "from an earlier school" of "political spouses" because of her "grandmotherly" or "motherly" style, albeit one with the occasional "acid-laced comment."[75] The unflattering juxtapositions demonstrated most vividly the lack of attractive options for political spouses in 1992; the wives were either portrayed as too politically intrusive and out of bounds ("Lady Macbeth") or too politically irrelevant and outmoded ("June Cleaver").[76]

The assignment of women to one category or the other (progressive or traditional) served an important authenticating function. Any attempt to conjoin tradition/progress or to move seamlessly across these categories disturbed the discrete juxtapositions that news frames helped affirm. As the coverage of Clinton showed, women are often judged as inauthentic for behavior that appears to cut across the entrenched binary. The *words* and *visual images* about gendered politics continued to reify sexist stereotypes even as the coverage also celebrated the Year of the Woman and women's political progress. The frames typically naturalized images that bind, privileging simplicity over complexity and clarity over abstraction.[77]

Just how enduring were the baseline news frames of Hillary Clinton from 1992? One way to evidence the staying power of these frames is to turn to the coverage of Hillary Clinton during the 1996 presidential campaign. After four years as first lady, how would the frames evolve now that Clinton represented the role of the incumbent's spouse and that of the sitting first lady? In 1996, Clinton would also face a candidate's wife in Elizabeth Dole whose career path of political achievement topped that of her own; Dole had already served as both secretary of transportation and secretary of labor under the Reagan and Bush administrations, respectively, in addition to running the Red Cross by the time she took on the role of presidential candidate's spouse.

Hillary Clinton's Baseline Frames—Four Years Later

For the news media, contrasting Hillary Clinton and Elizabeth Dole occupied more airtime than the comparison between Clinton and Bush in 1992. Both Clinton and Dole represented successful career women in their own right—a mark of distinction for the 1996 presidential campaign. Consequently, frames that featured the bifurcation of tradition and progress seemed more outmoded and inadequate by 1996. Even as tenets of the "cat fight theme" remained, the news organizations would be forced to reconstitute notions of tradition/progress in more unconventional ways. In a previous study with David S. Kaufer and Beata Beigman Klebanov, we demonstrate how the news media were compelled to keep up with the changing roles of Hillary Clinton. Clinton's unprecedented actions helped disrupt the news media's stereotypical framing of her.[78] These conclusions were dependent on Judith Butler's theory of "gender performativity," which posits "that materialization is never quite complete," with bodies seldom complying completely "with the norms by which their materialization is impelled." The actual political performances of women allow for hard-won "rematerialization" over the passage of time.[79] The actions of women like Clinton thus can help promote more progressive coverage in the press even as the frames of tradition resist such progress.

Language most aptly displays the stereotypical and can evidence the struggles of language users to keep up with women's actions in real-time political practice. Susan Gal shows how political practice and the language used to define it can restructure commonplace binaries through a process of "recalibration." Gal demonstrates such linguistic fluidity through the public-private divide as private resonances can open up in discourse (both verbal and visual) about the public, and public resonances can suddenly appear in discourse marked as private.[80] Bill and Hillary Clinton's public event can be recalibrated (or reframed) as a private moment, for example, as the couple whisper into one another's ears even as they stand before television cameras. Conversely, the Clintons' privacy can be easily invaded by the television camera or open microphones, turning an intimate backstage exchange into a public moment broadcasted across the public airwaves.

Within the 1996 coverage, the presence of two progressive and successful career women could seemingly make the stereotype of the traditional political spouse more obsolete. While both Clinton and Dole were portrayed as progressive career women by the U.S. news media, a space of the traditional nevertheless opened up within these news themes of progress for Elizabeth Dole in particular. Such recalibrations allowed for changing themes that were nevertheless slowed by the pull of tradition. As John Fiske argues, "meanings within the text are structured by the differential distribution of textual power . . . [and] exist in relations of subordination or opposition to the dominant meanings proposed by the text."[81] Unquestionably, the 1996 coverage of Hillary Clinton and Elizabeth Dole showed a greater level of acceptance of the candidate spouse as career woman and political partner. Yet, the coverage of Clinton in particular reified some of the same negative frames associated with feminism's perceived causticity, contributing to the corresponding need to discipline the feminist. The coverage ultimately revealed the lack of plasticity associated with Clinton's feminist representations. As Michelle M. Lazar contends, "[h]egemonic structures," while "fragile," can also be quite "resilient."[82] Any perceived deviation from feminist commitments, of course, would once again raise questions about Clinton's authenticity.

RECALIBRATING PROGRESSIVE POLITICAL WOMEN

In 1996, one theme that played across news organizations was the idea of presidential wives as "running mates"—a title typically reserved for the vice presidential nominees. This theme reinforced the idea of powerful candidate wives advancing their husbands' presidential campaigns. As previously shown, running mate references were made of Clinton in 1992. But by 1996, the "running mate" theme had become an even more popular expression, especially for Elizabeth Dole especially.[83] Drawing on this theme, Paula Zahn of CBS News alleged on August 1, 1996, that when they mentioned "Bob Dole's running mate . . . we mean the mate he's run with since 1975 and who, if Dole is elected in November, would be the new first lady."[84] Relying on similar symbolism, Chris Bury of ABC's *Nightline* indicated in October 1996 that "Bob Dole's other running mate will make eight campaign stops in six media markets."[85] Lisa Myers of NBC also argued that Dole appeared "as a third candidate" on October 21, 1996, elevating Dole's status from that of running mate to presidential candidate. As Myers explained, Dole functioned as an advisor to her husband on "issues" related "to debate strategy," necessitating her own staff of more than forty people.[86] In February 1996, Bob Schieffer of *CBS Evening News* offered a more generalizing statement reflecting the seemingly changing times for political spouses: "In the politics of the '90s, the candidates' wives are finding themselves in the spotlight."[87] These frames typically omitted the more evaluative connotations linked to Clinton's outspoken and out front campaign role in 1992, illustrating one way in which a more empowered political wife appeared less incendiary by 1996.

In certain respects, the contributions that the political wives brought to the campaign were discussed in more celebratory fashion as the election neared in the fall of 1996. Linda Douglass of CBS News observed in October that "this year voters are flocking to see the candidates' wives—each powerful, politically skillful."[88] Lisa Myers also observed that "never before have we seen two political partners with such star power."[89] NBC's Tom Brokaw punctuated the precedent-setting dimensions of the 1996 campaign given that "two of the most fascinating people of this campaign are not in fact going to win or lose office. Elizabeth Dole or Hillary Clinton. Two of the strongest candidate wives ever."[90] A similar theme was invoked by Bernard Shaw of CNN when he opened up an hour-long broadcast comparing the two women with the following introduction: "They are both highly educated. Both have high-powered resumes; both are smart and savvy. Hillary Rodham Clinton and Elizabeth Hanford Dole—two women with very much in common."[91]

While accentuating both women's high-profile careers, the news media in effect seemed prepared to put to rest the more traditional model of the first lady whose career evolved around being a supportive political spouse. CNN's titling of its October 13, 1996, *Democracy in America* special captured the presumed obsoleteness of the conventional first lady role while also resurrecting a baseline frame from 1992: "They Don't Bake Cookies." Further reflecting the changes in the spousal role, Bernard Shaw of the same CNN broadcast noted that "historians tell us first ladies have always wielded power behind the closed doors of the White House. But Hillary Clinton blew those doors open."[92] The precedent-setting dimensions of the 1996 campaign were further substantiated by Bill Schneider of CNN on November 3, 1995, when he offered the following summary about Clinton and Dole: "Presidential politics is finally catching up with reality. The reality is, most married women work these days. Hillary Rodham Clinton broke one barrier when she became the first president's wife with her own professional career. Now, another barrier may be broken, and by a Republican this time." Had Bob Dole been elected president, Elizabeth Dole had pledged to pursue what no other first lady ever dared, Schneider claimed, which was to "work full-time outside of the White House"—returning to her post as head of the American Red Cross.[93]

The news media by 1996 thus appeared willing to open the door a bit wider in praising the career accomplishments of the political wives; even Hillary Clinton's political contributions were extolled by certain journalists. Focusing on Clinton's speech before the Democratic National Convention in August 1996, Bob Schieffer of CBS News drew on the spatial exposure themes (e.g., front and center) from 1992. Yet, he would do so with a less disapproving tone than many journalists from four years earlier: "She's going to be front and center. Tonight will be Hillary Clinton's night . . . What is also clear . . . is that campaign strategists have decided that, controversial or not, Hillary Clinton is one of their best assets. Politics is politics. If they did not believe that, she would not be front and center tonight."[94] The day following her speech, ABC's Jim Wooten introduced the reactions of delegates to Clinton's primetime convention speech: "And the delegates were still celebrating today," Wooten observed, as a young girl pronounced that "Hillary's speech was definitely a 10. It was awesome." An adult woman then delighted, "It was very exciting. Very energizing."[95] Of Clinton's public performances during the week of the convention, Linda Douglass of CBS summarized the reactions more descriptively, eliding the condemnatory tone of 1992. Even though "[t]here had been talk that she would soften her image" during the convention, Douglass contended, "instead the first lady let it rip in a rousing feminist speech to women celebrating their right to vote" in the days leading up to her primetime speech.[96] Most interestingly, references to Clinton's "feminist speech" did not produce the scolding and threatening judgments that most vividly marked the 1992 campaign coverage.

Of course, the press also pointed out that the empowering role of political wives would come at a political cost. These statements recognized the unfair expectations placed on candidate's wives, particularly Hillary Clinton. In a separate CBS News broadcast from February 17, 1996, Douglass normalized the idea of a political partnership—a residual frame from 1992: "Hillary Rodham Clinton has discovered the age of chivalry toward first ladies is over. Equal partners with their husbands, they are facing equal scrutiny." Echoing a similar theme at the end of the same broadcast, Douglass also relied on the same partnership frame from 1992: "The Clintons promised the country two for the price of one," yet "the tough new job of first lady may be more than anyone bargained for."[97] From October 18, 1996, Jeff Greenfield of ABC's *Nightline* provided an expanded sense of sacrifice that women like Clinton made for their political husbands:

> When Hillary Rodham was president of her class at Wellesley, she gave a speech that was featured in *Life* magazine, a commencement speech, the first student ever invited to do that at that college. A lot of people thought they were looking, if not at a future president, at least at a future senator, and I think to have invested all this time and effort in her husband's career, with all of those sacrifices and frustrations, to now find herself kind of looked at by some in that campaign as, "Well, we've got a little problem here, but go out among the faithful," you're dead right, that's got to be really frustrating for her.[98]

These news constructs exuded a more lamenting tone that successful career women were stymied in their role as political partners. Ted Koppel reinforced such sentiments when he began his *Nightline* broadcast with the following qualification in October 1996: "Before we begin congratulating ourselves on how much progress has been made in leveling the playing field for women in this country, consider the current presidential campaign." Noting that "the wives of the two major candidates might, arguably, make stronger presidents than the men they're married to," the broadcaster demonstrated that both women were pressed into "what the campaigns believe we want them to be," which involved singing with children (Dole and Clinton), riding motorcycles with Jay Leno (Dole), and going to Disney World (Clinton).[99] As two strong career women consequently competed to become the next first lady, news organizations did ponder the seemingly unfair restrictions binding strong political women. This change in tone showed how the news media were attempting to keep pace with the progressive changes in women's political involvement. The coverage accordingly illustrated the impact of the historical context on public texts and the importance of women's lived reality on cultural representations.[100]

PRESERVING THE TRADITIONAL IN FRAMES
OF PROGRESSIVE POLITICAL WOMEN

Yet, within such rhetorics of women's political progress remained an allegiance to the traditional, revealing the recalibration processes at work in the progress-tradition relationship. As Clare Walsh argues, "the gendered nature of the public-private dichotomy has been reproduced *within* the public sphere."[101]

In a head-to-head competition between Dole and Clinton, Dole typically prevailed in garnering more positive news coverage. She prevailed because of her perceived softer and more graceful style—a personal grace Clinton seemingly lacked. Elsa Walsh, a *New Yorker* author speaking on ABC's *Nightline* in April 1996, argued that "we see Elizabeth Dole as being the much softer person than Hillary Clinton. Part of that is Hillary's style." Walsh concluded that "Elizabeth Dole, in contrast . . . doesn't have the same sort of . . . arrogant tone that Hillary tends to take on, or self-righteous tone."[102]

These themes were expressed by linguistic frames that coupled images of empowerment with softer, flowery symbolism steeped in gender stereotypes. Dole's press persona as a "steel magnolia" most vividly expressed this sentiment.[103] Dole's steeled strength—the epitome of empowerment and progress— was thus tempered with a symbol of southern beauty and elegance, evidencing a blossoming of the traditional within the framing of Dole's political achievements. And CNN's Bernard Shaw, in emphasizing Dole's important career accomplishments, did so in competitive fashion with Clinton, utilizing a feminine language that seemingly helped mollify Dole's feminist advancements: "Americans have a hard time accepting power in the hands of a first lady. But when it comes to powerful women in Washington, Elizabeth Dole is high-heels above the rest. She was breaking glass ceilings before Hillary Clinton even bumped her head on them."[104] Although acknowledging both women's political achievements (e.g., breaking glass ceilings), the construct made Dole's femininity a visible feature within her gender progress; a feminine language of tradition, through word pictures of high heels, thus re-emerged in the recalibrated rhetoric of Dole's impressive career accomplishments.

Lisa Myers's stories from *NBC Nightly News* on August 15 and August 27, 1996, furthered these traditional resonances in a language of women's political progress, especially for Dole; Clinton conversely continued to suffer from insinuations that her style was too cold and too aggressive. Myers talked about Dole in the following ways: "She is polished. She sugar coats everything . . . So even though she is a powerful woman, she is somebody who manages to . . . hide her formidability in her sweet-talking southern style." Although hinting that this softer style masked the true Elizabeth Dole, Myers ultimately concluded that the sweeter style helped account for Dole's effectiveness because "she is not seen as threatening."[105] Clinton, on the other hand, Myers claimed, was viewed as "more forceful in her expression" and less "sensitive because she is direct." In interviewing a group of women about their perceptions of the candidates' wives, Myers wondered aloud if "some people find" Clinton's style more "threatening." In response, the women concluded, "Yes, very much so." In synthesizing the criticism, Myers explained how Hillary Clinton was portrayed by the group in more mixed terms, as one who was "smart and savvy, aggressive, sometimes insincere." The group contrastingly awarded Dole more uniformly positive attributes: "self-assured, bright, professional . . . classy." Dole's softer style was clearly preferred among the women assembled. As one concluded: "Elizabeth Dole does have . . . more experience, a lot more grace, a lot more style."[106] Rhetorical scholar Karlyn Kohrs Campbell offered a similar explanation, arguing that Clinton, unlike Dole, typically omitted "virtually all of the discursive markers by which women publicly enact femininity." This logic suggested that because Clinton's persona was aligned more with feminism than femininity, she attracted greater animosity.[107] Dole instead appeared more immune to charges of feminism because of her perceived softer style more commonly associated with authentic womanhood.[108] Within Dole's frames of progress emerged a rhetoric of tradition that seemed to blunt Dole's political threat.

Hillary Clinton's baseline frame as a more controversial feminist with an aggressive style made it more difficult for her to break free of such image confinements. Jeff Greenfield of ABC's *Nightline* drew on the memory of the Tammy Wynette and cookies and teas moments to reinforce Clinton's stabilizing image as a feminist from the 1992 campaign. As Greenfield suggested, Clinton appeared as a "symbol to some of hard-edged feminism, with a single offhand remark about why she had practiced law." Immediately following Greenfield's statement, ABC re-aired Hillary's cookies and teas utterance and the Tammy Wynette clip, further conflating these two decontextualized media moments. Greenfield then equated Clinton with the "political equivalent of nitroglycerin," given the ways she was treated by the Clinton campaign, suggesting the aura of danger surrounding Clinton.[109] This coverage reveals that once a woman is framed as a feminist, the possibilities of altering the initial impressions are very difficult in the world of press frames.

The recalibration efforts also evidenced a level of confusion over women who appeared at once as progressive *and* traditional. In October 1996, David Lewis of CNN made the following observation about the confusing and competing images of Clinton and Dole, furthering the notion that simplistic bifurcations of progress and tradition provided a source of clarity and comfort:

> Hillary Clinton is sometimes perceived as a very aggressive, ambitious feminist, while Elizabeth is seen as the more traditional. The irony is, in fact, that Hillary is the one who's been more traditional in her life. She gave up a promising career in Washington to move to Arkansas, she's the one who's had a child, which Elizabeth Dole hasn't. So there's a tremendous irony there.

In introducing this story, Bernard Shaw asserted that "Elizabeth Dole's life has been anything but traditional."[110] In a separate CNN broadcast, David Lewis raised similar questions about the inconsistent images of Dole: "Elizabeth Dole has a very traditional appeal. She combines a personal grace with her professional strength in a way that confuses some, and leaves others wondering if that grace is a just a façade."[111] Bewilderment seemingly arose from the disruption of the linguistic stereotype that graceful women were typically women of tradition and empowered women stereotypically lacked any sense of personal grace.

While the 1996 coverage showed a level of progress that worked against the stereotypical binaries, it also demonstrated the strong pull of traditional stereotypes. News indices drawn from feminism and masculinism reflect what Bernadette Barker-Plummer refers to as the "liberal and masculinist underpinnings of news" at the turn of the twenty-first century.[112] Press confusion can be further enhanced by political performances that move against the grain of tradition. How could Hillary Clinton emerge at once as a feminist and a woman of tradition (mother and trailing political spouse)? How could Elizabeth Dole appear as more traditional stylistically yet live a life without the typical trappings of gender tradition (motherhood)? The confusion over Clinton of course drew on the age-old assumption that feminists hated men and loved women;[113] it stood to reason that the Clinton marriage was viewed in political rather than relational terms given that presumption. The confusion also demonstrates how the traces of the traditional represented a recalibrated feature of progressive frames. Reified stereotypes can clearly inhibit recalibration efforts. Efforts that destabilize such binary thinking can also raise questions about political authenticity.

THE REAL HILLARY CLINTON OF 1996—CAUSTIC OR INAUTHENTIC?

As in 1992, Hillary Clinton was still framed as a threat to her husband's candidacy in 1996, eliciting what some in the press suggested was the need for further disciplinary action by the Clinton campaign. Greenfield's aforementioned reference to Clinton as the "political equivalent of nitroglycerin" framed that danger in very acute terms. Reflecting a linguistic frame from 1992, NBC titled an October 22, 1996, newscast "The Hillary Factor" to underscore the problems that Clinton brought to her husband's re-election campaign.[114] ABC's *Nightline* would revise the linguistic frame and identify this phenomenon as the "Hillary problem," which, according to Ted Koppel, represented Clinton's struggle "to deal with a public image . . . of being too strong, too intelligent, too driven." Because of Clinton's image problems, *Nightline* writers claimed that the Dole campaign was debating how Elizabeth Dole could "be seen as a strong partner but not as Hillary Clinton."[115]

Clinton's threatening attributes were reinforced with the re-emergence of the "lightning rod" metaphor in 1996. In the context of the 1996 Democratic National Convention, Linda Douglass of CBS News argued that Clinton had become a "lightning rod for conservative wrath."[116] Lisa Myers also used the same construct for Clinton during the same time period, noting that such controversy was to blame for women's doubts about her: "Most of these women rooted for Hillary when she became first lady but that was before she became a lightning rod for controversy."[117]

These stalwart images demonstrated once again the authenticating force of a feminist news frame—a frame with tremendous staying power revealed in the persistency of Clinton's baseline frames from the first campaign to the second. Once authenticated, the frame made it more difficult for Clinton to move across the fields of career and motherhood/wife or progress and tradition. As Mary Douglas Vavrus explains, "The more naturalized and hegemonic ideologies are, the more difficult their articulations are to challenge."[118] When Clinton was acknowledged for her outspokenness *and* for her role as wife, it was still in very incendiary terms, as CNN noted her reputation as "the boss's wife from hell."[119]

And as in 1992, any sense of deviation from the image of an outspoken and out-front feminist (symbolized by the Tammy Wynette and cookies and teas frames) tended to produce allegations of Clinton's inauthenticity. ABC's *Nightline* broadcast from April 1996 featured Elsa Walsh's claim that "Hillary Clinton . . . has swung wildly between I'm more like Barbara Bush than unlike her and I'm no Tammy Wynette, 'Stand by your man' . . . people don't know who she is."[120] Ted Koppel of *Nightline* put the emphasis on her campaign makeover, remarking that "she, too, has reverted to the more traditional role of a 1950s-style first lady, more the helpmate than the professional equal," evidencing how Clinton and even Dole were forced "to masquerade as something they are not."[121] CNN's Kathy Slobogin called Hillary "a national Rorschach test" because "her images" were "as numerous as her hairstyles." To reinforce the changing and thus inauthentic images of Hillary Clinton, CNN re-aired both the *60 Minutes* clip and the cookies and teas stock footage as a reflection of the Hillary Clinton from 1992; yet they also showed Clinton welcoming people to the White House in a more traditional and hostess-like fashion. For CNN, these visual juxtapositions captured her inconsistent images. Author Gene Lyons traced the authenticity issues back to Arkansas when Hillary changed her hair and her clothes: "It was like a complete makeover, as they say in the women's magazines." Slobogin provided a summarizing character judgment of Clinton that emphasized her personality problems: "Put aside political detractors and overzealous reporters, and there may be something about Hillary Clinton herself that prolongs the scrutiny. Her strong sense of mission, of her own rightness, may have blinded her to appearances, made her resistant to challenge, creating an impression of someone who is guarded and evasive."[122] As Clinton sought to retreat from high levels of public visibility, she was consequently condemned for her changing image, resulting in questions over the veracity of her character.

The authenticity questions persisted as the 1996 campaign came to a close in October 1996; disciplinary frames accompanied these character questions. As Election Day neared, NBC News offered a retrospective of Hillary Clinton, juxtaposing the Hillary of 1996 with that of 1992. Gwen Ifill disclosed: "We asked for an interview. No dice. A far cry from 1992 when Bill Clinton was convinced his high-powered lawyer wife could only help." NBC then aired the cookies and teas statement as Ifill's skepticism shone through: "Now she only talks about baked goods when she's taking a tour" of bakeries and food factories. Tom Brokaw reinforced the image transformations in the same story, commenting: "This is a different Hillary Clinton than the one we saw in the 1992 campaign . . . This time she sticks closely to her very carefully prepared script." Reinforcing the disciplining of Hillary Clinton through her diminished role in the 1996 campaign, David Maraniss—Bill Clinton biographer—argued: "If she can raise money and keep quiet and not stir up too much controversy, I wouldn't call her a liability." Conflating her changed image with the redisciplining of Clinton in 1996, Ifill concluded: "This election year," Clinton was "on view as the loyal wife and mother, almost entirely under political wraps, out of reach of controversy and Republican attacks."[123]

Once Clinton's image was viewed in more traditional terms, her liability to her husband's campaign seemed to dissipate in the news narratives from both 1992 and 1996. Scholar John Sloop offers an explanation for such rhetorical occurrences, maintaining that "cultural expectations and mechanisms continue to discipline each of us to practice 'proper' gender behaviors."[124] Yet, Hillary Clinton was presented with a difficult dilemma: if she remained outspoken and out front, she faced a rhetorical disciplining; if she fulfilled the expectations of authentic womanhood, she faced a rhetorical inquisition into her authenticity.

Conclusion

David S. Kaufer and Brian S. Butler contend that "if writers do not add additional individuating texture to . . . stereotype[s]," audiences "will never move past the type to an individual."[125] Journalists seem content, as political actors themselves influenced by the ideological structures, to live in a world of predictability that frames provide; the accumulative effect of image reifications across news organizations and across time offers a staying power and stubborn reaffirmation of the political image.

Consequently, the authenticated Hillary Clinton came to personify the rigid tenets of feminism not only in 1992 but also in 1996 and 2008—tenets that suggested Clinton violated traditional notions of authentic womanhood. This coverage revealed a gendered nation much less hospitable to women aligned with feminism than to those reflecting at least some of the tenets of authentic womanhood. Through a journalistic recalibration of the progress-tradition divide, Elizabeth Dole faced less criticism for her progressive past because of her perceived personal style that personified a woman of tradition and grace. The coverage of Clinton in particular seemed more resistant to similar recalibration efforts. Instead, the coverage evinced a lingering expectation that most women would exude the qualities of progress *or* tradition. To embody an image that displayed both furthered a sense of political confusion, suggesting the ideological force of role distinctions, behavioral expectations, and character consistencies prescribed in the rhetoric of gendered nationalism. Campaign makeover frames in particular raised the likelihood of Clinton being labeled as a political imposter, attempting to mask her true self in order to advance her husband and herself politically. As Claude S. Fischer suggests, "The authentic self presents, in principle, one consistent, honest personality to the world."[126] Trying to appear progressive *and* traditional seemingly violated this one personality principle.

The allegation that Clinton was trying to change her feminist image also helped explain why assumptions about her lack of authenticity abounded during the 2008 presidential campaign. As shown in the beginning of this chapter, some charged that Clinton had swung too far in a different direction, leaving behind her authenticating mantle of feminism in favor of political masculinity. Clinton's true political image thus was reduced to her feminism, making it hard for her to appear genuine if she departed at all from the stereotypical images of that routinely debased depiction. The coupling of political wife with feminism made her appear from the start as a political aberration given the long-held moniker that feminists hate men and love women, implicitly, at least, conflating feminism and lesbianism. The entrenched stereotypes were that most political wives served as supportive helpmates while most feminists stereotypically shunned the trappings of heterosexual matrimony. The latter construct in particular helped reify the Clinton marriage as a *political* partnership.

As this chapter has shown, the baseline frames that first emerged in the national press coverage of Clinton in 1992 continued to frame her political actions in the presidential campaigns of 1996 and 2008. They included the stock frames of Tammy Wynette and cookies and teas, as well as residual and linguistic frames that fell under the auspices of the "Hillary Factor" and her persona as a radical feminist. In speaking more historically about public assumptions of character, Scott E. Casper contends that "one's performance or actions on the public stage *revealed* one's character (true self), and at the same time they *fixed* one's character (reputation) in others' eyes."[127] The U.S. news media, predictably, played an important role in helping to fix Clinton's political image through their news practices.

As Hillary Clinton prepared to enter the East Wing of the White House after the 1992 presidential election, Lynn Sherr of *ABC World News Tonight* asked the following question: "is she now free to be Hillary Clinton, the first first lady who's had her own career, or must she fit into a more traditional role?"[128] The following chapter sheds light on this all-important question of political authenticity as Clinton moved into the legislative spaces of the nation's health care debate and the judicial spaces as a defendant accused of illegal and unethical wrongdoing.

CHAPTER 2

Hillary Clinton as Legislative Activist and Legal Defendant

Health Care Reform and the Whitewater
Investigations—1993–1995

From the moment that Hillary Clinton entered the 2008 presidential campaign, her candidacy was framed by the memory of her involvement in the Clinton administration's health care reform efforts from 1993 to 1995. With the presidential campaign well underway in early 2007, journalists often reminded the viewing public of Clinton's most memorable political failure. Andrea Mitchell of *NBC Nightly News* dubbed this policy issue as one of Hillary Clinton's "biggest mistakes."[1] Jim Axelrod of *CBS Evening News* referred to it as Clinton's "spectacular political failure,"[2] and Richard Wright of ABC's *Good Morning America* similarly called health care Clinton's "first spectacular failure" as she took on the "signature issue of her husband's campaign."[3]

Many blamed Clinton's failed health care efforts on Hillary Clinton's comportment during the hotly contested debate. In separate broadcasts during the fall of 2007, ABC correspondents characterized Hillary Clinton's leadership as "rigid" (Timothy Johnson), "confrontational" (George Stephanopoulos), and "uncompromising" (David Wright).[4] Axelrod of CBS also called her approach similarly "unyielding,"[5] and Wright of ABC said she pursued the initiative with "hammer and tongs."[6] These negative attributes were all ideologically consonant with the framing of Clinton's feminism from 1992. Most troublesome, many claimed, was Clinton's lack of openness. In discussing Carl Bernstein's book on Hillary Clinton (*A Woman in Charge*) in June 2007, its author and Sean Hannity of Fox News agreed that the Clintons handled the health care process with "secrecy and subterfuge."[7] A few months later, CBS's Axelrod summarized the legislative process in ways that recalled the memory frames from the early years of the Clinton presidency: "It's been thirteen years since Hillary Clinton's first health care reform effort bombed. It still fuels Clinton's critics, who saw her as the leader of an arrogant, overreaching attempt to implement socialized medicine."[8]

During the 2008 presidential primary season, news outlets reinforced Hillary Clinton's sense of unprecedented power for a first lady during the health care debate, culminating in charges of her abuse of power and reminders of her stylistic mannerisms. Reflecting Clinton's sense of power and political savvy amidst the reform efforts, columnist Joel Mowbray argued on CNBC in May 2007 that "the woman is shrewd, she is smart . . . and she knows how to use power."[9] For others, Clinton's calculating style of leadership raised doubts about her trustworthiness and magnified her authenticity difficulties. As Republican strategist Mike Murphy argued on ABC's *Nightline* on January 22, 2007, "She's tough, she's mean, she's ruthless, you can't trust her. That's the baggage . . . she carries" from the health care debate into the 2008 presidential campaign.[10] And Meredith Vieira of NBC's *Today* show addressed Clinton's perceived lack of cordiality and authenticity in a broadcast from August 2007: "Political opponents have long questioned her warmth and sincerity."[11]

Recollections of Clinton's involvement in health care were also fused with memories of the Whitewater controversy as the two public issues collided in the earliest years of the Clinton presidency; both foreshadowed the political hurdles that Clinton would have to surmount during her 2008 presidential bid. Bernstein argued on Fox News in June 2007 that the "egregious" actions of the Clinton administration's "first two years . . . were attributable to Hillary Clinton" and involved "health care" and "answering the questions or not answering them about Whitewater."[12] Andrea Mitchell of NBC News also entangled the two issues in a retrospective of Hillary Clinton's early years as first lady during a January 22, 2007, report. Because "Americans don't like what they see," Mitchell concluded, Clinton's 2008 campaign staff tried to "erase first impressions." To help recall the Hillary Clinton of 1992, NBC began the broadcast by showing archival clips of Clinton's Tammy Wynette and cookies and teas video as revelatory of Clinton "selling herself as two for the price of one." Next, Mitchell identified two other damaging media memories for a Clinton candidacy—"failing to reform health care . . . and being too secretive about Whitewater." Journalist Chuck Todd subsequently reinforced the negativity of these remembrances in the same NBC broadcast: "Every moment that we remember that's famous is a negative moment for Hillary Clinton."[13]

The coverage from the 2008 presidential contest revealed other media memory frames that were holdovers from the Clintons' first years in the White House. These linguistic residuals framed Clinton's involvement in health care with a rhetoric of violence, particularly from 1993 onward. Cynthia McFadden of ABC's *Nightline* noted in January 2007 that Clinton's decision to feature health care as a signature issue for her presidential campaign was "ironic" given that "health care . . . gave Hillary Clinton such a black eye in the first term of her husband's presidency."[14] McFadden attributed Clinton's decision to front health care in 2008 as a strategy to beat President George W. Bush "to the punch," as he sought to unveil a new health care proposal of his own. Clinton's own framing of her involvement in the debate illustrated the rhetoric of violence that permeated the framing of this public issue. On September 17, 2007, Clinton argued, "I have tangled with this issue before, and I've got scars to show for it."[15] Reflecting the consequences of such a volatile debate, Kate Snow from ABC's *Good Morning America* concluded in 2007 that even Clinton administration staffers viewed Hillary Clinton as "damaged goods" by the end of the health care controversy.[16]

This chapter returns to the recycled and newly produced news frames that emerged from the health care and Whitewater controversies—frames that subsequently influenced the coverage of Clinton during her own political campaigns. In particular, this chapter examines how the news media covered Hillary Clinton as she simultaneously traversed two different political fields of controversy—one centered in the legislative spaces of health care reform and the other in the judicial sphere as a legal defendant in a battle that predated her time in the White House.

In the process, this chapter demonstrates the re-emergence of familiar patterns in the news framing of Hillary Clinton. From the outset of the health care debate, Clinton was given a leadership role in ways that reflected the co-presidency themes of 1992. Correspondingly, many of the baseline frames from the 1992 campaign were still operative between 1993 and 1995, revealing similar patterns in the authentication and inauthentication of Clinton as first lady. Even as Clinton was lauded by some in the press for her ability to take on an important leadership position in her husband's administration, warning bells were rung by the Republican opposition, journalists, and the American public once she stepped into the legislative arena. Eventually, the news media emphasized that Bill Clinton's advisors restricted Hillary's visibility and public power in ways that mirrored the Hillary Clinton "campaign makeover" in 1992. In voicing the concerns of presidential advisors, the press reasoned that Clinton's overexposure and outspokenness threatened her husband's political viability once again. From the campaign to the legislative and legal controversies over health care and Whitewater, condemnation mounted because of charges that Clinton overstepped the boundaries and norms of the gendered nation.

One issue of contention related to questions over Clinton's moral character. As discussed in the introduction, women have historically been expected to serve expediency ends by making politics more ethical. Constructions of Hillary Clinton's leadership style seemingly defied such authentic notions of womanhood as her image became one of corruption linked with secret meetings on health care and lies about Whitewater. The visual images of Clinton in television news broadcasts during the Whitewater controversy in particular helped reinforce a portrait of a malevolently deceptive woman; decontextualized facial images of a smiling Hillary Clinton seemed counterintuitive to the serious ethical and legal charges she faced. The collapsing of two public issues by the news media—health care reform and Whitewater—ultimately suggested that Clinton should not be trusted with such a powerful role in legislative matters—particularly as a president's wife flouting conventions of first lady tradition.

Clinton's alleged abuse of power involving health care and her questionable ethics in Whitewater resulted in the linguistic disciplining of Hillary Clinton. A rhetoric of violence framed the health care debate in particular and contributed to such disciplining efforts, with images of war and death becoming commonplace in the news vernacular. Seemingly unable to withstand the strain of battle, Hillary Clinton was portrayed once again as seeking refuge from the political spotlight and retreating to the shadows of her husband's administration.

In explicating these themes, this chapter first examines the television news coverage of the health care debate followed by an analysis of the Whitewater coverage; it ends with an assessment of the rhetoric of violence that contributed to the redisciplining of Hillary Clinton in ways that eventually reflected a cycle of domestic violence by the time that Clinton stepped into the 2000 U.S. Senate race from New York (chapter 4).

Framing Hillary Clinton's Leadership on Health Care Reform

Only days into his first term in office, Bill Clinton demonstrated that his administration would be different from all the others. He would do so by awarding his wife a leadership role in health care reform. As he expressed on January 25, 1993, "I'm grateful that Hillary has agreed to chair this task force, and not only because it means she'll be sharing some of the heat."[17] The early coverage of the debate emphasized the expansion of the first lady position in the Clinton White House in ways that portended the danger that lay ahead—a danger that

Bill Clinton even jokingly acknowledged in his press conference. The initial critiques of Hillary Clinton's role in health care reform, however, were more tepid compared to the level of enmity that eventually surfaced as the debate unfolded, ending with the failure of the Clinton reform efforts by 1995. The evolving news coverage of the health care dispute predictably resulted in the disciplining of Hillary Clinton for her political and gender transgressions as the nation's first lady. Although evidence of Clinton's linguistic disciplining was visible in the 1992 news frames, the health care debate showed a growing level of vitriol over an empowered first lady, culminating in a rhetoric of violence that reflected the historical and ideological underpinnings of U.S. nationalism.

The framing of politics with a rhetoric of violence is certainly not a new phenomenon. Some trace the conflation of U.S. war and politics to the Jackson era when the passion of party politics became increasingly viewed through the prism of war and violence. As Perry M. Goldman explains, "Politicians" from the era of "[Andrew] Jackson perceived . . . that politics was war carried on by other means."[18] Certainly, the partisan clashes in the antebellum period leading to the nation's only civil war furthered the fusion of party politics and war imagery.[19] These imagery clusters included linguistic references to the opposing party as an enemy combatant. Murray Edelman contends that depicting the opposition as the enemy centers attention on the "character of the opponent," which often leads to the branding of adversaries as "evil, immoral, warped, or pathological." According to this logic, the "threat" that enemies pose persists regardless of the actions taken or the battle's outcome; the enemy's activities, public and private, are perceived as dangerous to the moral and political stability of the nation.[20] The conflation of a language of politics with a language of war makes it seem nearly unimaginable to talk about politics in any other way. Once naturalized, Edelman contends, these rhetorical depictions (politics as war) help produce "the political 'realities' people experience."[21] One consequence is that this divisive rhetoric makes political compromise seem nearly impossible; domestic "enemies" often struggle as much as wartime foes to broker resolutions and compromises during policy debates. Predictably, war rhetoric escalates, culminating in a rhetoric of violence that serves hegemonic and disciplinary ends.[22]

MAKING SENSE OF A FIRST LADY AS A LEGISLATIVE TASK FORCE LEADER

From the outset, the news media interpreted Bill Clinton's decision to put his wife in charge of a health care task force as proof of the Clinton co-presidency. *CBS Evening News* reporter Bill Plante referenced the co-presidency baseline frame in a January 25, 1993, broadcast entitled "The Hillary Factor." According to Plante, "Hillary Clinton began generating heat early in the campaign. 'Vote for him,' she said, 'and you get both of us.' When that didn't go over well, her role as advisor was played down." The residual and decontextualized nature of the co-presidency theme was most exemplified by the fact that Bill Clinton rather than Hillary Clinton made the original utterance; by 1993, CBS was attributing the idea of a co-presidency to Hillary instead of Bill Clinton. The theme of controversy that permeated this announcement was reinforced by CBS as former labor secretary Lynn Martin pinpointed what she saw as the biggest problem associated with Clinton's leadership on health care: "It's hard to fire your wife. It's also hard . . . for White House staff to ever tell a president he's wrong . . . The only harder thing might be telling the president's spouse that she's wrong."[23]

The depictions of health care revolved around questions of spatial politics in the nation-state. Hillary Clinton was framed as putting herself and the office of the first lady squarely in the contentious spaces of political action—a pattern resembling her intrusion into the campaign spaces of 1992. NBC's Jim Miklaszewski observed in January 1993 that "Hillary Clinton sat front and center because the president put her in charge." To help visualize her centrality to the reform efforts, NBC aired video of Clinton surrounded by a group of male cabinet officials and administrative staffers.[24] The novelty of such empowerment was further pinpointed as the press referenced Hillary Clinton's creation of two offices for herself—one spatially located in the East Wing (the space of first lady tradition and authentic womanhood) and another located in the West Wing (the space of the presidency and authentic manhood and the nerve center of political action). Bill Plante of CBS News accentuated the shifting of the first lady role from social to political power in a January 25, 1993, broadcast: "Traditionally, first ladies preside over an office in the East Wing of the White House, which oversees social events . . . But Hillary Clinton has an office in the West Wing, where the president and power are, and that's a first."[25] This unprecedented move, Jim Wooten of ABC News argued, reified Clinton's defiance of first lady tradition—invoking another 1992 baseline frame: "But Hillary Rodham Clinton is anything but traditional. She's the first first lady with two official offices—the usual one in the East Wing where parties are planned, and one in the West Wing where policy is made." In discerning parties from politics, ABC gendered the offices through the colors featured for their verbal captions—pink for East Wing and blue for West Wing. These color choices visually marked policy making as a male preserve and party-planning as a female tradition.[26] Multiple bifurcations surfaced in ABC's storyline: East Wing/West Wing, social/political, and feminine/masculine.

In subsequent broadcasts, NBC reinforced the theme that Hillary Clinton was reshaping the spaces of the White House and breaking from tradition to do so. Tom Brokaw characterized Clinton's unprecedented actions in the following way in February 1993: "It's no secret . . . that Hillary Clinton has unprecedented power for a first lady, more than just the last word with the president at night, first word in the morning." This depiction relied on the stereotyped image of first lady power as confined to the presidential bedroom where the president's wife enjoyed the power of "pillow talk."[27] Because Hillary's power moved out of the bedroom and into the political boardroom, Brokaw contended, "She's rewriting the role, maybe forever."[28] In his editorial commentary for NBC News during the same February newscast, John Chancellor suggested the need to even reconceptualize the title of the position: "First lady doesn't fully describe the position that Hillary Rodham Clinton holds in the White House. First mate may be more accurate, or . . . executive officer. She interviews nominees for the cabinet. She lobbies on Capitol Hill. She runs the giant task force on health reform."[29] A renovation of the first lady post led *Nightline* guest Ellen Goodman to dub Hillary Clinton as the "the world's most visible independent wife," conflating images of progress (independence) and tradition (wife).[30]

Once she assumed this new role as an independent wife, the press struggled with how to refer to Hillary Clinton's leadership on health care. Tom Brokaw experimented with several different titles over the early months of the debate. Emphasizing a level of autocratic power shared with no others, Brokaw first called Hillary Clinton the "health czar,"[31] which assumed more masculine connotations. Into the fall of 1993, Brokaw's titles became less incendiary, as he referred to her as the "captain of health care"[32] and also the "president's architect of health care reform."[33] ABC reporter Jackie Judd likewise referred to Clinton as "architect of the administration's health care plan."[34] None of these titles, however, seemed to stick.

Over time, the press worked hard to pinpoint the functions that Hillary Clinton would perform in a Clinton White House, with the Clinton administration directing these definitional efforts early on. The concept of "advisor" caught on because the White House used that term. ABC News aired a statement by George Stephanopoulos, then White House communications director, explaining that Hillary would "serve as a close advisor to the president." During Stephanopoulos's statement, ABC visualized the advisory role through a generic image bite of Hillary Clinton whispering in her husband's ear. During the entire exchange, Bill Clinton sat in a chair as Hillary Clinton stood over him yet slightly behind and to his side.[35] Bill Clinton was never shown responding to his wife verbally but instead listened to her with his head turned slightly toward her. Although this video was initially shot during the presidential transition period as Bill Clinton made initial cabinet selections, it offered a telling visualization of Hillary Clinton's public and private role as advisor—an image that would reappear over the next months of the health care controversy. The underlying message was that Hillary assumed control over this private exchange staged within this public setting. She was portrayed as front and center in such political spaces as she talked privately to the president in a very public moment. He listened until she ended the conversation and exited the room. This advisory role assumed a level of insider status and power—the kind of access that allowed the first lady to offer advice to the president as he made important policy decisions.

For other news organizations, the concept of policy "advocate" was a more apt term for Clinton's White House role because of the first lady's more activist tendencies. Tom Brokaw compared Bill Clinton to John F. Kennedy and Hillary Clinton to Martin Luther King Jr., as he set up an insider/outsider conception of Bill and Hillary's power dynamic: "Today, Bill Clinton is cast in the JFK image—the politician's politician, while Hillary, like Dr. King, has worked outside the system—an advocate for the forgotten." Brokaw grounded his impressions in Hillary Clinton's work in Arkansas as that state's first lady. Of her former position, Brokaw noted that "many in Arkansas think she is the better advocate of the two." Simultaneously, NBC aired clips of Clinton taking on one of her husband's gubernatorial opponents, Tom McRae, directing her comments to the cameras that captured this confrontational moment: "Tom . . . it's ironic to me that before you were a candidate, many of the reports you issued not only praised the governor on his environmental record but his education record and his economic record."[36] This historical footage showed Hillary Clinton as an outspoken advocate on behalf of her husband's gubernatorial administration, allowing Bill Clinton to govern while Hillary Clinton derided the opposition publicly.

ABC furthered the analogy between the Clintons and the Kennedys, with Hillary's advisory role compared to Robert Kennedy's service in his brother's administration. For ABC's Jim Wooten, the most important difference between the Kennedys and the Clintons was that "for this president, it's a woman's voice."[37] With gender functioning as an important differentiation for Clinton's involvement in legislative battles, the press questioned whether or not she could truly juggle these competing roles as presidential wife and task force leader. Once again, the press struggled to comprehend a woman who might perform more traditional first lady duties while also serving a clear political role in her husband's administration.

The administration seemed prepared for the likely backlash that would follow Hillary Clinton's more integrated performance of the first lady role. White

House staffers insisted that she could make multiple contributions to the administration—social *and* political. A number of pro-Clinton supporters were interviewed by the press, suggesting very unambiguously that Hillary Clinton was up to the task because of her credibility and experience. Ruth Harkin—spouse of Senator Tom Harkin (D-IA)—argued on *CBS Evening News* in January 1993 that Hillary Clinton "is a significant and . . . trusted advisor to . . . her husband and always has been. And so I think it's just a natural progression that she would be doing this." To further Clinton's ethos, the White House, according to Bill Plante of CBS, put out twenty-one pages of newspaper articles from when she oversaw the 1983 Commission on School Standards in Arkansas, "as if to prove that the first lady is qualified for the job."[38] To reinforce such a view, former Governor Bill Clinton's chief of staff, Betsy Wright, offered the following testimony to Garrick Utley of NBC News in January 1993:

> Hillary Clinton is the best sounding board, devil's advocate, and advisor that any of his professional staff or he will have. I would have given my right eye teeth to have had . . . her down the hall in an office when he was governor. She is going to have a great deal of influence because she is so smart and so valued and the American people should be thrilled to death that she is there.[39]

Hillary Clinton's staff was also quick to emphasize that she could traverse the divide between the East and West Wing, promoting an image of Clinton as a multifaceted multitasker. Clinton's social secretary, Ann Flock, contended: "I think she'll be very involved in the dinners. It's something that she enjoys doing . . . it's just one of the many facets of what she does."[40]

Even members of Congress seemed amenable, at least early on, to Hillary Clinton's empowered role in health care reform. In talking to reporters inside the Capitol, Richard Gephardt (majority leader—D-MO) commented approvingly in February 1993: "She's very effective and very believable on this subject. She knows it, she's dealt with it, she cares about it, and the members are very relaxed and enthusiastic about her participation in this."[41] In a subsequent gathering with U.S. senators later that spring, Republican Thad Cochran of Mississippi even seemed upbeat about an ability to reach a compromise with Hillary Clinton as head of the health care task force: "We ought to be able to achieve a result . . . that the American people will applaud by the end of the year."[42]

Despite the insistence that Clinton could successfully integrate the political and social, some journalists raised questions about this dual role; the linguistic tendencies to bifurcate the traditional and the progressive would persist in the early months of 1993. Drawing on a stock frame from 1992 and 1996, Jamie Gangel of *NBC Nightly News* wondered aloud whether the traditional and the progressive could indeed be integrated—a feat that preoccupied the attention of the press during the 1992 campaign: "Can she bring home the bacon . . . and still serve tea and cookies?"[43] NBC's Tom Brokaw also noted in the fall of 1993 that Hillary Clinton served as "first lady and captain of the president's effort to get health care reform through Congress." Emphasizing the uneasy mix of these two roles, Brokaw observed that "those two titles commanded a great deal of attention and a little tension."[44] Most visibly demonstrating the divide between the East Wing and the West Wing, between the social and the political, and between traditional and progressive, Linda Douglass of *CBS Evening News* raised the following question on February 4, 1993: "But does the country want its first lady to be in charge of policy? The White House clearly was unsure. So far there have been conflicting signals about which Hillary Clinton will be shown to the country—the sharp politician or the conventional first lady."[45]

Attempting to merge the traditional and the progressive once again raised questions about Clinton's authenticity and veracity. In 1992, the debate was over whether Clinton could perform the role of a traditional wife *and* outspoken campaign surrogate given the bifurcation of such positions. In 1993, the tension played out over whether Hillary Clinton would be a traditional first lady who reified the ideologies of authentic womanhood *or* an activist first lady who reconceptualized the first lady role by speaking out in the halls of Congress.

Attempting to fuse the progressive and the traditional once again not only challenged Clinton's genuineness but also foreshadowed the danger that loomed over her defiance of tradition. *Nightline*'s Bury linguistically framed the attempt to serve as a policy advocate and a first lady hostess as a "high-wire act" in his story on the "international curiosity" of Hillary Clinton as first lady, stressing the danger involved in seeking to couple both roles.[46] NBC's Jamie Gangel stressed the "high risk" of "Hillary's high profile" in February 1993. "If she fails," Gangel concluded, "there will be no one else to blame."[47] In a separate NBC commentary from 1993, John Chancellor referred to Hillary Clinton's leadership on health care as "either an act of breathtaking political audacity or a very dangerous political move." The breathtaking audacity became even more pronounced given Clinton's unprecedented role in what Chancellor called the "health care mess," which he defined as the "meanest monster in town."[48] These dangerous political maneuvers necessitated, the news media implied, acts of surveillance to capture any Hillary Clinton misstep in her leadership role on health care.

THE SURVEILLANCE OF HILLARY CLINTON AS HEALTH CARE TASK FORCE LEADER

In order to capture this dangerous "high-wire act" in real time, members of the press implied that that they were going to establish round-the-clock surveillance of Hillary Clinton and her never-before-attempted political maneuvers. CBS referred to their coverage as "The Clinton Watch" in February 1993, promoting the sense that their news cameras were on the scene, following Hillary Clinton's every move. The intensified coverage was justified because of the public's keen interest, CBS proclaimed: "Across the country, Americans are ... talking about the new first lady."[49] CBS's title for their more in-depth feature stories—"Eye on America"[50]—furthered the aura of surveillance. During the same month, NBC News used the phrase "Clintonwatch" in their day-by-day coverage of the first lady, particularly when covering her first congressional trip as task force leader.[51]

As part of the Clinton watch, NBC's cameras followed Hillary Clinton around for a full day on Capitol Hill. We seldom were able to hear Clinton speak; instead, we gained glimpses of her walking in different spaces of power as shown on numerous monitors in NBC's studio. Like a high-security nerve center keeping watch over spaces of threat, NBC's multiple camera shots and multiple monitors connoted a surveillance stakeout of Clinton's audacious policy acts. Brokaw narrated the Clinton watch: "Hillary Clinton was all over Capitol Hill today, talking about health care reform. First stop, a meeting with House speaker Tom Foley and majority leader Richard Gephardt." NBC then took viewers behind the scenes with Hillary's infiltration of the legislative spaces; we could see her walking the halls of the House of Representatives with Tom Foley (D-WA) and Richard Gephardt (D-MO). This shot was followed by a split screen. On one side, Hillary was delivering a speech; on the other, she sat at a long table with Gephardt as other political leaders looked on. Brokaw then mapped Hillary's trail from the Democratic side of the House to the Republican side: "Next, across the aisle. Minority leader Bob Michel [R-IL] and other Republican leaders." NBC then featured a video clip of Clinton sitting in a chair, flanked by men positioned all around her. She was leaning toward one as he talked and gestured. This picture next moved to the top right of the screen and was accompanied by two smaller video images. These pictures were subsequently frozen in place; the video stopped running so that three still shots filled the screen: (1) Clinton meeting with Representative Foley; (2) Clinton sitting at the luncheon table surrounded by congressional leaders; and (3) Clinton interacting with Republican leaders. Brokaw concluded: "And finally, the Republican task force. The first lady said it was time to face reality about the costs of health care."[52] The visual images that accompanied Brokaw's day-in-the-life of Hillary Clinton showed the organization's ability to track the unprecedented movements of the first lady, filling a watchdog role for the nation.

Moving from the traditionally social spaces of the East Wing to the political spaces of Congress in February 1993 represented, for some, a wide and gendered chasm for Hillary Clinton to cross. Sexualized images of Clinton began to appear in the news coverage once she crossed over from the East to the West Wings. As journalists previously noted during this debate, the spaces of the Capitol were often marked as a male political preserve. ABC made this designation most explicit when talking about the leadership of the House on February 16, 1993. Jim Wooten asserted: "And her visit took her into the usually exclusively male conclaves of the House leadership, Speaker Foley's inner sanctum, and Republican leader Michel's private suite. And although she holds no official office, Mrs. Clinton seemed neither out of place nor ill at ease."[53] Chris Bury of ABC's *Nightline* also contended on March 10, 1993, that Clinton seemingly "crashed the all boys leadership club, lobbied both sides of the aisle." These representations portrayed Clinton as invading the private spaces reserved for "men only" rather than visiting public offices of the leaders conducting the nation's business. Bury also referred to Hillary Clinton's "honeymoon" with the male leaders of Congress—a reference also used by NBC's Jamie Gangel.[54] Such a linguistic frame—whether consciously or unconsciously—sexualized Clinton's private interactions with multiple men, constructing Clinton in more promiscuous ways as she engaged congressional males in their private suites.

Even though first ladies had entered the congressional arena before (see introduction), the press portrayed Clinton's entrance into the male political spaces as uncharted territory—a unbeaten path fraught with difficulties for a first lady. When Clinton visited the U.S. Senate, Linda Douglass of CBS News observed on February 4, 1993, that "it was an unprecedented moment. The president's wife paid a visit to some powerful senators—not a social call but to do a piece of tough political business." The obstacles that Clinton faced were magnified by the issue under consideration. Douglass maintained that "the mission of Hillary Rodham Clinton is one entire governments have failed to complete." Characterizing her immense power, CBS aired shots of Clinton on Capitol Hill interacting with congressional leaders as Douglass contended: "[T]he president made Mrs. Clinton the most officially powerful first lady in history, overseeing six cabinet secretaries on the issue of health. She's charged with solving one of the country's most urgent and complex problems, a job for a political pro."[55]

Taken together, the filming techniques portrayed NBC and CBS as on scene prepared to capture any relevant political moment of this precedent-setting first lady traversing the spaces of male power. According to John Fiske, surveillance helps empower the news media to form judgments about their political observations that are dependent on "the power to speak, the power to know, and the power to see."[56] Michel Foucault likewise links surveillance with disciplinary power, arguing that "hierarchized surveillance . . . leaves no zone of shade and constantly supervises the very individuals who are entrusted with the task of supervising."[57] That surveillance would intensify with the increasing controversy over health care reform efforts.

Problems arose of course when the news media felt hindered in their surveillance efforts. The persistent complaint by many in the press was that Clinton held secret meetings, raising suspicions that she was hiding information from the U.S. public and the press. When NBC's Tom Petit talked about a "news blackout," NBC showed images of the Old Executive Office Building where the secret meetings on health care were taking place in February 1993. This image connoted that even though NBC's cameras were in place, their access was blocked during the meetings.[58] A similar complaint was issued by other news organizations. *CBS Evening News* noted that "no cameras were allowed" when Hillary Clinton held meetings with U.S. governors.[59] Questioning the ethics of a news blackout in March 1993, ABC News argued that the "health care reform plan remains shrouded in secrecy," an actuality that led some in Congress, Brit Hume contended, to "say making policy in secret is wrong and, in this case, even illegal."[60]

Clinton's secret meetings eventually did become a legal matter. Tom Brokaw of NBC noted on March 10, 1993, that the first lady had "drawn fire" because particular "interest groups" had been "shut out of the decision-making process."[61] Even though a court ruling in June 1993 stipulated that the proceedings could remain private because Clinton was a private citizen, the battles over the legality of closed-door meetings would persist throughout the Clinton presidency. These news themes ensured that the linguistic framing of Clinton's secrecy reverberated across both terms of her husband's administration.[62]

And even as Clinton's private meetings were upheld legally in the spring of 1993, questions about her secrecy and empowerment on health care led some to worry that Clinton wielded too much power in her husband's administration. Ted Koppel of *Nightline* raised the question that would dominate the March 10, 1993, broadcast: "how much power should the first lady have?" Justifying the episode's theme, Koppel characterized the concern as the "uncontrolled exercise of power." Imelda Marcos from the Philippines represented the international equivalent for Koppel—a woman whose husband's presidential administration was viewed as one of the more corrupt in that country's history. And although Imelda Marcos held elective office after leaving the presidential palace, she also was remembered for the number of shoes she purchased while her husband was president.[63] Both women were treated as gender and political anomalies. And both women epitomized the concept of the "power wife" for ABC, exhibiting an integration of the linguistic divide—the progressive and traditional, the political and the social. Yet, this integration was problematized throughout a *Nightline* episode from March 11, 1993, with power wives depicted as unacceptably domineering. When a clip from *Saturday Night Live* was aired, the male voiceover for ABC quipped that Hillary Clinton was "skewered as the overbearing wife."[64]

A rhetoric of fear ultimately resulted from images of an overbearing and powerful wife deeply involved in partisan politics. John Cochran of *NBC Nightly News* argued in March 1993 that "a lot of people in Congress admire [Clinton] and just about everyone is scared of her. Scared because she has real power and isn't afraid to use it." Cochran then coupled the fear over Clinton's power with her feminism, reifying one of the oldest stereotypes about women in power: "A lot of congressmen are also spooked because it is politically incorrect in this feminist age to suggest that possibly the first lady has too much power."[65] Cochran's statement magnified most visibly the fright of having a feminist invade the masculine halls of Congress.

The fears over her aggressive style and overreach of power would culminate in sexualized images when Clinton visited the private offices of congressional leaders. Cochran, in summarizing the objections of anti-ERA activist Phyllis Schlafly, noted that Clinton was perceived as too "pushy." Ed Rollins, a Republican strategist, echoed the alarm that Clinton would exhibit too much "aggressiveness," which led Cochran to conclude: "And that really is the question. Will Hillary Clinton be judged on whether she is pushy or on the programs she pushes?" These depictions were enhanced as ABC aired a photograph from *Spy Magazine* that featured a smiling Hillary in whips and chains—epitomizing a dominatrix that sexualized Clinton with a promiscuously aggressive and dominating hue.[66] The integration of tradition and progress, women and power, thus resulted in the manifestation of a powerful woman who sought to dominate men sexually—promoting a combination of fear and fascination.

The *Nightline* story revealed most explicitly the sexualization of women in the spaces of politics and news—the legacy of the nineteenth-century construct where public women were construed in more prostitute-like ways. The appearance of the dominatrix image in a story about Clinton's political power showed the recalibration of the traditional within the discursive spaces of the progressive, fusing power and sex. These demeaning images undercut Clinton's serious attempts to help the nation reform its health care policies and instead positioned Clinton's body in seemingly unnaturalized spaces for women. Gendered portrayals of space, Gillian Rose maintains, constitute "women as embodied objects to be looked at"—as women are "caught in the analytical stare of geography, caught inside spaces, speaking in places" marked by "patriarchal power."[67] For women politicians in particular, their "sex is always on display" across news texts and political contexts of the nation-state.[68]

Yet, Hillary Clinton confounded these constructs because she was perceived as a highly competent "policy wonk" with experience in successfully negotiating difficult compromises on complicated issues. As the debate grew in intensity, how would the contested leader of health care reform—at once praised for her skill yet feared for her overreach of power—fare in such a masculine quagmire of legislative unrest? NBC similarly puzzled over the issue of a "Feminist as First Lady" during its February 8, 1993, broadcast.[69] The following section examines the construction of the health care context and the changing frames of Hillary Clinton's comportment in the rhetorically charged political battle.

The Escalating Debate over a First Lady in Charge

The fear and fascination over Hillary Clinton's re-envisioning of the first lady post helped exacerbate the intensity of the news coverage. Throughout, journalists continued their surveillance, turning into fact checkers of the proposed health care plan as they maintained a close eye on the drama surrounding the debate. Although the Clintons had hoped to unveil a health care policy for congressional scrutiny within their first one hundred days in office, the plan's unveiling was delayed until the early fall of 1993 because of the growing controversy surrounding this third-rail issue. As deliberations persisted through the remainder of 1993 and into 1994, the prospects of its passage grew dimmer with even Democrats coming to question the fiscal practicality of a more universalized system of health care. By the summer of 1994, Democratic senators were beginning to predict publicly that the Clinton plan would fail if taken before a congressional vote.[70]

The Clintons though were dogged in their determination to make health care the administration's signature issue. Bill Clinton spoke directly to the American people in support of the health care plan. Both Clintons took the issue directly to the public through town hall meetings and bus tours. Hillary Clinton also met with congressional committees and members of Congress; and she lobbied stakeholders, particularly doctors and other health care professionals. Yet, such public relations activities would prove far too tepid against the oppositional forces the Clintons faced in reforming the U.S. health care system. The news media helped elevate the vitriol surrounding the debate through their use of war imagery, complete with violent images of death. By early 1995, with the Clinton plan no longer viable, journalists offered retrospective assessments of the plan's death; the primary culprit, not surprisingly, would become Hillary Clinton and her style of leadership during the health care controversy.

As Bill and Hillary Clinton embarked on a series of efforts to take their health care campaign to the American people, the press tried out a variety of linguistic frames to define the administration's rallies. Initially, Hillary Clinton's campaign efforts were portrayed more as a road show, akin to an entertaining sales pitch. CBS, for example, talked in "barnstorming" terms. These linguistic frames were historically linked to popular air shows featuring high-flying airplanes as well as short-term yet intensive political campaigns—both of which attracted inquiring crowds eager to take in the spectacle.[71] In setting up the story in February 1993, CBS's Linda Douglass maintained that Hillary Clinton "will barnstorm through hospitals and clinics, urging changes in a health care system which has left millions sick or broke." Elaborating further on the broader efforts to fashion public opinion, Douglass concluded that the "first lady will wage a full blown, Clinton-style campaign, bouncing from town halls to hospitals."[72] Borrowing on another more populist theme, Diane Sawyer of *ABC World News Tonight* referred to the bus trip as "the Clintons' health care bandwagon" in April 1994,[73] implying a level of entertainment designed to mobilize public favor. Tom Brokaw of NBC relied on a similar entertainment-based theme on February 11, 1993, suggesting that Hillary Clinton "put on her own road show today."[74] Later in the same month, CBS portrayed the campaign in more religious terms, calling it a "traveling health care crusade . . . the mirror image of her husband's own cross-country populist campaign" that resulted in his election.[75] The entertainment assumptions of the barnstorm, bandwagon, and road show in particular weakened any sense of the didactic function the campaign might serve. Yet, Clinton seemed undeterred in her mission to gain information from the public about their health care exigencies as well as raise awareness of the health care crisis facing the country. Both goals were designed to set the stage for the congressional showdown over the bill.[76]

By the spring of 1994, Bill and Hillary Clinton would intensify their campaign to drive up support among the American people as a means to foment congressional action on the bill. In framing this stage of their efforts, CBS in particular marked the events as media spectacles. Rita Braver of the *CBS Evening News* referenced the "carefully crafted photo opportunities" that were "designed to get on television" during Bill Clinton's trip to a rural part of North Carolina in April 1994. CBS then reinforced the idea of the media spectacle visually by showing all of the news cameras in the room covering the president's remarks. Braver commented that Hillary Clinton "was selling health care today" in her trip to New York. The goal for both Clintons, Braver concluded, was "to get airtime for their side."[77] CBS reinforced the same message in July 1994 as Hillary Clinton participated in a cross-country bus trip dubbed the "Health Security Express." CBS interviewed Tom Oliphant of the *Boston Globe* who suggested that the efforts of the Clintons to ramp up support for their health care initiatives were falling flat with audiences. He concluded derisively: "What they should have realized is that this is not theater, this is media politics, and in media politics there are no second acts."[78]

Such contempt for media spectacles demonstrated the double bind that the news organizations faced. Producers and journalists wanted to engage in surveillance of all things political, particularly in terms of health care reform, but they wanted to do so on their own terms. They preferred to observe uninhibitedly the behind-the-scenes machinations of the process rather than to become conduits in the public relations activities of a presidential administration. With the latter, the news media, as an integral feature of media spectacles, would prove instrumental to the Clinton health care campaign; their cameras and microphones were used by the Clintons to sell their policy initiatives—airtime, some complained, paid for by taxpayer dollars. CBS seemed determined to stir up ill will toward these media spectacles—spectacles that news organizations helped create—by warning the American people that their taxpayer dollars were at work in the PR moves of the president. As Braver of CBS stressed, "The government is paying for TV production and satellite time to broadcast the president's message live."[79]

In addition to framing the Clinton campaign as an entertaining spectacle, the press also began to portray the health care debate in more violent and warlike terms. These constructions portended the inevitable failure of the Clinton administration's health care campaign. How could embarking on a road show, a bandwagon, or a media spectacle stand any chance in an all-out political war of such great magnitude? A clear disconnect consequently existed between the linguistic frames of Clinton's tepid PR campaign designed to achieve health care reform in a political context construed as an all-out war.

From the outset, NBC framed the Clinton plan to reform health care as a "revolution," suggesting the enormity of the political changes sought and the linguistic link to war. On March 9, 1993, Andrea Mitchell of NBC News posited that the "Clintons are taking on the doctors, the trial lawyers, the hospitals, and the insurance industry. They know that what they're proposing is nothing short of a health care revolution."[80] NBC used the caption—"The Health Revolution"— on April 30, 1993, and again on September 21 of the same year,[81] demonstrating the repetition of linguistic framing by a news organization across the span of a single political issue. Changing such frames, Robin Tolmach Lakoff argues, "seems counterintuitive," and once stabilized, frames consequently become difficult to alter because of the order and predictability they offer.[82]

NBC extended a language of war and violence to capture the revolutionary actions of those involved in the battle. When introducing the story on February 24, 1994, Brokaw referenced "the real battle" of the health care debate taking place "behind the scenes." Andrea Mitchell would push the battle theme even further, introducing the story with the following rhetoric of war: "Today, the front line of the health care war was in Connecticut, led by the commander-in-chief. Along with his top general, they are fighting on the ground and in the air, struggling for the hearts and minds of the American people." Although Hillary Clinton was designated as the "top general," her contributions were downplayed by Mitchell's contention that "the real battles are being fought where you can't see them by White House lieutenants and the foot soldiers of the health care war, lobbyists for the drug companies, the hospitals, the insurance industry . . . big business, the elderly, all trying to influence key members of Congress."[83] NBC extended the war frame in yet another broadcast entitled "Back in the Trenches" in July 1994, talking about a "full-scale assault" on the Clinton plan during their August 10, 1994, broadcast.[84] In the end, NBC extended the linguistic frames of war, suggesting that the Clintons had already "lost much of the war."[85]

NBC was not the only news organization to use a discourse of war in framing the health care debate. *CBS Evening News* anchor Dan Rather contended on May 4, 1994, that the president is "taking increasingly heavy fire about his version of health insurance reform. What's more, some of it is now coming from inside his own party."[86] According to this framing, the Clintons were taking on friendly fire from their allies, showing the expansion of the assault on their reform efforts. Hillary Clinton would draw on war-like images herself when talking about the opposition they faced: "You do what you have to do. Come visit us in the bunker sometime."[87]

ABC and NBC also conceptualized the debate over the Clinton health care plan through a fighting discourse that furthered violent images. In the summer of 1994, Peter Jennings, the anchor of *ABC World News Tonight*, also referenced how the political leaders "will duke it out," when paraphrasing the statements of congressional leaders. Jennings normalized this violent fare when he claimed, "'that's called democracy' . . . a very messy and complicated process as various factions try to promote their particular interests."[88] ABC furthered the fighting frame, with Jim Wooten observing: "Worried that time is running out, Mrs. Clinton wants committees to agree on almost any health care bill so that the final bruising fights can begin on the floors of the House and Senate."[89] NBC also drew on this fighting imagery in their coverage of the debate, with Brokaw asserting that "the battle in Congress over health care reform . . . is already brutal . . . the president's plan is taking a beating but the Clintons are not giving up."[90]

This rhetoric of violence—derived from warring factions and bruising fisticuffs—helped spawn linguistic death and killing frames when the press depicted the final outcomes of the health care debate. In March 1994, Bill Plante of CBS News reported that Republicans "who led the opposition in the House today say the Clinton plan was already long dead."[91] NBC News followed in kind, with Brokaw calling the plan "dead in the water." Asking and then answering his own question, Brokaw queried: "Can it be revived? Not easily."[92] ABC similarly referred to the bill as "dead on arrival" in August 1994—connoting that it was dead long before it could arrive on the Senate floor—the only hospital-like body that could resuscitate it.[93]

The death frames took on a different connotation when NBC resorted to a killing aesthetic. Using a more toned down conception of ritualized killing, Andrea Mitchell argued that if the House did not vote on the bill in the summer of 1994, as Tom Foley projected, "that could kill any chance of passing a bill this year."[94] In a July 1994 story, NBC relied on the narrative theme of a car wreck rather than the imagery of war in their promulgation of death themes. Brokaw introduced the story in this way: "Bill Clinton and the Democrats are calling for a fresh start but that loud crash heard in Washington last night was the wreck of the Clinton health plan. It was totaled." Lisa Myers then talked about a plan with employer mandates, which "probably will be killed," she conjectured. The death connotations were furthered by the captions on the screen: "Life Support." Over the words "Employer Mandates," NBC featured the words "Probably Killed." Over the words "Mandatory Alliances" and "Universal Coverage," NBC inserted the word "Dead."[95] Although the shift from war to car wreck and death to killing offered distinct connotations, the underlying assumption was the same—the bill was anthropomorphized and it ultimately died a violent death.

The Clintons themselves responded in kind, drawing on their own rhetoric of violence in depicting the opposition's approach to their reform efforts. On August 10, 1994, Hillary Clinton complained that the Republicans and business leaders had promoted a "kill it, kill it, kill it, kill it drumbeat against health reform."[96] And Andrea Mitchell of NBC paraphrased Bill Clinton's allegation that "even though Congress has buried his health reform plan, the president insisted it wasn't a case of murder, more like assisted suicide."[97] The consequence of framing politics with such language helps naturalize the violent symbolism, making it difficult to recognize a full range of alternatives during policy disputes. James Dawes talks of how words like "killing" function as a "cliché," which "manipulates reality to fit a predetermined form . . . that immobilizes thought" and limits "interpretive patterns."[98]

The infusion of violent language throughout the coverage of the debate constituted a political climate that valued aggression over cooperation, animosity over good will, and a battle of winners and losers over a dialectic leading to compromise. Certainly, a bandwagon or barnstorming campaign faced little likelihood of success in a context that called for a violent and bloody revolution. These frames reinforced what NBC's overall message communicated across these latter stories—the Clintons themselves were ill-equipped for such a battle and were ultimately the cause of their own bill's death.

Other news organizations would draw the same conclusion—that the Clinton administration was to blame for the ultimate defeat of the health care reform efforts. Britt Hume of ABC News concluded his story on April 5, 1994, with the following observation: "The view here is that the problem on health care has not been the Clinton plan but the selling of the plan."[99] CBS also subtly reinforced the idea that the failure of the bill rested with the Clintons because of their lack of clear direction. Bob Schieffer of CBS News closed his broadcast on July 22, 1994, by discussing Hillary Clinton's bus tour: "But with all the confusion now over what the president really wants and what . . . Congress will approve, the real question is, where exactly is this bus heading?"[100] In a separate CBS broadcast from September 15, 1994, Linda Douglass seemed to suggest that part of the problem pertained to Hillary Clinton's comportment and her intrusion into the spaces of politics: "And Mrs. Clinton didn't hesitate to become a political figure in her own right, blasting health care opponents, negotiating with senators, testifying alone to Congress."[101] The latter assertion implied that Clinton, as a woman and particularly as first lady, had no business entering the masculine congressional spaces *alone*. By doing so, she seemingly violated notions of authentic womanhood as a lone woman surrounded by a large group of men in clearly marked masculine spaces. This nationalism rhetoric reinforced the ongoing division of gendered spheres—a divide that the first lady ought not to have breached.

Hillary Clinton's style consequently became a source of media concentration, with some praising her style and others insinuating that it contributed to the downfall of the reform efforts. Early on, Clinton's style was portrayed in more positive terms, accentuating her ability to fight hard on important issues where she exuded a level of compassion. Linda Douglass asserted in February 1993 that "politician Hillary Clinton mixed toughness with compassion" when "she talked mother to mother with a woman who feared losing coverage for her two sick children."[102] The following February, Douglass once again emphasized Clinton's more integrated style when she asserted that she mixed "soft photo opportunities with hard words for opponents of the Clinton health care plan."[103] John Cochran of NBC News also referenced Clinton's compassion and prudence, maintaining on February 11, 1993, that Clinton was "trying to blend compassion with the practicalities of a cost accountant."[104] And, Jackie Judd of ABC News depicted Clinton as someone who could make "the case for reform in personal terms."[105] In these instances, the press showed a more integrated Hillary Clinton who could serve as the policy wonk promoting health care reform through a more compassionate communication style.

Yet, there were also instances where that integration clearly broke down, resulting in critical assessments of Clinton's aggressive style more consonant with the negative stereotypes associated with feminism. Jackie Judd of ABC News offered the following characterization of Clinton's changing style in less than flattering terms, particularly when comparing Clinton to a dog breed known for its aggressiveness: "She is always the cheerleader and sometimes the pit bull."[106] The seemingly irreconcilable images of a cheerleader, marked as feminine, and a pit bull, often connoted for its hyper-masculine power or threatening female aggression, suggested a sense of abnormality with Hillary Clinton's style. Senate minority leader Bob Dole (R-KS) charged more boldly that Hillary Clinton represented the primary obstacle to achieving compromise. He urged her to "cool off a little bit and let us take our time, study this very carefully," rather than resorting to "a lot of partisan sniping."[107] These constructions suggested that Hillary Clinton needed to back off and stop talking—pegging her overexposure and outspokenness in the health care negotiations as an important impediment. House opposition leader Dick Armey (R-TX) reinforced the negative impressions of Clinton's style during a hearing on health care covered by CBS News, when he laughingly quipped: "I have been told about your charming wit, and let me say, the reports on your charm are overstated and the reports on your wit are understated."[108] Assessing the overall impression of Hillary Clinton's style, Doris Kearns Goodwin argued on a separate CBS broadcast from 1995 that Clinton's "opinions were less compromising than his, and that made both of them look bad."[109]

Downplayed in the "death" narratives was the influence of the large and loud opposition to the idea of a nationalized health care program. The press instead reasoned that the Clintons, particularly Hillary Clinton, had to absorb the primary blame for the plan's demise. Accordingly, Hillary Clinton's style—a style clearly at odds with the ideals of authentic womanhood—would bear the brunt of the blame. After all, who would want to debate a serious public issue with a sniping pit bull lacking in charm and incapable of compromise?

With less than high marks for her leadership role on health care, Hillary Clinton would be forced to traverse two separate fields simultaneously as she increasingly became caught up in a controversial legal battle over Whitewater. The news media as well were compelled to cover Clinton's navigation of the legislative and judicial fields concomitantly, which often led to a conflation of the two issues. The press thus struggled to tell the complicated stories of health care reform and of a land deal gone bad in a more compact and synthesized way. The fusion of these issues intensified the political exigencies facing the first couple during their first years in Washington, D.C. As Andrea Mitchell of NBC noted on August 3, 1994, "For the Clintons, the timing was awful. Their administration was being hammered on Whitewater just as they needed all their political clout to save health reform."[110] The twin preoccupations also necessitated that the news media step up their surveillance efforts. As Dan Rather of *CBS Evening News* promised during the summer of 1995, "Bob Schieffer is on the Whitewater watch."[111]

Framing Hillary Clinton on Whitewater

The concept of "Whitewater" became a catch-all term that referred to a 1970s land deal that involved the Clintons when Bill Clinton was governor of Arkansas. The term also represented the subsequent fallout of the land transaction that persisted throughout the 1980s and into President Bill Clinton's second term in office. Part of the fallout related to Madison Guaranty's bankruptcy in the 1980s; this savings and loan company oversaw the investment deal resulting in what the Clintons reported was a loss of money from the transaction. Further complicating the matter, this bankrupt company was headed by James B. McDougal—a former business partner of the Clintons. McDougal was ultimately charged with legal irregularities associated with the failed savings and loan company. When Madison Guaranty went into bankruptcy, then-Governor Clinton appointed regulators to oversee the legal process. The controversy intensified because Hillary Clinton and her Little Rock law firm had legally represented the company for a brief time. Some also charged that McDougal had illegally collected campaign support for Clinton's gubernatorial races and then reimbursed the donors. The Clintons would consistently claim they had no knowledge of any wrongdoing.

The news networks began reporting on the Whitewater allegations during the 1992 presidential campaign. By 1994, an independent counsel was appointed to investigate the matter (Robert Fiske in May followed by Kenneth Starr in August). By May 1995, as the health care debate came to an end, the U.S. Senate ultimately set up a special committee to investigate the matter (Special Committee to Investigate Whitewater Development Corporation and Related Matters). What was a land deal gone bad during the Clintons' time in Arkansas had now become a significant political issue for the Clintons in the White

House—an investigation that would later focus on Bill Clinton's relationship with a White House intern, resulting in only the second presidential impeachment in the nation's history (see chapter 3).[112] This section examines how a first lady's alleged unethical and even illegal behavior during Whitewater was treated by the news media as the press grappled with her unprecedented leadership on health care reform.

Because Hillary Clinton was accused of at best ethical wrongdoing and at worst illegal business practices, the coverage of Whitewater addressed questions of Clinton's morality and character. Character judgments have historically served as a key ingredient of an individual's authenticity (see introduction), particularly prevalent in the evaluation of the nation's political leaders.[113] The press consequently served as the barometer of Clinton's character during the coverage of health care and Whitewater. Even the hint of ethical lapse could undermine perceptions of Clinton's character given women's perceived superiority on all things moral. Allegations of Clinton's wrongdoing furthered her violation of authentic womanhood—ideals expected to enhance rather than erode the morality of family and nation. Hillary Clinton emerged from this period as one known for her secrecy—a personal subterfuge that masked her abuse of power (health care) and her ethical wrongdoing (Whitewater). The visual news strategies reinforced images of her questionable character by conflating these two controversial issues. The alleged character flaws that surfaced in both health care and Whitewater once again resulted in the disciplining of Hillary Clinton; a rhetoric of violence was ultimately targeted toward the transgressive one who flouted the norms of authentic womanhood. Predictably, with Clinton silenced, sidelined, and engaged in the traditional activities as the first lady, the press would again frame the alleged transition from progressive feminist to traditional first lady as evidence of Clinton's inauthenticity, individualizing her character flaws as an inherent part of her press biography.

CLINTON AND WHITEWATER: THE ALLEGATIONS AND THE DEFENSE

From the beginning, questions of Clinton's morality represented the central topic of conversation with Whitewater as attention turned to the ethical and legal fallout. In the spring of 1994, Dan Rather of CBS raised questions about the comparison between Watergate and Whitewater, beginning with the following teaser: "Tops on the White House agenda, trying to halt any comparisons to Watergate and any suggestions of cover-up." Bob Schieffer in the same CBS broadcast explained the potential connections between the two presidential controversies, paraphrasing Representative Jim Leach (R-IA) to do so: "It's no longer about an obscure real-estate deal in Arkansas but about the possibility of a White House cover-up that could amount to a felony violation, says Leach of Iowa."[114] From the vantage point of the press, the ethical and legal controversies from Whitewater spilled over into Clinton's leadership on health care. As Connie Chung of *CBS Evening News* charged in March 1994, "Some of the latest Whitewater stories to hit the headlines are splashing mud in Hillary Clinton's direction. This could be taking some of the shine off her power and prestige and her role as a key player in issues such as health care reform."[115] These allegations put further pressure on the Clintons, particularly Hillary Clinton, to address the charges forthrightly. As Tom Brokaw of NBC News argued on March 15, 1994, "Whitewater won't go away until some questions, many questions are answered—many of them having to do with Hillary Clinton."[116]

This pressure forced the Clintons to repeatedly address the allegations surrounding Whitewater. When the controversy about Whitewater intensified, Hillary Clinton first dismissed the charges in a more defensive way, implying a level of political sabotage directed toward the Clintons during December 1993: "My husband's presidency speaks for itself and what he has done for America in just one year . . . ultimately that's how the American people are going to judge, not some story that somebody promotes for their own financial gain or because they have a political vendetta."[117] By the following spring, Bill Clinton was addressing the allegations more forcibly, defending his wife's morality in the process: "People can ask whatever questions they want, and we will do our best to comply. But I'm just telling you, the American people can worry about something else. Her moral compass is as strong as anybody's in this country."[118]

The questions would persist despite the president's insistence on his wife's moral superiority as the nation's first lady. Hillary Clinton ultimately held her own press conference on Whitewater in hopes of quieting the rumors. On April 22, 1994, Clinton appeared before reporters; rather than standing behind a podium, Clinton sat on a makeshift stage in the State Dining Room of the White House and answered questions in a more conversational style. NBC's Brian Williams responded to the press conference in the following way, accentuating another precedent-setting moment for the president's wife: "A first of its kind appearance by First Lady Hillary Rodham Clinton . . . Mrs. Clinton held a formal news conference, facing 140 of the reporters who normally grill the president . . . No bombshells but it was a first and Mrs. Clinton earned high praise for her poise."[119] Although Hillary Clinton received much praise for her comportment during the one-of-a-kind press conference, the attention to Whitewater did not subside anytime soon. The press coverage of Whitewater and Clinton's response would further challenge her authenticity; the visual techniques reinforced concerns about her true character.

THE MANY PORTRAITS OF HILLARY CLINTON

A common visual technique of broadcast news is to feature a portrait-like image of the story's subject behind the anchor as the news segment is introduced. In some instances, the images are an actual portrait photograph that political leaders make available on their websites or for use in the press. In other cases, the news media simply freeze an image of the person from stock video footage and frame it in ways that resemble a portrait photograph. These practices are a routine part of American journalism, serving as a visual "framing" device that promotes the salience of *face politics* to journalistic practice.

For centuries, the face has served as a barometer of character, with portrait painters trained to capture the "essence" of the individual through their artwork. During the Enlightenment period especially, people conceived of a facial portrait and the subsequent photographic portraits as an art form that could either mimic or mask reality. The great painters and photographers, the logic suggested, could unveil the mask and reveal the authentic individual that the face was sure to reveal. As Alison Conway explains, "The success of a portrait depends on its movement between the question of physical resemblance and the larger truths manifested by the sitter's character, a movement that defines the portrait as both private and public, particular and general." As the portrait moves out of the private spaces and into the public sphere, Conway contends, it "takes the individual into the arena of public judgment."[120]

The historical association between the face and character is revealed in a pseudoscience called physiognomy and its relationship with phrenology.[121] Although addressed during antiquity and attributed to Aristotle's students, the popularity of physiognomy grew in the West from the late eighteenth century through the latter part of the nineteenth century. As Lucy Hartley explains, physiognomy posits an understanding of "the inner meaning of human nature from the observations of actual appearances—facial expressions are used in this context to tell us about the kind of person we see," as types "of emotion" are equated with "a standard type of character." Because physiognomy became a means to discern the authenticity of an individual's character, its influence was most visible in popular culture (e.g., poetry, plays, novels) and served as common teachings for portrait artists. Although the height of physiognomy's popularity began to wane by the end of the nineteenth century, Hartley contends that the legacy of physiognomic assumptions is still visible in our "present age" because the "attempt to describe the core of our nature . . . continues to arouse an . . . unbridled curiosity."[122]

Face politics correspondingly serves as a key dimension of political authenticity. The face, such logic presumes, acts as an indicator of a political leader's honesty or deceitfulness given the adage that the face cannot lie. As the news media seek to get behind the promises and the slogans to locate the real candidate, the face represents the primary avenue into the leader's authenticating soul.[123] The legacy of physiognomic assumptions helps explain the prevalence of close-up facial shots in the press. Visual facial shots accordingly allow for the interrogation of the seemingly private or the authentic, demonstrating, Reginald Twigg argues, how the private is constituted as a "hidden mystery to be explored by the camera," with access often marked as "an exclusive privilege."[124]

In the process of offering the face for viewer inspection, the news media assume a level of authority in the selection of portrait shots and video images to represent the news subject. There are undoubtedly multiple factors at play in the visual selection processes. Some are more deliberate, others inadvertent, and still others having to do with the rush of news to air. Intentional or not, the interaction between verbal and visual messages offers insight into the mediated modes of political authenticity. One of the more questionable practices of face politics involves the common news practice of decontextualizing images from one news story and recontextualizing them into another.[125] In these practices, Hillary Clinton's face functioned as an implicit marker of her character and a means by which to unravel the mystery of her inner thoughts and being.

As the Whitewater controversy unfolded, video from the health care debate often stood in for images of Whitewater because the former images were more readily available; Whitewater activities took place nearly a decade before the Clintons came to Washington, D.C., and no signature video existed to exemplify the issue. To demonstrate a routine decontextualization-recontextualization practice involving both issues, I turn to an observation that Joe Klein made on CBS news about Clinton "working for the Rose Law firm, which did legal work for Madison and also for federal agencies investigating Madison." As Klein's statement was aired, CBS inserted an image bite of Hillary Clinton testifying before Congress as the head of the task force on health care reform; she was seen but not heard, which obscured the context of the original footage. One could argue that the image functioned in a more innocuous way because of its fleeting nature. Yet, rather than acknowledge that she was testifying on behalf of the presidential task force, CBS implied instead that she was speaking about a legal matter pertaining to her own wrongdoing. Klein's subsequent statement framed the image in more sinister ways: "And now there is the possibility that the Clintons might have wanted to impede those investigations. The Clintons may have done something seriously wrong back in Arkansas. They may be trying to cover it up now. Then again, there may be nothing here—just a dust storm of opinions."[126] This particular framing suggested that the news media may have caught Hillary Clinton in a cover-up—visualized by her speaking into a microphone surrounded by onlookers capturing her every word. The recontextualization of Clinton's health care testimony would commonly stand in as stock footage for Whitewater across multiple news broadcasts and news organizations. Such practices showed the free-floating nature of news footage that can be used, regardless of context, to visualize any story being told.[127] In the process, the footage added a sense of presentism to a decade-old subject and implied that Clinton had already testified about her alleged wrongdoing.

That Hillary Clinton's face would become a preoccupation during Whitewater is evidenced by another CBS News storyline; zoomed-in facial shots of Clinton, again extracted from health care footage, were offered as a means by which to explore her candor over Whitewater. CBS's Linda Douglass made the following observation in March 1994: "Though she's been praised for her work on health reform, some in Congress complain there's been a lack of follow-through and critics charge her political judgment on other issues has been uneven. She argued against responding to early stories on Whitewater. Unanswered questions gave the story life." During this statement, CBS showed video footage of Clinton meeting with people on health care issues. Even though the photos originated from her health care activities when she met with doctors and patients, the camera panned in slowly to feature a close-up image of her face as the story turned to a focus on Whitewater. Such a slow-moving camera zoom allowed viewers time to draw conclusions on the truthfulness of her statements about Whitewater, which were ostensibly visible in that one facial shot in that one particular public moment.[128] The isolated face of a political leader, regardless of context, becomes an opportunity for political judgment; the zoomed-in shot can signal to the viewer the need to scrutinize the face for clues of public or personal deception.

The portrait images of Hillary Clinton served as another means by which to gauge Clinton's character, lending evidence to her guilt or innocence on Whitewater, depending on how one read the facial cues. While individual judgments of images can certainly differ,[129] the news media can direct viewers toward a particular judgment through the selection of visual images, captions, and words. In certain stories, frozen and framed facial images assume the appearance of a mug shot, connoting a semblance of guilt. One such example appeared in a December 19, 1995, *ABC World News Tonight* broadcast, where Peter Jennings opened the story in the following way: "At the Whitewater hearings in Congress this week, there has been increasing attention paid to Mrs. Clinton's credibility." Correspondent Barry Serafin then summarized the details of the allegations, noting that "Mrs. Clinton has said she played a very limited role in representing Madison Guaranty before state regulators." Yet, evidence also existed, ABC reported, that challenged the veracity of Clinton's statement. According to Serafin, "The Senate Whitewater committee has released notes taken in 1992 by Susan Thomases, a lawyer and close friend of the first lady, indicating that Mrs. Clinton did far more work for Madison Guaranty than previously acknowledged."[130]

As Serafin talked about the notes, a black-and-white image of the Rose Law Firm appeared on the screen; photos of handwritten documents symbolizing the notes in question were then superimposed on top of the Rose Law Firm photograph. Next, a picture of Hillary Clinton slid in from the left side of the screen. The image was extracted from her 1994 press conference on Whitewater. Frozen in time, ABC's makeshift facial portrait of Clinton assumed the appearance of a mug shot because ABC transformed it from bright colors (Hillary wore pink during the press conference) to more washed out black-and-white hues. In the frozen portrait image, Clinton looked straight toward the camera with a serious look—common features of a mug shot displayed across the news. Her eyes were dark in color, squinty in appearance as if more blinded by the flash, and her hair was darkened around the edges. Underneath her portrait the words read: "HC had numerous conf,"[131] signposting that Clinton had been caught in a lie. The contours of the mug shot image and its accompanying captions made one wonder, could the first lady really be trusted?

Clinton's facial shot in the above example was also double framed to resemble a picture frame. The portraiture style that dominates news coverage draws on a familiar visual aesthetic that typically enhances an aura of affection. Most people who decorate their homes with portraits feature photographs of loved ones that foster a sense of intimacy with those pictured on their walls, tables, and mantles.[132] With the case of ABC's image, however, a level of incongruity existed; the aesthetic framing of the "portrait" defied the appealing qualities expected of photographic images. Contrastingly, the facial features of the image—the unpleasant expression, squinty eyes, and the overall darkened color—connoted a mug shot more than a family member's portrait. If the assumption persists that the face stands in as a character metric, Clinton's portrait during this ABC broadcast reinforced the message of alleged deceit and wrongdoing—the same implication offered through ABC's news narrative.

There were other ways in which the news media wittingly or unwittingly projected a level of character incongruity through the use of portrait images. In these instances, portraits were featured of a smiling and perhaps taunting Hillary Clinton, which stood in sharp contrast to the serious allegations involving Whitewater. Such a disconnect between the image and the story challenged the first lady's character, suggesting a malevolent Clinton eager to hoard power. An ABC *Nightline* broadcast represented a case in point. In addressing Clinton's alleged relationship with the failed savings and loan company, Ted Koppel introduced the December 1995 story with a facial portrait of Clinton smiling and looking just to the left of the camera in more traditional portrait-like fashion; Clinton's facial expression of happiness made the image more aesthetically pleasing than the black-and-white mug aesthetic ABC used in the example above. Given its glamorous trappings, the *Nightline* photograph may well have been issued by Clinton's office for use in the press. The issue, though, was that the portrait served as the backdrop to Koppel's discussion about Clinton's alleged illegalities with Whitewater. The incongruity between the image and the narration was furthered by Jeff Greenfield's contextualization of the exigency: "This is a cover-up without a crime. It's Watergate without the break-in . . . As Whitewater once again hits the front pages, we're beginning to get a sense of what Republicans believe may be at the heart of the matter and who."[133] Because she was the targeted one for the investigation, Clinton's smile appeared perplexing, raising questions about her perceived expression of pleasure as she faced legal and ethical charges. CNN likewise featured an aesthetically pleasing portrait of Clinton as Jeanne Meserve informed the viewing audience that "a member of the Whitewater special prosecutor's team reportedly has told an appeals court that First Lady Hillary Rodham Clinton could be indicted." The smiling Hillary in this portrait was looking to the left of the camera and boasted a lime-green shirt decorated with pearls. CNN added the caption "Whitewater" to the photographic image,[134] reifying a disjuncture between the potential charges of an indictment and a smiling picture of Hillary Clinton in pearls preparing to confront criminal charges.

Clinton's character thus was exemplified through a combination of visual images and verbal prose. Her morality was challenged through the Whitewater allegations—allegations aggravated by a smiling first lady who connoted a sense of malevolence most unbecoming a national role model. These recontextualized images depicted Clinton as a woman who was at best unphased by the proceedings, and at worst, enjoying the cat and mouse game with Congress, exuding no shame for her alleged wrongdoing.

Visual images consequently enhanced questions about Clinton's authenticity as uncertainties over her character loomed large in the framing of Whitewater. Authenticity questions were furthered by what the press and the Republican opposition identified as her contradictory statements, secrecy, and cover-up, with some charging Clinton with outright lying to the American people. These constructs further eroded Clinton's moral standing as the national embodiment of authentic womanhood.

THE HYPOCRITICAL AND THE SECRETIVE HILLARY CLINTON

For some in the press, Hillary Clinton's handling of the Whitewater crisis reflected a brilliant performance that masked the truth about her alleged wrongdoing. During an April 26, 1994, broadcast of ABC's *Nightline*, Howard Fineman called Clinton's press conference a "masterful piece of political theater." She showed, Fineman claimed, "how to seem calm . . . in the face of a lot of questions." Both Michael Barone and Ted Koppel graded Clinton on her performance. "On demeanor" and "poise," Barone asserted, "she got an A," but on "content . . . a zero." Koppel also awarded Clinton a "brilliant, A+" in terms of her performance. Chris Bury summarized the underlying theme of the entire broadcast: "Mrs. Clinton deflected other difficult questions with all the spin and polish of a political pro."[135]

This divide between style and content led ABC to question Clinton's character directly. In situating the Whitewater scandal in the history of Clinton's fight against corruption in politics, ABC accentuated a level of hypocrisy. During a March 23, 1994, story on *ABC World News Tonight*, Jeff Greenfield opened the feature story with the following observation: "It's an idea that took hold in the late 1960s—the personal is political. If we want a better world, we have to start by being better people." After airing historical footage of protesters from the 1960s, an image of Hillary Clinton speaking to her peers at the Wellesley College commencement ceremony appeared. Greenfield then stated: "At her 1969 commencement, one student speaker talked about her generation's rejection of ambition and greed." Transitioning then to the contemporary political context, Greenfield noted Clinton's ongoing commitment to a principled politics: "Nearly 25 years later, Hillary Rodham Clinton was still speaking of some higher purpose, of a search for a politics of meaning." ABC next turned to footage of Clinton from 1993 uttering the following statement, aired without reference to its context: "How we can have a society that fills us up again and makes us feel that we are part of something bigger than ourselves?" Greenfield then juxtaposed Hillary Clinton's "politics of virtue" against Hillary Clinton's actions during Whitewater, pondering the following thought before the television camera: "Maybe a deep belief in your own good intentions makes it hard to see the tough questions others have about your financial dealings. Perhaps when you've been told since youth that you're a part of the most selfless generation in history, it's hard to see how anyone could accuse you of involvement in a conflict of interest." Captions of newspapers appeared on the screen as this statement was delivered, with one caption reading: "First Lady, Defending President, Denounces 'Outrageous Attack.'"In furthering the hypocrisy between Clinton's rhetoric of virtue and her alleged questionable ethics, Greenfield closed the report with the following rhetorical question that insinuated Clinton's level of guilt: "And maybe it's the ultimate irony for a political leader. The more certain you are that you are on the side of the angels, the less likely you may be to notice what your behavior looks like to those outside your virtuous circle."[136] The hypocritical themes of course contributed to questions about Clinton's political authenticity, as they emphasized a juxtaposition between the public image that she projected and the politics that she practiced—a disconnect that furthered anxieties over her inauthentic character.

CBS also accentuated similar hypocrisy themes in a March 30, 1994, broadcast, touting how Clinton had been dubbed "Saint Hillary" on a *New York Times* magazine cover. Reinforcing an image of moral superiority, Richard Threlkeld noted that "it hasn't helped that both the Clintons have spent so much time preaching the politics of virtue." Explaining the quandary that Hillary Clinton faced with the Whitewater controversy, Sally Quinn asserted: "If you stake out a high moral ground, then you have to be perfect, and if you are shown to have any flaws, then people are going to turn on you."[137] Framing Hillary Clinton as the personification of political hypocrisy served to undermine her veracity and further undercut an image of a moral first lady—the symbol of authentic womanhood.

Clinton's authenticity was further challenged by the allegations that she appeared secret and guarded on Whitewater, promoting high levels of suspicion that the first lady was covering up the truth. Lisa Myers of NBC News stated in January 1994 that some of Bill Clinton's aides favored "releasing many or all of the docs" on Whitewater and "others do not." Characterizing the first lady's response, Myers said that "so far, Hillary Rodham Clinton adamantly opposes that." When talking about Whitewater, NBC aired the decontextualized clip of Clinton testifying before Congress on health care. Her voice was barely audible except for the following phrase, "we also believe," which NBC allowed to be heard, suggesting that she was defending herself and her husband against the Whitewater allegations.[138] The coverage of Clinton's Whitewater press conference was framed similarly by CBS; Linda Douglass highlighted that "the first lady, who so jealously guards her privacy, suddenly decided to open up today to answer any and all questions about her financial dealings and Whitewater."[139] An ABC news source returned to the use of the war frame when talking about Whitewater to evidence Clinton's guardedness. During a *Nightline* special of

April 22, 1994, ABC News interviewed John Brummett from the *Arkansas Gazette*, who noted that "Hillary Clinton has a bunker mentality, a sort of siege mentality whenever her husband . . . was criticized . . . [S]he . . . didn't like to concede a thing to critics and liked to maintain what she subsequently called a zone of privacy."[140] Clinton furthered her propensity for privacy when she explained during her April 1994 press conference why she had not opened up sooner about the Whitewater allegations: "I've always believed in a zone of privacy and I told a friend the other day that I feel after resisting for a long time, I've been rezoned."[141]

For many of the networks, notions of individual privacy were equated with political secrecy. When discussing Clinton's propensity for secrecy, they turned to decontextualized video footage to visualize the ways in which she guarded her privacy. These video images functioned as stock news frames. One common practice featured footage of Hillary Clinton wearing sunglasses to mark her guardedness. Elizabeth Vargus of ABC News reported that Hillary Clinton had been "deposed for five hours today at the White House by prosecutors from Ken Starr's office. This is the sixth time over the past several years that the first lady has been questioned, but this time there was a particular urgency about it." ABC then showed images of Clinton and an aide walking in a garden; the two appeared at a distance from the camera location, with no visual recognition of the camera's presence. Clinton was dressed in a yellow suit and was wearing sunglasses; the two appeared to be having a private moment that the camera just happened to catch.[142] This same image of Clinton sporting sunglasses would be used in other broadcasts as journalists spoke of the secrecy surrounding the Whitewater case. ABC used the same image in at least one other instance when talking about Whitewater in a retrospective story from 1997; CBS News also used it in a 1997 story about Clinton's fiftieth birthday. The sunglasses footage appeared as CBS emphasized how Clinton went into hiding in the aftermath of health care.[143] In yet another example with a different image of Clinton in sunglasses, Lisa Myers of NBC News indicated that Senator Chuck Robb (R-VA) called for a special counsel investigation; Myers then stressed that a such an inquiry "undercut the White House strategy of trying to dismiss the furor as an issue created and fueled by Republicans." Hillary and Bill Clinton were then shown walking together with Hillary once again sporting sunglasses.[144] Given the considerable latitude that the news media hold in selecting images to accompany their statements, it is revealing that more than one network opted to include stock images of Clinton in sunglasses to represent the idea that the Clintons, particularly Hillary, had something to hide. Sunglasses thus helped frame Clinton as unavailable for comment and in hiding from the press and her legal problems, furthering the formability of face politics. When the eyes are hidden, physiognomic logic suggests, the most revealing signs of authenticity are camouflaged, inhibiting the surveillance process.

Another visual marker of the privacy and subterfuge pertained to the use of images that featured Hillary Clinton whispering to her husband in a public setting. In a March 1994 broadcast entitled "Finger Pointing," NBC News addressed Bill Clinton's repeated defense of his wife's morality. Tom Brokaw stated: "President Clinton . . . insisting this is no Watergate. He also gave a spirited defense of Hillary." Bill Clinton was next shown arguing: "I have never known a person with a stronger sense of right and wrong in my life, ever, and I do not believe for a moment that she has done anything wrong." Andrea Mitchell next talked about the Clintons' release of Whitewater documents and questions over when Bill Clinton was told that an investigation was imminent. NBC then aired the stock footage referenced earlier from the Clinton transition period where Hillary was shown standing over, yet behind, the president-elect, whispering in his ear. The implication was that NBC caught on film the moment when news of the investigation broke and Hillary was disclosing the turn-of-events to her husband privately in a public setting.[145] This floating signifier of the whispering first lady exhibited her secrecy and her power, and perhaps even her involvement in the Whitewater cover-up.

News frames of Hillary Clinton's comportment on Whitewater (and even health care) thus punctuated an image of a private and secretive first lady who defied conventional morality expectations for the position. The Whitewater allegations ultimately led conservative newspaper columnist William Safire to label Hillary Clinton a "congenital liar"—a linguistic frame that circulated throughout network news. During a January 9, 1996, news story, NBC News resurrected a baseline linguistic frame by titling their story "The Hillary Factor," which featured an "in-depth" story on Whitewater. Lisa Myers began the story by indicating that a "storm" was "swirling around the first lady." As Myers spoke, NBC aired video footage of Bill and Hillary attending a church service and trudging through a snow storm to do so. Myers talked of how the "storm" centered on the "discrepancies between what Mrs. Clinton had said and what the record now shows." These discrepancies became the focal point of Safire's *New York Times* column from January 8, 1996, entitled "Blizzard of Lies," where he called Clinton "a congenital liar," Jim Miklaszewski reported. Miklaszewski added that such an insult brought a "White House spokesman out swinging." Bill Clinton once again defended his wife's honor, as his press secretary, Mike McCurry, quipped: "President Clinton 'would have delivered a more forceful response on the bridge of Mr. Safire's nose.'"[146] Of course, Bill Clinton's repeated defense of Hillary Clinton's morality showed a level of traditional chivalry where a husband fights for his wife's honor, serving as one mediated step toward her redisciplining; the Hillary Clinton who circulated on the media stage gradually lost the agency to fight on her own behalf.

In the end, the portrayal of twin controversies involving a botched health care reform effort and a muddled legal matter led some to spotlight the dangerous consequences of an empowered first lady. During a *CBS Evening News* broadcast from March 30, 1994, anchor Connie Chung argued that "few first ladies over the years have earned as much attention as Hillary Clinton." Richard Threlkeld billed the story with the war frame "under fire," returning to the beginning of Clinton's time on the national stage: "Even in the presidential campaign, you could see this first lady was not going to be traditional." CBS then played the stock news image of cookies and teas as Threkeld uttered: "Quite the contrary." To show the violation of tradition, the emergence of a new stock frame became one of Clinton touring Congress with Senator George Mitchell during the health care debate. Threlkeld's use of the image foretold the story that "Hillary Rodham Clinton took over the East Wing of the White House and health reform." Although he noted that Clinton "wowed them in Congress" for being "smart, articulate, her husband's equal partner, the most powerful and public first lady ever," the story soon turned to the consequences of defying tradition. Threlkeld next paraphrased media analyst Ellen Hume, who argued that "much of the current furor over Mrs. Clinton and Whitewater stems from her attempts to rewrite the first lady's job description." The conflict developed, Hume argued, because "she collided with the myth that the first lady also has to be the first hostess." The end result, Threlkeld maintained, was that "the Whitewater affair . . . called into question her competence, her judgment, even her ethics." Even though Threlkeld ended the story by asserting that "Hillary Rodham Clinton has forever changed the role of first lady, no matter what comes of Whitewater,"[147] these broadcasts speculated that Clinton's morality breaches were caused by the dangerous expansion of power for a first lady. After all, as Sheila Tate—press secretary for Nancy Reagan—argued in January 1996, Clinton "put herself really quite squarely in the political cross hairs when she took on health reform,"[148] seemingly necessitating a redisciplining of Hillary Clinton and a return to first lady tradition.

Disciplining the First Lady . . . Again

Increasingly the political talk reverted back to the summer of 1992 commonplace that Hillary Clinton was becoming a liability to her husband's political standing. The liability stemmed this time from her inappropriate leadership on a controversial policy initiative and her alleged wrongdoing and cover-up of Whitewater.

A distinctive news language began to surface during this period of controversy, reflecting the growing animosity toward Clinton's public actions and political image. The rhetoric of violence that permeated the debate over health care began to target Hillary Clinton directly, culminating in threats of violence directed toward her that served as another means of gender disciplining. According to press accounts, the consequences of Clinton's aberrant behavior and the threats of violence would lead once again to a silencing of Clinton, at least on public policy matters. The press would emphasize her return to a more traditional role as a political wife—mirroring the makeover from the 1992 campaign. Any changes in Clinton's comportment would predictably reinforce images of her inauthenticity, with the press making clear that Hillary Clinton could never be the embodiment of authentic womanhood. Press videos from her past would stand as proof of the real Hillary Clinton—no stand by your man woman and no hostess serving cookies and teas.

THE CONSEQUENCES OF AN OUT FRONT AND OUTSPOKEN FIRST LADY

The assumption that Hillary Clinton was a liability to her husband's administration would once again take hold during the Whitewater controversy especially. Linda Douglass of *CBS Evening News* foreshadowed the controversies to come in a story from early March 1994: "Mrs. Clinton's defenders say she is one of the president's greatest assets. But as the Whitewater controversy grows, she could also become a liability."[149] ABC featured a storyline with the same theme during the same month, with the on-screen caption questioning: "Is she a political liability?" The controversial issues pertained not only to Whitewater but also to her expanded power as first lady. ABC surveyed the titles of news articles during the 1994 broadcast, picturing one caption that read "Power Through Wedding" and the second one entitled "Hillary's Power." ABC reporter Michele Norris then registered the consequences of Clinton's inflated power: "All of this is starting to chip away at the first lady's image." Poll numbers were then displayed, which showed Clinton's favorable ratings had dropped 12 percent and her unfavorable ratings had risen 13 percent. As Norris contended, "This could hurt Mrs. Clinton's ability to serve as an effective spokeswoman for health care reform."[150]

The theme of Clinton as a liability for her husband and his policies would dominate another ABC News broadcast nearly two years later. In recounting Clinton's biography, Jim Wooten used stock frames from the 1992 presidential campaign to emphasize Clinton's true character and the problems originating from her enhanced power in the Clinton political marriage. Wooten began this segment with Clinton's 1992 cookies and teas footage. As this video played in the background, he first turned to the memory of the Tammy Wynette comment to authenticate the real Hillary Clinton: "As she herself explained during her husband's campaign, she was never the little woman, never the conventional political spouse." ABC next re-aired what had become for the press Clinton's most authenticating statement: "I suppose I could have stayed home and baked cookies and had teas, but what I decided to do was to fulfill my profession, which I entered before my husband was in public life." Explaining the contours of her progressiveness, which, arguably, also served as a source of her problems, Wooten observed: "She had her own career, her own ideas and, as it turned out, her own ethical problems and political baggage." In continuing his press biography of Clinton, Wooten transitioned to Whitewater, where he reviewed the ways in which she was dishonest—"not a crime, just not the truth." The arc of Wooten's narrative about Clinton's life in politics was the danger she posed to her husband's administration. Wooten concluded: "None of this is particularly helpful to the president's re-election campaign. By her own choice, Mrs. Clinton's profile is nearly as high as his own and her ethical problems could become his political problems as well."[151]

As the political intrigue surrounding Whitewater intensified, a rhetoric of violence began to permeate the press frames, reflective of the war and death metaphors circulating during the health care debate. *CBS Evening News*, for example, created a special series entitled "The White House Under Fire," with one broadcast devoted to "Hillary Rodham Clinton" and her role in Whitewater.[152] NBC also returned to a common linguistic war frame in their coverage of Whitewater too, titling one broadcast "The Home Front," a story that aired as Bill Clinton traveled around Europe during January 1994. In setting up the broadcast on Whitewater, Lisa Myers argued that "most of the president's damage control team remained back at the White House searching for a way to stop the hemorrhaging."[153] Ultimately, the Whitewater saga came to an end in September 2000 with no charges brought against either Bill or Hillary Clinton. To mark the moment, NBC News anchor Tom Brokaw opened the story with the following prognostication: "And although it may never die in the hearts and minds of hardcore Clinton bashers, tonight Whitewater, as a legal issue, is officially dead, killed by the special prosecutor."[154]

With a rhetoric of violence such a naturalized part of the political and press vernacular, it should come as no surprise that controversial figures in American politics like Hillary Clinton become potential targets of physical violence. To be sure, U.S. history is filled with the painful memories of assassinated political leaders; others have been fortunate enough to survive such violent attacks. For Hillary Clinton, threats of violence contributed to her disciplining in ways that were not as visible in the 1992 campaign press coverage. During an August 24,

1998, episode of *Nightline*, a writer for the *New Yorker Magazine*, Jane Mayer, made the following revelation: "Her taking an actual policy role [with health care] . . . started a huge backlash and that chapter really came to an end in . . . 1994 when she became so unpopular . . . that there were actual very real death threats against her. And I think she was shocked at the level of animosity she had stirred and basically began to retool her role."[155] In a separate *Nightline* broadcast from January 1996, Chris Bury associated the increased threats against Clinton with the intensity of the rhetoric about her role as first lady: "Threats to Mrs. Clinton have increased, we are told, as the rhetoric about her role [in health care] becomes more shrill."[156] These symbols of violence became public in the summer of 1994 when Connie Chung of CBS News reported that Hillary Clinton had been burned in effigy: "The White House said today 'it's time to tone down the rhetoric reacting to the burning in effigy of Hillary Rodham Clinton.' The effigy was doused with gasoline and set on fire in a weekend rally at Owensboro, Kentucky. It was sponsored by tobacco activists opposed to an increase in cigarette taxes to pay for the Clinton health care plan." Footage from the effigy accompanied the narrative, featuring a stick figure with legs and a makeshift head that contained the semblance of hair; the stick figure was dressed in green clothing—the color of the suit that Clinton wore during the health care hearings in Congress. As the stick figure burned, a crowd of white men and women smoking cigarettes gathered around the burning symbol in protest.[157]

Some scholars connect the dots between a language of violence and a culture of violence. James Dawes, for example, argues that in "societies structured by asymmetries of power speech functions to perpetuate violence against the disenfranchised."[158] On one hand, Hillary Clinton could not in any way be construed as disempowered because of her race, class, sexuality, and status as first lady. On the other hand, by entering the political spaces of masculine authority as an outspoken woman defying the nation's gender traditions, she became embroiled in the ideological bog of hegemonic masculinity that women in politics have confronted since the nation's founding.[159]

Hillary Clinton discussed the threats of violence in her autobiography. While on the bus campaign—the "Health Security Express"—Clinton wrote of how local radio hosts had encouraged protesters to disrupt each rally. When she arrived in Seattle during July 1994, for example, more than 4,500 protesters met her bus. While she had been encouraged to wear a bulletproof vest for some time by her security team, she reportedly complied with security requests on this occasion given the elevated threats of violence. Clinton recounted the fury in the following way:

During the rally, I could hardly hear my voice over the booing and the heckling. After the speech ended and we were driving away from the stage, hundreds of protesters swarmed around the limousine. What I could see from the car was a crowd of men who seemed to be in their twenties and thirties. I'll never forget the look in their eyes and their twisted mouths as they screamed at me while the agents pushed them away.[160]

The political debate against the Clinton reform efforts had moved from the floor of Congress to the nation's streets, culminating in acts of aggression targeting the first lady's leadership on health care reform. The press frames consequently became part of the pernicious political process that contributed to the linguistic disciplining of Hillary Clinton for her political transgressions.

The consequences demonstrate an emerging pattern in the news frames: Clinton's expressions of political and gender power were followed by a discursive disciplining. In assessing Clinton's treatment as first lady, Robin Tolmach Lakoff contends that the repeated attempts to interpret, misinterpret, and over-interpret Clinton served as the best means to "neutralize her."[161] In 1992 and even in 1996, the outgrowth of such disciplinary forces resulted in disempowering and silencing Clinton. During the health care and Whitewater controversies, the press frames became even more venomous, culminating in a rhetoric of violence directed toward the first lady. A rhetoric of violence—though not a form of physical aggression—nevertheless exacts an emotional toll that can be frightening and debilitating, exacting material consequences. A language of violence, Dawes contends, can "function as a corporeal disciplinary mechanism regulating motor dispositions."[162] This perspective understands language as action where the body, Judith Butler contends, is "sustained and threatened through modes of address."[163]

SUFFICIENTLY DISCIPLINED AND INAUTHENTICATED

The news coverage of Hillary Clinton thus followed a familiar pattern first noticeable on the national stage during the 1992 presidential campaign. Clinton initially served as a publicly visible and outspoken advocate on behalf of her husband's election bid and then as a task force leader on his signature health care issue. Conceived as outspoken and overexposed, Clinton was framed as exhibiting too much power—as flouting tradition and the tenets of authentic womanhood and fronting her true feminist disposition and activist mission. Her alleged abuse of power on health care and her reported moral transgressions with Whitewater illustrated for some in the press and the Republican opposition what predictably would happen when political wives assumed too much power in the family and the nation. Even as certain journalists seemed motivated to recalibrate images of tradition and progress during the health care debate, such constructs often bowed to tradition—repeating the framing patterns from the 1992 and 1996 presidential campaigns.

A growing consensus tended to emerge in the press coverage that Clinton needed to be barred from the policy debates for overstepping the bounds of her role. In September 1994, CBS aired a statement by a man on the street who objected to Clinton's inflated power: "She acts like she's the president, and actually she's not the president. She wasn't elected to office." Even those who were supportive of Clinton, Linda Douglass contended, "believe she should become a spokesperson for key issues, but give up trying to shape legislation." Reaffirming the natural order of the presidency, historian Doris Kearns Goodwin argued that "it's very tough to become . . . an internal political decision maker when your husband is president and when it jumbles up the whole lines of authority." Douglass suggested that the realignment of gender power in the White House had seemingly been achieved: "These days Mrs. Clinton is less visible in Washington, and sources say she's less involved in White House personnel decisions."[164]

Yet, when Clinton performed the more traditional roles of first lady, she was routinely chastised as an imposter first lady. Few accepted Clinton playing the part of the traditional first lady performing the trappings of authentic womanhood. The real Hillary Clinton instead represented the outspoken and the politically front-and-center progressive woman from 1992. As Kearns Goodwin insisted: "You can't take that passion, that fight, that personality out of you unless you're truly muzzled . . . Hillary Clinton can't suddenly shift herself into something that she's not."[165]

The press frames emphasized once again the pitfalls associated with crossing the tradition-progress divide. Traversing such cavernous terrain appeared nearly unimaginable for a presidential wife. Clinton therefore had to pick one role and stick with it. ABC's Jackie Judd demonstrated the continued bifurcation between progress and tradition for first ladies in late 1994: "This Christmas at the White House, Hillary Clinton seems very much the traditional first lady, not the barnstorming brains behind national health care reform."[166] On CBS News, Representative Susan Molinari (R-NY) summarized the problem by juxtaposing most plainly the public-private roles of the first lady in traditional fashion: "The first lady can't have it both ways . . . Do you want to be a public figure or a private figure? You can't mix the two roles. It just isn't fair to the American public." Journalist Richard Threlkeld then questioned: "Be one or the other?" Molinari retorted: "You have to be one or the other."[167] Linda Douglass of CBS noted in November 1994 that Bill Clinton's advisors clearly favored the traditional: "Advisors are urging [Hillary Clinton] to focus on children's issues, already one of her passions and a traditional first lady's cause." Yet, in foreshadowing the future, Douglass made clear that Hillary Clinton would not be satisfied in her more constrained role as first lady: "Most who know her say she will not be forced to stand on the sidelines."[168]

Conclusion

As the opening pages of this chapter demonstrated, the legacy of the news frames from the health care and Whitewater controversies carried over into the news coverage of Clinton's 2008 presidential bid. Journalists continued to raise questions about Clinton's character and her personality problems during 2007 and 2008, comparing the Clinton of the early 1990s with the Clinton of the new millennium. During a May 25, 2007, MSNBC *Hardball* story on Carl Bernstein's book, Chris Matthews read a passage that emphasized Clinton's personality flaws: "Hillary's own personality and her . . . moral superiority killed . . . the greatest program effort of the Clinton presidency." That Hillary's personality alone "killed" the bill raised hard questions for Matthews about Clinton's personality and underlying character. Matthews then pondered whether or not Clinton possessed "the best character to be president." In answering his own question, Matthews expressed doubt, suggesting that she "will do what it takes" to become president, revealing her "ruthless" tactics in the process.[169]

To try to overcome such personality and character flaws, the press pinpointed again what many journalists saw as Clinton's attempts to remake her image.[170] In recalling Tammy Wynette, cookies and teas, health care, and Whitewater in 2007, Andrea Mitchell summarized the key concerns for Clinton aides, who worried that too "many people think Hillary Clinton is too cold and calculating." In response, Mitchell said Clinton was now pursuing a "softer, chattier, conversational" style in hopes that "people will like the new Hillary better than the one critics remember."[171] Through their surveillance coverage, journalists like Mitchell clearly felt most adept at uncovering evidence of political transformations and inconsistencies, revealing the inauthentic nature of the individual. Their vaults of old video allowed them to turn historical footage into authenticity proofs—a practice that ensured the recirculation of stabilizing historical frames across issues and time as a means to detect image fraud.

Yet, as this chapter has also shown, the news media play fast and loose with the video contained in their vaults. News actors routinely recontextualize video images in ways that fit the narrative they wish to tell, creating new storylines with floating visual imagery. Even as journalists condemn political leaders for inventing and reinventing their own images, the news media simultaneously invent and reinvent the meaning of free-floating political images at their creative disposal.

In the process, the news media help protect the borders of tradition for the nation-state, scrutinizing acts of gender progress and change and interrogating proper first lady comportment. These frames—composed of words and visual images—act as a primary means of disciplinary action through their recirculation and edification. As Judith Butler argues, "Language govern[s] the regulation and constitution of subjects," influencing the "exercise of agency." It is through "repetition" that "linguistic tokens of a community" take hold.[172]

Once removed from the media spotlight of health care and Whitewater, Hillary Clinton would reassert her political agency in a new political context as many predicted, pursuing a role as international envoy. In the process, she would tour more than seventy different countries during her time as first lady. Yet, the frames from 1992 through 1996 would accompany her movement across issue lines and national borders. While Hillary Clinton was serving a more diplomatic role on behalf of her husband's administration, another crisis would soon grip the first family and the nation at large. Clinton would once again find herself the subject of news surveillance. The media attention would derive not from questions about her political leadership or her legal troubles but from her status as a scorned wife. The context of her husband's marital infidelity would become a new staging ground for re-evaluating Clinton's authenticity and promoting her linguistic disciplining within the gendered nation.

CHAPTER 3

Hillary Clinton as International Emissary and Scorned Wife

Diplomatic Travel and the Clinton-Lewinsky Scandal—1995–1999

As Hillary and Bill Clinton faced what was arguably the biggest crisis of their marriage in the summer and fall of 1998, one of the key news frames of Hillary was that of a victim. From that summer forward, she was routinely framed as the scorned wife suffering the consequences of a philandering husband who had an illicit affair with a twenty-one-year-old intern named Monica Lewinsky. Yet, nearly ten years later, when rumors spread that Clinton would enter the 2008 presidential contest, that frame would be drowned out by one focused on the politically ambitious Clinton—the woman who had her sights set on the White House and would do anything to achieve that goal, even if that meant staying married to her habitually cheating husband of more than thirty years.

Not only was Hillary Clinton no longer framed as a "victim" by 2007, some charged that she preferred this label for political reasons; others maintained that she actually knew about the affairs all along, even serving as an occasional accomplice in the cover-up of Bill Clinton's indiscretions. Dick Morris, former Bill Clinton aide and outspoken critic, was one who claimed that Hillary welcomed the victim label during his Fox News interview in the spring of 2007: "A victimized wife. But that's what she wants" because it will help her politically.[1] Others would reinforce the "Hillary Clinton is no victim" mantra, going so far as to suggest that she actually was an accessory to her husband's deceit. In summarizing Carl Bernstein's book, *A Woman in Charge*, in May 2007, *Hardball*'s Chris Matthews alleged that "both Clintons went to great lengths to keep the lid on his infidelities." The pattern, according to Matthews's summation of the book, was for friends and attorneys of the Clintons to coach the adulterous women on handling the sexual allegations, getting them to sign statements that denied a sexual encounter with Bill Clinton. On one occasion, Matthews charged, "Hillary Clinton was present for the questioning." The takeaway for Matthews was that "it does get to their marriage, but it also gets to their political partnership."[2] Far removed from the image of the suffering wife, Hillary Clinton by 2007 and 2008 was perceived as working on behalf of her husband's political legacy and her own presidential ambitions by helping to silence her husband's mistresses.

For the news media, Hillary Clinton's presidential ambitions reached back years and even decades. Recollecting the co-presidency frame from 1992, radio talk show host Melanie Morgan made the following observation during the same *Hardball* broadcast: "We never doubted for a moment that Hillary Clinton was going to run for president . . . She and Bill Clinton bragged about it, two for one presidency."[3] The presumption of Hillary Clinton's presidential ambition was the subject of other books that were published during the lead-up to the 2008 presidential campaign, including Sally Bedell Smith's *For Love of Politics*.[4] When talking to John Gibson of Fox News in November 2007, Smith contended there was a plan for a sequential Clinton presidency. Gibson asked, "Back-to-back?" Smith responded: "Eight and eight." Smith went so far as to charge that their "friends . . . were talking about it as long ago as the '70s."[5] These themes built on the co-presidency residual frame from 1992. Yet, by 2008, co-presidency no longer just meant that Hillary would serve as Bill's co-president; it now meant that he in turn would serve as her co-president. This logic provided the answer for why Hillary Clinton—the outspoken feminist—opted to stay with her husband even after he admitted publicly on August 17, 1998, that "I did have a relationship with Miss Lewinsky that was not appropriate."[6]

The assumption that politics served as the bedrock of the Clinton marriage furthered the mystery surrounding their marital union throughout the course of Hillary's presidential bid. In an October 23, 2007, interview with CBS's *The Early Show*, Smith spoke to the mystery of the Clinton marriage, arguing that "their marriage is so unusual . . . people . . . called them Billary" back in "Arkansas."[7] On his Sunday morning talk show from October 2007, Chris Matthews raised questions about the real Hillary Clinton. Matthews asserted: "Nobody really seems to have a fix on Hillary, who she is. We know she's sixty years old. But we don't know her happiness level in her personal life." In response, David Gregory implied that Clinton engaged in a sense of purposeful subterfuge in terms of her marriage: "And I don't think she wants you to know. And I think that's part of her answer on the marriage, which is, 'Marriage is complicated.'"[8]

Yet, certain journalists seemed more than willing to fill in the knowledge gaps of the mysterious Clinton marriage during the 2008 presidential contest; some furthered the idea that the Clinton marriage was a sham to camouflage Hillary's political ambitions. Others viewed it through a gender lens, as a woman simply in need of a man. John Gibson led off his broadcast with the following question as he introduced Smith's book with a familiar reference to Tammy Wynette—was Clinton "really standing by her man . . . or just playing the game of politics knowing that she . . . might run for president one day?"[9] The 1992 stock frame involving Wynette would gain even further media traction during the Clinton-Lewinsky scandal as the press wondered whether or not Clinton was Tammy Wynette after all. Others, however, simply zeroed in on the political calculations in 2007, seemingly bent on exposing the counterfeit marriage. On ABC's *Good Morning America* from October 25, 2007, author Gail Sheehy made the claim that "everything . . . Hillary Clinton says is quite calculated." Sheehy detailed Clinton's strategy, suggesting that the goal was to bring "up the idea of romance in connection with her husband" and then to always "look happy and assured about it." This plan, Sheehy concluded, would go "a long way to reducing some of the suspicions that people still hold."[10] David Gregory, appearing on *The Chris Matthews Show* in October 2007, gave voice to the women who questioned Clinton's decision to stay in the marriage: "I think there are a lot of women who say, 'You were humiliated. You're a fool for staying. And then we don't really know who are you. You're doing it because you want to be president.'"[11]

That Hillary Clinton did run for the presidency affirmed the journalistic image of her as a politically ambitious co-president seeking her own unprecedented political goals. In stark contrast, however, the press coverage between 1995 and 1999 would also portray Clinton in ways more consonant with the ideology of authentic womanhood. The changes in coverage coincided with her comportment as a diplomatic first lady championing women's and children's causes and as a scorned woman victimized by her husband.

This chapter steps back in time to the television news coverage of Hillary Clinton from 1995–99 by first examining her role as a national mother, tackling issues affecting women and children at home and abroad. During this period of Clinton's press biography, the first lady was framed as coming into greater compliance with the more traditional norms as first lady, aligning her with the strictures of authentic womanhood as never before in her national press coverage. These news frames also sent the message that she had been sufficiently disciplined from entering the spaces of politics. Clinton continued to attract news coverage in her travels internationally, yet she was much more likely to be seen but not heard during short summations of her global excursions. Authentic womanhood was thus marked by a speechless woman who befittingly smiled or looked appropriately pained according to the prevailing ceremonial moment. Yet, when Hillary Clinton's words were actually aired, it became clear that she was serving as an outspoken advocate for women's and children's issues, gaining valuable political and diplomatic experiences that helped launch her future political career. Her outspokenness would be magnified momentarily by the press when she became the object of political intrigue during the 1995 World Conference on Women in China. Because the U.S. news media did not cover the expansiveness of her international activities as closely, she gained greater political freedom as an outspoken advocate without the constant scrutiny of the U.S. press. Consequently sidelined from the spaces of domestic controversy and more attentive to what were perceived as traditional first lady issues, Hillary Clinton would enjoy soaring approval ratings.

Clinton's framing as the humiliated and wounded wife during the Clinton-Lewinsky scandal further strengthened her alignment with the ideologies of authentic womanhood. These themes drew heavily on the 1992 stock frame of Tammy Wynette, suggesting that perhaps the real Hillary Clinton was a traditional wife after all, standing by her cheating man. From 1992 to 1995, Clinton was disciplined for overstepping the boundaries of the first lady position and thus the confines of authentic womanhood. From 1995 to 1999, she was featured as the smiling first lady and concerned national mother navigating the waters of international and diplomatic politics. In the private sphere of marriage, she was portrayed, at least for a brief time, more as a silent and scorned wife than the confident and outspoken political partner who led a task force on health care reform. These press frames epitomized a more normative portrait of authentic womanhood for U.S. women historically. Rather than viewed as a political anomaly, Clinton had finally joined the first lady club of ceremony and tradition more in line with Mamie Eisenhower and Jackie Kennedy than Eleanor Roosevelt, Betty Ford, and Rosalynn Carter. She also had become part of the sorority of scorned women suffering the consequences of a philandering husband, a sorority that included other first ladies like Roosevelt and Kennedy. The disciplining of Hillary Clinton would continue, this time through the intensive emphasis on her husband's betrayal and her own accompanying humiliation. She had finally reached the summit of authentic womanhood by serving in what some in the press saw as a selfless role of averting a national crisis by saving her marriage and thus her husband's presidency.

Bill Clinton of course was the marquee character in the news drama over his scandalous affair with a young White House intern. Even though he was impeached for perjury and obstruction of justice in December 1998,[12] the press and his supporters, including Hillary herself, seemed to hold Bill Clinton less responsible for his marital indiscretions. Those held most responsible seemed to be the women in his life: Hillary Clinton for traveling too much and leaving him alone too often; Monica Lewinsky for preying on the sexually susceptible president; and Bill Clinton's mother and grandmother for failing to offer the stable and nurturing environment he needed to thrive as a child. The visual images and the camera angles during the Clinton-Lewinsky drama visually reinforced Clinton's male gaze, further substantiating the traditional ideologies of authentic manhood. This cultural logic implied that the patriarchy of the presidency had been appropriately reinstantiated, reifying the age-old assumption—"men will be men"—and apparently—"presidents will be presidents."

In the end, as Hillary Clinton opted to stand by her man *and* to run for the U.S. Senate (chapter 4), the press frames rather quickly reverted back to the sentiment of the Clintons' *political marriage*. These frames reinforced the inauthenticity of Hillary Clinton and her marriage while also tarnishing her own political bids. This chapter first centers on the press coverage of Hillary Clinton's contribution to women's and children's issues at home and abroad from 1995 to 1999 before turning to the news treatment of Clinton's response to her husband's presidential affair from 1998 to 1999.

Hillary Clinton—Reframed as the Embodiment of Authentic Womanhood

Once Hillary Clinton was nudged from the political spotlight in the aftermath of the health care debate, journalists centered their attention on just how she would set about revamping her political image. This time, the news surveillance would have to follow Hillary Clinton around the globe as she re-envisioned her role as a diplomatic aide, stepping out of the domestic political spotlight and entering the glare of the global media watch.[13] Yet, with U.S. news organizations shrinking their international coverage, Clinton often received scant attention, being seen but not heard in many news accounts. The file footage aired was likely supplied by the first lady's media team or other news organizations if journalists from the networks were not dispatched to cover her daily movements. The press more often spoke for Hillary Clinton rather than allowing Clinton to speak for herself in their increasing use of "image bites" across political news stories.[14] As a result, Hillary Clinton's new role as an international diplomat was often narrated by a journalist who provided voiceover commentary on Clinton's actions in these international regions.

Specifically, Hillary Clinton's quiet smile and presence in such international spaces of pomp and ceremony reified her role as the nation's mother, embodying notions of authentic womanhood, freed from controversy and condemnation. Yet, when Clinton's outspokenness became the subject of international scrutiny during her participation in the 1995 Fourth World Conference on Women, the news media returned to more surveillance patterns. With such increased coverage of her trip to China, the press frames quickly reverted back to Clinton as a controversial first lady, where her "talk" could now threaten the peace and stability of U.S.-Sino relations. Once she became embroiled in international politics, Clinton's image as an authentic woman was quickly deflated by her outspokenness more consonant with her feminism expressed in the 1992 baseline frames. Hillary Clinton nevertheless took advantage of this time to travel the world and promote a human rights agenda for women and children outside of the U.S. media limelight. In the process, she gained experiences that would help launch her into elective office and lay the foundation for a robust political career of her own.

HILLARY CLINTON'S NEW AUTHENTIC WOMANHOOD ROLE

With Hillary Clinton out of sight and no longer the easy target of surveillance, the U.S. news media pondered her next move as the press turned the focus once again to her image adjustments. In January 1995, *NBC Nightly News* explored the question: "Is Hillary Clinton trying for a softer image?" In anchoring the broadcast, Tom Brokaw referenced "Mrs. Clinton's makeover mission for 1995," as she sought "to get out of the line of fire." Such coverage punctuated the familiar pattern for Clinton: her authentic outspokenness and overexposure (framed through a rhetoric of violence) was followed by an inauthenticating image makeover. NBC answered its own question through the title of the story—"Kinder, Gentler." NBC's Gwen Ifill drew on the war frames from the health care debate as well as the past frames that reinforced Clinton's propensity for backroom secrecy during the health care and Whitewater controversies: "The war over Hillary Clinton's image is a fierce one. Some despise her and the president's political enemies fuel that fire, although she often wins behind the scenes." Beyond depicting the controversy through a rhetoric of war, NBC also re-aired the image of Clinton burning in effigy from the health care deliberations, recirculating symbols of violence directed toward her.[15] Given this backlash to the real Hillary Clinton—feminist and political activist—what would be her next move?

ABC News helped answer this question by broadcasting a story on the first lady's newspaper column—reminiscent of Eleanor Roosevelt's "My Day" writings.[16] ABC displayed a photograph of Clinton who looked more like Ann Landers or Jackie Kennedy, with teased hair that curled upward at the bottom edges. Ann Compton of ABC News emphasized that Clinton was experiencing a time of great introspection over her image controversies. "There is a distinct edge of frustration in the column," Compton maintained, reflecting Clinton's struggle "'to recognize the Hillary Clinton that other people see.'" In the face of such harsh criticism, Compton portrayed Clinton as eager "to project a warmer, more personal side."[17] This framing held out the possibility that even Hillary Clinton seemed uncertain about her true self and the persona she wished to project; even she seemed to acknowledge her own past missteps as first lady. Since 1992, Clinton had been portrayed as the colder, harder-edged feminist rather than the warm and graceful woman more consonant with first lady comportment. Her goal, these stories implied, was to project a greater sense of warmth as a means of warming public sentiment toward her.

The press consequently emphasized Clinton's aim to recenter attention back on the issues that children faced—issues more normalized in the performances of first ladies (introduction). In referencing Clinton's continued work on behalf of children in October 1997, Martha Teichner of *CBS Evening News* claimed that Clinton clearly abandoned the spaces of politics for the social expectations of her gendered position: "Doing her best no longer means working the halls of Congress. Instead, she meets with children and encourages individuals, rather than government, to work for change." Clinton was clearly rewarded for such image transformations; Teichner reported that her approval rating had climbed to 69 percent, illustrating that "Americans like Hillary Clinton better now that she's softened her image."[18] Within this role as national mother, Clinton hosted a symposium on child development in April 1997. As Peter Jennings of ABC News noted, in "Mrs. Clinton's words," they were there "to talk about baby talk." ABC then featured Clinton's admonition that "a child's earliest experiences . . . [and] the challenges they meet, determine how their brains are wired."[19] CBS covered the same White House summit and also commented on Clinton's changed image. Rita Braver reported that "sources close to the first lady say she has chosen the popular issue of children and families as a safe place to rebuild her reputation, damaged by Whitewater and the president's failed health care plan."[20] This framing suggested that choosing more traditional causes became an ideal way to repair her unbecoming persona in the aftermath of the health care and Whitewater controversies. And the use of the words "safe place" was particularly revealing, connoting that Clinton had been in danger, warranting her seclusion from the perils that threatened her. This symbolism implied that Clinton needed to shield herself from such intense animosity and threats, reflecting a level of fear that undergirds the logic of disciplinary rhetoric.

As Hillary Clinton entered the safe world of children's issues, the news media's surveillance began to wane. She was often pictured in more traditional spaces of first lady conduct where she was seen but not heard. In her role of national mother, Hillary Clinton confronted the issue of violence on television in May 1995, appearing on *Oprah Winfrey* and chastising television talk shows for their lack of sensitivity to children's needs. According to Tom Brokaw of NBC News, "Mrs. Clinton slammed TV talk shows, saying their content plus other television violence, quote, 'changes the way that children feel about themselves in a very damaging way.'" "She said," Brokaw continued, that "all Americans should be ashamed if we can't help children have better lives."[21] Even though we could see Hillary Clinton speaking in this video clip, Brokaw voiced her words. As Clinton performed the time-honored role as first lady more aligned with authentic womanhood, her own voice was increasingly muted in the growing use of image bite coverage. Clinton's outspokenness on less controversial children's issues also led to more limited coverage. And this diminished coverage would become even more pronounced as she gave up the contested political terrain at home for her wide-ranging excursions around the globe. The news media would certainly track her movements; yet, the most newsworthy moments resurfaced when her level of "talk" became the subject of political and international intrigue.

HILLARY CLINTON AS INTERNATIONAL ENVOY

Hillary Clinton would travel the globe after the health care defeat, visiting such countries as Pakistan, Senegal, and Paraguay. More routinely, especially when compared to coverage of Clinton prior to 1995, we could not hear the words she spoke. We instead saw her positioned in such spaces of ceremony and diplomacy. As the embodiment of authentic womanhood—a featured component of U.S. nationalism—the smile would become the signature symbol of first lady comportment as the news media narrated Clinton's travelogue.

To exemplify the new trends in Hillary Clinton's coverage, *CBS Evening News* captured Hillary and her daughter Chelsea in Lahore, Pakistan, on March 27, 1995, as Connie Chung offered a travel narrative of the Clinton women, who "had another day of sightseeing and consciousness-raising in Pakistan." Chung recounted that "Mrs. Clinton urged a greater role for the women of Asia. Later they watched some traditional dancing. They'll go on to India tomorrow."[22] The visuals that accompanied the story pictured Hillary and Chelsea smiling broadly and interacting with girls in a school setting. The story was descriptive, benign, and without controversy, suggesting that traditional women should be seen but not necessarily heard. ABC News similarly covered Clinton's March 1997 trip to Goree Island in Senegal. Forrest Sawyer framed the story in this way: "In Africa today, Hillary Rodham Clinton began a two-week visit to the continent . . . in a place laden with symbolism for Americans." In this story, Clinton's facial expressions fit the tragedy of the hallowed site. As she encountered chains and manacles from this wretched period in U.S. slave history, she expressed a look of seriousness and genuine sadness. Yet, as she greeted crowds of supporters during the same broadcast, she once again exuded a level of merriment through her broad smile. As Sawyer concluded: "Mrs. Clinton is on a trip to broaden American awareness of African people and its new democracies."[23] In these instances, the news media served as Clinton's vocal surrogacy, featuring images that reinforced her appropriate demeanor as a diplomatic envoy. Clinton's voice would be audible in an ABC News follow-up story from the following day, yet her words represented mere pleasantries: "Good morning. Good morning. How are you?" In her national motherhood role, we see a smiling Clinton surrounded by children as Sawyer narrated the exchange: "And she was delighted by a group of children at a Soweto orphanage."[24] Such broadcast patterns reflected the assumption that issues affecting women (and children) often fell outside the boundaries of politics, requiring scant attention.[25]

CNN, as a twenty-four-hour news service with an international bureau, offered noticeably more expanded coverage of Clinton's travels with actual journalists on location covering her daily activities. During these stories, excerpts from Clinton's substantive statements were more routinely aired, demonstrating a politically active first lady on the world stage, advocating for human and civil rights. One of Clinton's key themes focused on the promotion of human and civil rights, particularly for women and children. *CNN World View* conducted an exclusive interview with Clinton after she visited several countries in Africa. Clinton summarized her political agenda accordingly in April 1997: "I believe strongly, as I have said in many different settings . . . that women's rights are human rights, and that societies which invest in girls, as well as boys, and give women incentives to be economically and politically and socially involved, will be more prosperous in the future."[26] Similarly providing a more substantive report on Hillary's trip to the Ukraine in November 1997, CNN aired Clinton's strong endorsement of democratic values: "We must build a civil society where democratic values live in our hearts and minds, where people stand up for what is right, and where the rule of law not the rule of crime and corruption prevail."[27]

Although promoting controversial positions on women's equality and human rights in the host countries, the controversy surrounding Clinton's outspokenness on the international stage gained minimal attention in U.S. news.[28] As Carole Simpson of ABC News observed on March 21, 1999: "Tomorrow, [Clinton] begins campaigning on behalf of her favorite causes—human rights for women and girls' education. A pleasant respite from Washington."[29] Once disciplined out of the domestic spaces of politics, First Lady Clinton took her political agenda to the world stage where she re-envisioned her political contributions before a U.S. press conditioned to view human rights as a cause far removed from partisan politics.

HILLARY CLINTON AS AN INTERNATIONAL THREAT

Everything would change suddenly when the first lady's international excursions became the subject of controversy. The moment that Hillary Clinton hinted she would attend the UN's Fourth World Conference on Women, conflict swirled around her possible participation. Some of the criticism related to the imprisonment of Harry Wu, a human rights activist held by the Chinese government. Others thought Clinton should boycott the trip given China's human rights record. An unidentified critic of Clinton's trip raised his objection before NBC's news camera on August 26, 1995: "It's like having a human rights conference in Bagdad. It's like having an NAACP rally at a KKK event. It's ludicrous."[30] CBS News also highlighted the partisan dimension of the objections by raising the issue of China's record on abortion. Bill Plante explained on August 20, 1995, that "conservatives distrust the aims of the women's conference, fearing that it could endorse abortion and birth control. The Republican congressional leadership wants the U.S. to boycott the gathering altogether."[31] Three days later, CBS's Plante would characterize the controversy this way: "Critics continue to say that . . . a high-profile visit by the first lady would send exactly the wrong signal" on matters of human rights.[32]

Hillary Clinton would defend the trip on the grounds that the United States needed to address human rights issues even if that meant participating in a conference hosted by China. CBS aired Clinton delivering the following statement on August 26: "Health care, education, economic opportunity, political freedom and participation, and human rights. The conference will raise awareness about the challenges and burdens women face."[33] Even though Harry Wu's release in late August 1995 would clear a major roadblock for Clinton's attendance, the controversy was far from over.

As Hillary Clinton arrived in Beijing for the conference in early September 1995, the press frames returned to a familiar focus on Clinton's presence in spaces of political controversy. In a segment called "Hope and Fears," NBC's

Andrea Mitchell introduced the story by noting that Clinton arrived in Beijing "at the height of the storm."[34] John Roberts of CBS News framed Clinton's arrival similarly, asserting that Clinton "landed right in the middle of a controversy over stifling Chinese security measures and over demands that she speak out about human rights."[35] Playing up the "Risks and Rights" in a separate broadcast, NBC returned to a popular image from the health care debate about Clinton's risky political maneuvers. Giselle Fernandez maintained that she would be "walking a political tight rope,"[36] foreshadowing the dangers that lay ahead.

Initially, the criticism involving Clinton's attendance centered on the rumor that she did not plan to criticize China's human rights abuses. CBS interviewed Richard Dicker of Human Rights Watch, and he leveled a charge against Clinton's silence on these matters: "For her to be silent on that would effectively give the Chinese just what they want."[37] Andrea Mitchell also emphasized the conflict surrounding Clinton's proposed nonresponse to China's human rights abuses: "The first lady will speak out on ways to improve the lives of women, children, and families and leave any direct criticism of China to the diplomats, and their chief interest is in making up with China's leaders."[38] In earlier controversies, Clinton's talkativeness became a major source of her problems. Now, her decision to go silent on human rights abuses punctuated a level of hypocrisy for rights activists and the attentive press—an implication derived from the move toward "making up" with China over matters of human rights. That Hillary Clinton traveled the world speaking out on human rights issues only intensified the scrutiny over her reluctance to condemn China.

The critique, though, quickly changed when Clinton opted to issue a human rights rebuke against the host country. The press returned to the familiar memory frames where the source of Clinton's problems related to her outspokenness. In this case, her outspokenness could now actually prompt a foreign policy crisis with one of the country's most complicated adversaries. NBC suggested that Hillary Clinton was once again venturing into uncharted territory by serving in a delicate diplomatic role as the wife of the president. According to NBC's John Palmer, "Hers is a mission that would tax the most experienced diplomat." Presidential historian Michael Beschloss reinforced Palmer's insight, arguing that "this could be a case in which she is substantively involved in diplomacy in a way that she has not been before."[39]

Even though Beschloss did not see a "down side" to the expansion of Clinton's diplomatic role, other stories would emphasize the danger of Clinton's outspokenness. On September 5, 1995, Dan Rather of CBS exuded an alarming tone when he argued that Clinton "waded into controversy today. She jolted the UN Women's Conference in Beijing with a blast at governments and cultures that violate the human rights of women. Among the chief targets were her Chinese hosts." Rather's use of the words *blast* and *target* reflected a sense of war-like alarm. Martha Teichner extended the war rhetoric by cloaking Clinton's words in a language of explosives: "Given the fragile state of U.S.-China relations at the moment, the first lady's human rights bombshell was unexpected and risky. She did not mention China by name, but there was no doubt that China was supposed to get the message." To evidence the riskiness of Clinton's "bombshell" message, CBS aired what was presumably one of Clinton's more incendiary passages: "Let me be clear. Freedom means the right of people to assemble, organize, and debate openly. It means not taking citizens away from their loved ones and jailing them, mistreating them, or denying them their freedom or dignity because of the peaceful expression of their ideas and opinions." Rather than critique Clinton for her silence on human rights, the consternation now returned to the potential consequences of her outspokenness. As Teichner concluded: "When the first lady of the United States breaks her silence in so dramatic a way, it is no longer just a women's issue—it is foreign policy with potential repercussions."[40] This statement punctuated the memory frame of Clinton's outspokenness as a source of political controversy and reinforced the adage that women's issues ranked lower on the list of political priorities. Most significantly, CBS suggested through its rhetoric of war that Clinton's condemnatory remarks ratcheted up an already intense relationship between the United States and China.

The notion that Hillary Clinton violated first lady comportment was also an important theme for ABC News. Ann Compton implied that Clinton was tone deaf in refusing to listen to her "critics." Not only did she go to China in spite of such warnings, she issued an inflammatory denunciation of the host country in a way that violated diplomatic protocol: "By coming to China, Hillary Clinton ignored critics who argued human rights abuses here are so bad, the U.S. should not send a delegation much less the wife of the president. But Mrs. Clinton delivered a surprisingly forceful attack on China. Without mentioning the conference host by name, she condemned a long list of abuses known to occur in China, from forced abortion to violence against women and girls." The implication for ABC was similar to the one invoked by CBS; both questioned Clinton's statements in light of her position and the complicated political terrain. As Compton brought the story to a close, she contended that Clinton "has waded through plenty of domestic controversy, but she has never taken such a bold step into international controversy."[41] One day earlier, the critique centered on her silence. Yet on this day, she would now be chastised for breaking that silence, demonstrating the "double bind" that Clinton faced.[42]

The coverage of Clinton's international travels suggested that when she confined herself to the conditions of women and children—framed as nonpolitical issues—she pursued more traditional topics that fell within the parameters of her role as first lady and the sphere of authentic womanhood. Yet, as soon as she moved away from such issues and tackled more seemingly significant *political* matters, she once again defied the prescriptions of her role. The U.S. news media would predictably recall the memory frames from the health care debate by referencing past "domestic controversy." To carry her propensity for political controversy from the domestic to the international spaces, the press conjectured, could risk an international incident of considerable magnitude.

The themes that Clinton addressed in China, however, reinforced the same human rights messages she delivered in many other countries, representing one of her signature campaigns as first lady. Hillary Clinton's message had not changed so much as the intensity of the coverage had shifted. Hillary Clinton was much more likely to experience a level of disciplining with heightened levels of media surveillance; she seemly enjoyed greater political freedoms without it. For a time, she would arguably perform the trappings of authentic womanhood based largely on the issues that *appeared* more appropriate and customary. The accompanying visual images of a smiling first lady engaged in acts of ceremony further reified cultural expectations of a more "appropriately" gendered woman representing the nation-state. This apparent transformation gained the approval of the press and the American people given the lack of controversy and her improving poll numbers.

As the crisis over the Clinton marriage began to take shape in 1998, Clinton's respite from media surveillance would come to an end. Other authentic womanhood themes would emerge, however, during what the press often dubbed as her period of public humiliation, where she would be forced to help salvage the presidency of her cheating husband.

Hillary Clinton as Public Defender and Scorned Wife

The year 1998 would open to rumors of Bill Clinton's affair with a young White House intern named Monica Lewinsky. Bill Clinton vigorously denounced the rumors on January 26, 1998. Most who were politically tuned in during this period can readily visualize the moment when the president of the United States notoriously shook his finger before the television cameras in a demanding and decisive way, professing his innocence: "I want you to listen to me . . . I did not have sexual relations with that woman, Miss Lewinsky. I never told anyone to lie . . . These allegations are false. And I need to go back to work for the American people."[43] The following day, Hillary Clinton's appearance on NBC's *Today* show would become another formative media moment for Clinton and another stock frame for the press. Within the interview, Matt Lauer, coanchor of the morning program, asked Clinton, "If an American president had an adulterous liaison in the White House and lied to cover it up, should the American people ask for his resignation?" Clinton offered a more definitive and reassuring response: "If all that were proven true, I think that would be a very serious offense. That is not going to be proven true."[44]

From that moment onward, Clinton would again be framed as her husband's defender because of her unwavering public support for him. In 1992 as in 1998, she would come forward to defend her husband and her marriage in convincing ways that helped lessen the anxieties over Bill Clinton's character issues. In spite of strong denouncements by the Clintons, the rumors persisted throughout the spring and early summer of 1998. And when independent counsel Kenneth Starr produced Lewinsky's famous semen-stained blue dress in the summer of 1998, the president would have no alternative but to come clean. DNA evidence could now scientifically rebut his denials.[45]

Hillary Clinton's decision to "stand by her man," the press emphasized, furthered the evidence that she was Tammy Wynette after all, despite her disavowals in 1992. For some journalists, Clinton's decision to stay married in the face of public humiliation and pain helped salvage the presidency. Through her steadfast support of the president, Hillary Clinton was lauded by some in the press for guiding the American people in their own forgiveness of the president. Clinton's demonstration of public grace reinforced the ideological commonplaces of authentic womanhood by selflessly putting the nation's interests above her own torment. These frames, however, would serve as yet another means of disciplining Clinton; her outspokenness came in the form of publicly defending a wayward husband who violated their vows of marriage in the most public of ways. As a scorned and disciplined first lady, she would attract more positive reviews in the press and higher approval ratings from those polled. Throughout this time, the press surveillance would intensify, turning to Hillary Clinton's decontextualized face as a barometer of her emotional response to her husband's illicit affair.

HILLARY CLINTON AS PUBLIC DEFENDER OF HER CHEATING HUSBAND

The legacy of the 1992 memory of Tammy Wynette would become a prevailing press frame for Hillary Clinton's response to her husband's personal betrayal. Matt Lauer reminded Clinton of her Wynette comment during the January 27, 1998, *Today* show interview: "You said at the time of the interview, a very famous quote, 'I'm not some Tammy Wynette standing by my man' . . . Six years later you are still standing by this man." Drawing on the *60 Minutes* interview from 1992, Lauer then asked if Clinton believed her husband "would admit that he again has caused pain in this marriage." In response, Hillary Clinton answered, "Absolutely not," affirming that Bill Clinton had nothing to apologize for. Instead, she diverted attention to the possibility of a "vast right-wing conspiracy" designed to bring down her husband's presidency: "We know everything there is to know about each other, and we . . . love each other. And I just think that a lot of this is deliberately designed to sensationalize charges against my husband because everything else they've tried has failed." Lauer would pursue another angle on the same theme, addressing the matter of Hillary Clinton as her husband's "chief defender." Lauer asked: "There have been reports that you've taken charge at the White House and decided to be the chief defender of your husband, of the president, and deflect these charges. How much of a role are you taking in this?" In answering Lauer's latest question, Clinton boldly vowed to "defend my husband." Yet, she also denied any official role in his defense: "I am by no means running any kind of strategy or being his chief defender. He's got very capable lawyers . . . and a lot of very good friends outside the White House." Referring to Hillary Clinton as her husband's "most credible defender," Lauer reified the sense that the wife of the president served as a moral compass. The assumption was that if the wife of the president stood by her man—the person who seemingly knew her husband better than anyone—the remainder of the country could more confidently follow. Hillary Clinton reaffirmed her role as a character judge for her husband by arguing, "I probably know him better than anybody alive in the world, so I would hope that I'd be the most credible defender."[46]

From the moment that Clinton's *Today* show interview ended, the news buzz centered on her public defense of the president. Popular frames from 1992 re-emerged in the coverage, including the stock frame of Tammy Wynette as well Clinton's need to be "front and center" in political activities. Some re-employed a rhetoric of war in the process. The *CBS Evening News* broadcast from January 27, 1998, assimilated all of these past frames into a matter of a few sentences. In introducing the story, Dan Rather asserted: "As the latest and most serious political trouble of Bill Clinton's career plays out here in Washington, Hillary Clinton has put herself in a familiar role, front and center, not just standing by but standing up for a husband under withering fire." After placing Clinton in the forefront of the "fire," Rather transitioned to a report by Rita Braver with the following words: "first family's first line of defense." CBS next re-aired part of the *Today* show clip where Clinton asserted: "We know everything there is to know about each other." A sound bite from the 1992 *60 Minutes* interview came next as Braver framed the latter media moment accordingly: "Those words today had a familiar ring. Remember this *60 Minutes* interview during the 1992 presidential campaign in the wake of charges that the president had an affair with Gennifer Flowers?" Braver ultimately extended Rather's war theme when offering her own narrative arc to the story: "And so Mrs. Clinton is taking on the job that she has in so many other times of personal and political crisis, rallying the president's staff and helping design an overall battle plan." CBS's banner headline throughout the Clinton-Lewinsky and impeachment scandal reinforced the use of this militaristic language: "White House Under Fire."[47] Even while recalling Clinton's Wynette utterance, CBS suggested that her comportment was anything but that of a traditional wife given her positioning on the front lines of another all-out war against her husband.

NBC Nightly News would use similar framing, including references to Clinton's role as her husband's public defender through the use of military imagery. NBC relied on a similar visual heading that connoted the magnitude of the controversy: "White House Crisis." Beginning the broadcast on January 27, Tom Brokaw invoked battle imagery from the beginning of the story: "A war is underway between the president, Mrs. Clinton, and Whitewater prosecutor Kenneth Starr after Mrs. Clinton said the current White House sex scandal is driven by a right-wing conspiracy. It's a war of words so far with no clear winner." Later in the same broadcast, Andrea Mitchell guided viewers through the *Today* show interview, segment by segment. She began with Hillary Clinton's part in the defense, surveying her many public and private roles: "New York City before dawn, wife, mother, first lady, first defender, emphatically denying charges about the most intimate details of her marriage." Mitchell ended the story by recalling the front-and-center frames from the 1992 campaign and the 1993–95 health care debates: "So tonight, she'll be front and center, no matter what else may be true, fiercely believing that her husband is the target of one of history's greatest conspiracies."[48] CNN's framing of Hillary Clinton's public role would resemble the crisis rhetoric of the other networks. During the broadcast from January 28, 1998, journalist Bob Franken set the stage: "There is a rescue operation going on . . . And of course, the first lady, Hillary Rodham Clinton, who seems to be leading the whole operation, is doing her own speeches."[49] These metaphorical constructions portrayed Hillary Clinton as a woman rescuing her philandering husband—a defensive stance she would take routinely throughout the Clinton marriage, such press frames suggested.

To keep alive the image of Hillary Clinton defending her husband, CBS put its momentous *60 Minutes* broadcast from January 1992 back on the air. CBS first re-aired the January 1992 clips during its January 30, 1998, broadcast of *CBS Evening News*. On February 1, 1998, CBS then recycled the *60 Minutes* broadcast with never-before-seen backstage clips in an episode entitled "Another Look." This second look allowed the 1998 audience to decide whether or not Hillary Clinton resembled Tammy Wynette more than she ever wanted to admit.[50]

As the time period neared when Bill Clinton finally went public with his admission of guilt for an affair with Monica Lewinsky on August 17, 1998, Hillary Clinton would again be depicted as one of her husband's primary advisors and defenders. In the days leading up to Bill Clinton's Map Room speech, Andrea Mitchell of NBC News noted Hillary Clinton's role in preparing her husband for his public defense. On August 14, Mitchell stated: "And I think that she is helping to . . . advise every step of the way."[51] As Mitchell uttered this phrase, video was shown of Hillary Clinton whispering something into her husband's ear as they appeared together in a ceremonial setting. Reading Hillary's private whispers to her husband in a public setting was presented once again as evidence of her advisory role. Lisa Caputo, a former staffer for Hillary Clinton, reaffirmed such an advisory position in an interview on CNN's *Larry King Live* from August 17: "I'm sure she helped prepare the statement tonight . . . and I think that right now all of her attention is on Chelsea and her husband."[52] Clinton's role as behind-the-scenes advisor would transition to that as public defender rather quickly. ABC's *Nightline* titled its story from August 24, 1998, "First Lady First Defender."[53] CBS used similar language when Dan Rather opened up his September 29, 1998, broadcast with the following sentence: "Hillary Clinton is going to . . . new lengths in her role as first lady and first defender of the president."[54]

Framing Hillary Clinton as a public defender suggested that she soldiered through this difficult period with public displays of strength; these frames emphasized Hillary Clinton's agency in taking control of her family's delicate situation—serving on the front lines in the battle involving the defense of her husband. In this role, she acted as a source of support and professional counsel to her husband in a time of considerable need; she also represented a pillar of strength for her daughter during this familial crisis. Yet, the coverage would also accentuate the level of humiliation that Hillary Clinton faced, which introduced the notion of Hillary Clinton as a victim and scorned wife, lacking in agency and unable to control her wandering husband and the public scandal swirling about her.

HILLARY CLINTON AS SCORNED WIFE

Hillary Clinton as an advisor would take control of the situation and not allow anyone to view her as the helpless wife, acted on by her cheating husband. Hillary Clinton as a victim, however, would lack the agency to control the situation, making her the source of national pity in the face of her husband's betrayal.[55] The images of Hillary Clinton as a scorned woman aligned her more with traditional notions of authentic womanhood. She would become one among many women facing life with a man who severed the promises of their marital vows. Clinton, as a character within this press drama, would assume the mantle of gender tradition that attracted sympathy and high approval ratings. Assessing Clinton's emotional state, though, necessitated an enhanced media surveil- lance effort and a more microscopic examination of Hillary's face as a pathway to her inner emotions.

As the media emphasized Hillary's public role in defending her husband, they simultaneously zoomed in on Hillary Clinton's private pain and humili- ation. ABC's story from August 17, 1998, would emphasize both. On the day of Bill Clinton's public admission of guilt, Peter Jennings framed Hillary Clinton's response in the following way: "It's just obvious to everybody in the country that this has been an enormous strain for Mrs. Clinton and for Chelsea to have the president come out after all this time and say that he had not been telling the country the truth." Clinton friend and religious counsel Jesse Jackson confirmed Clinton's emotional turmoil while still portraying her as an important source of support and advice for her husband and daughter: "Hillary's amazing strength and love is exemplified by the fact that yesterday, while there is some pain and some humiliation on her part and embarrassment on the president's part, she was in the strategy room, helping to map out strategies for today's sessions." Ultimately, Jackson surmised, Hillary Clinton demonstrated an "unconditional love" for her husband and a "commitment to their marriage."[56] NBC News cov- ered Jackson's statements to the press as well, putting less emphasis on Clin- ton's agency and more on her fragile emotional state. David Bloom, reporting from the White House, contended that "Jackson says Mr. Clinton is in pain and embarrassed; his wife, humiliated."[57]

CNN offered a more extensive discussion of both Clintons, taking an inward turn when discussing Hillary. Garrick Utley interviewed David Gergen, former Bill Clinton advisor, for this segment of the broadcast. Transitioning from the public Clintons to the private Clintons, Utley observed: "As lawyers, both are trained for confrontation. As politicians, both have disciplined themselves to keep smiling, no matter how bad it gets. But what happens when the cameras are not running?" In characterizing Hillary's response, Gergen asserted that "she has been more . . . hurt . . . more emotionally vulnerable." Utley responded: "That, too, may not be apparent on the surface."[58] This assumed lack of surface-level emotions would signal for the press the need to engage in an internal interrogation of Clinton's emotional state, warranting a return to face politics to do so.

The television news camera became an important means for the news media to comprehend the mysteries and unanswered questions about Hillary Clinton. During the Whitewater controversy, the camera's explorations pertained more to Hillary Clinton's honesty. During the Clinton-Lewinsky scandal, the camera's explorations were more focused on capturing the true emotional state of this deeply private and publicly scorned woman. Presumably, such emotions could be captured by careful attention to her facial clues, visible through the magnifying lens of the news camera.

ABC's *Nightline* used its camera to steer the viewer to Hillary Clinton's face as a measure of her emotional condition. Once Bill Clinton admitted his guilt, he would travel with his family to Martha's Vineyard to work through their personal issues. Former Clinton advisor James Carville suggested that Bill Clinton would "spend a little time in the woodshed" while on a family retreat.[59] As the Clintons were shown shaking hands with people waiting to greet them at the airport, Chris Bury of *Nightline* talked of Hillary Clinton's humiliation. As soon as he characterized the issue as a "personal" and "humiliating" one, the camera zoomed in for a tighter shot on Clinton as if to allow viewers a close-up glimpse into what a humiliated Hillary Clinton might look like.[60] Even though Hillary Clinton was smiling in these shots, the continued discussion of her humiliation marked the smiling Hillary Clinton as a truly pained woman hiding behind her sunglasses and her Stepford wife facial expressions. In these instances, the press framed Hillary's smile as a mask for her true emotions. The press, accordingly, served the ends of physiognomy, which were designed to "struggle against dissimulation, secrecy, and hypocrisy . . . in favour of truth, clarity and openness."[61]

Another starker example of face politics would be practiced by NBC News, exhibiting further ways in which the news media conflate issues and decontextualize visual imagery. As discussed in chapter 2, from approximately 1993 to 1997, networks used footage from the health care debate to stand in for the Whitewater controversy. In 1998, NBC in particular relied on images from a memorial service for victims of U.S. embassy bombings in Kenya and Tanzania to stand in for an emotional assessment of Hillary Clinton and the Clinton marriage as the Clinton-Lewinsky crisis unfolded. The exchange of images could occur because the memorial service at Andrews Air Force base took place on August 13, 1998, four days before Bill Clinton's final admission of guilt.[62] The Clintons appeared together at the ceremony, looking emotionally pained, having just met with the victims of family members of the terrorist attack. The decontextualized images were specifically extracted during the part of the public ceremony aired on C-Span where the Clintons watched the flag-draped caskets being placed into waiting hearses.[63]

The most commonly decontextualized image from the memorial service was that of a close-up facial profile of Hillary Clinton. The backdrop was darkened, with no available clues as to the context of the image. Her face—shot from a profile position with the camera located to the side and slightly behind Clinton—filled the television screen, further obstructing any contextual markers. NBC's first known decontextualization of this memorial service shot occurred on August 17, 1998, when Andrea Mitchell narrated a segment on the private implications of Bill Clinton's affair on the Clinton marriage. As Mitchell punctuated Hillary Clinton's pain and humiliation, the recontextualized facial profile image appeared on screen: "She is right there at his side, smiling for the cameras, despite the biggest crisis of their twenty-three-year marriage. Over a weekend of public humiliation and private pain, sources tell NBC News she helped her husband prepare first to admit to adultery to Ken Starr, the man they both view as a mortal enemy."[64] With this shot, NBC turned a video taken during a public memorial service into a private moment of personal anguish. During the Clinton-Lewinsky period, NBC used that particular facial shot as an index of Hillary Clinton's emotional turmoil, suggesting that NBC caught Clinton in a backstage moment where her true emotions were unobtrusively displayed. This shot symbolized that NBC had presumably removed the mask of Clinton's plastered-on smile and discovered her true emotional anguish. The stock image frame would be used in subsequent NBC broadcasts and stood in as a short-cut reference to Clinton's condition during the controversy over her husband's public admission of guilt.

For NBC, Hillary Clinton's eyes in particular served as the site of greatest emotional disclosure. In a September 12, 1998, *Dateline* special entitled "The President and the People," Jane Pauley directed the viewers to Clinton's eyes as NBC edited the facial profile into this new narrative: "People are looking into her eyes for an idea of what she's going through as the release of the independent counsel's report draws near."[65] Physiognomically, attention to the eyes was believed by many to offer the greatest insight into the interior self.[66] Even though Clinton served as a public defender of her husband, her eyes and her face told a different story, NBC implied. Transforming a memorial service shot into an image of Clinton grieving over her husband's deceit gave NBC an attention-getting image by which to attract viewer interest. By suggesting that the NBC news camera had actually penetrated Clinton's public veneer, the narrative and the camera shot invited a sneak peek behind the image mask in order to interrogate Clinton's true emotional state.

NBC would extract other images from the memorial service that focused the camera's attention on the first couple. NBC used one shot from the service of the noninteractive Clintons looking emotionally distraught as they stood side by side, staring straight ahead. This image stood in as an indicator of the Clintons' marital strain. While it was clear that the Clintons were part of a public event, the details of the event were obscured, as they faced the cameras with a group of nondescript people filed in behind them. In the same August 17 broadcast, the image appeared as Mitchell referenced Lewinsky's blue dress that served as the smoking gun in the Clinton-Lewinsky affair: "This time, say the first lady's friends, there was potential evidence, impossible to ignore, leading finally to her husband's admissions this weekend."[67] Using an image of public pain as an instantiation of private strain reinforced the message that NBC seemingly sought to send—the Clinton marriage was anything but healthy despite the public pretenses they upheld.

NBC would use one additional image related to the memorial service to stand in for the state of the Clinton marriage. This one featured the first couple returning from the memorial service to the White House as they held hands and walked together across the White House lawn. Despite the fact they were actually touching, they were not interacting. Rather than looking toward each other, they were looking down instead, with Bill Clinton occasionally looking ahead. Hillary Clinton once again was sporting sunglasses, which connoted her efforts to hide her true emotions, according to prevailing press logic. The message of this image, though, differed from the one extracted from the memorial service. For NBC, the signature meaning of the White House lawn video was that even though the Clintons obviously experienced pain in their marriage, they were nevertheless still together—struggling through their marital discord. NBC's *Time & Again* episode from September 19, 1998, drew similar conclusions about the steadfastness of the Clinton marriage in spite of their ongoing problems. When Jane Pauley reported that the Clintons "relied on each other when times were tough," NBC inserted this particular post–memorial service video.[68] While the strain was clearly evident, NBC used it as a more hopeful image, suggesting that the Clinton marriage endured in spite of the pain Bill Clinton had caused.

The transformation of these public memorial service images into private moments involving the Clinton marriage would continue for at least another eighteen months. The facial profile image would be used by NBC in at least six different broadcasts through January 27, 2000. It not only stood in for the mysterious Hillary Clinton, attempting to capture how she was responding to her husband's affair, but it also was used in other mystery stories related to Clinton—whether she would pursue the Senate candidacy in 2000, and whether she would stay in the heated Senate contest once she became a candidate. The second image of the Clintons standing side by side during the memorial ceremony reappeared at least five more times in NBC's coverage. In all instances, the image epitomized their troubled marriage, regardless of the story's theme. The final image of the Clintons on the White House lawn would be used in at least four additional broadcasts. The meaning that NBC imposed on this memorial image was one of marital strain yet marital endurance.[69]

Decontextualization practices demonstrate most vividly the ways in which news organizations play fast and loose with video footage, engaging in acts of visual manipulation and distortion. The meanings of these images were transformed by the news media in order to substantiate the message of the moment. These visualization devices could also help attract viewers to the stories that the press wished to tell. The narrative such videos told was of a marriage in trouble—yet one where the couple stayed together in spite of obvious relational strain. The signature facial profile also connoted a privately grieving first lady who endured considerable pain privately yet maintained a face of strength and determination publicly.

That Hillary Clinton was able to put on such a brave and smiling face and stand by her man in spite of such personal pain would invoke greater admiration for Clinton in ways she had yet to experience on the national stage. Barbara Walter's expressions of sadness during a March 1999 episode of *Nightline* reflected the presumed disconnect between the public and the private Hillary and the amount of sympathy she attracted for her pain. "I'm filled with great sadness for her no matter what she may be showing," Walter acknowledged empathically. "I just think it's so sad."[70] An unidentified woman expressed similar sympathy for Clinton on *CNN World View* from August 2, 1999: "I kind of feel sorry for Hillary" because of the "Monica Lewinsky mess. The one thing it's accomplished is make people who ordinarily wouldn't be sympathetic to Hillary Clinton" be more "sympathetic."[71] Importantly, as Clinton exuded greater political strength, her poll numbers would dip. As she showed a clear sense of marital fortitude by staying with her cheating husband, her poll numbers would rise. As the scorned and sad woman attracting sympathy from others, Clinton would more closely resemble the traditional ideals of authentic womanhood.

HILLARY CLINTON AS AUTHENTIC WOMAN

As a woman standing by her man, Hillary Clinton would receive more praise than she was accustomed to as a political activist fighting for the election of her husband or the passage of his administration's health care bill. The admiration scores for Hillary Clinton would rise as never before as a privately suffering wife. In the press coverage, she served as a role model in helping the nation make sense of her husband's indiscretions. This admiration though was rooted in more traditional expectations for a wife who accepted her husband's marital waywardness and forgave him. Within this narrative, Hillary Clinton ceased to be Bill Clinton's equal in the marriage. Press coverage instead posited a more patriarchal view of the presidential relationship. By righting the hierarchy of a man in control of his marriage, Hillary Clinton was again sufficiently put in her place, attracting higher approval ratings for her status as a more traditionally authentic woman.

CNN communicated admiration for Clinton's "stand by your man" persona in the most explicit of ways. In a story entitled "Standing By Her Man," journalist Eileen O'Connor claimed on August 17, 1998, that "Hillary Rodham Clinton is doing what she always does and by all accounts will always do—stand by her man, and the public loves her for it." The first image CNN aired was of the Clintons walking on the White House lawn after the memorial service—engaging in the same practice as NBC of recontexualizing the memorial service images. Though walking together and holding hands, both look detached. When suggesting that the "public loves her for" standing by her man, CNN then aired video of Hillary Clinton surrounded by enthusiastic crowds. CNN further evidenced O'Connor's claim by interviewing two women. One commented that "you have to admire her . . . for the position she's in." A second one commended Clinton for being "courageous." CNN also turned to both Clintons' approval ratings as further testimony of how supportive the American people were of her decision to remain with her husband. Both Clintons had surpassed a 60 percent approval rating, which O'Connor dubbed as one of Hillary's "highest numbers since the first inauguration in 1993 and dead equal to her husband's." In addition to acknowledging Clinton's pledge to support her husband, O'Connor framed Clinton as a role model in the Clinton-Lewinsky drama: "By all indications, people will be looking to Hillary Clinton now more than ever, to gauge her reaction to her husband's testimony." Surprisingly, the president of the National Organization for Women (NOW)—one of the most well-known feminist organizations in the country—confirmed O'Connor's position. Patricia Ireland argued that "if Hillary Rodham Clinton is there, once again portraying this as something that is between them . . . that will help a lot." O'Connor responded: "In fact, it could make all the difference."[72]

To affirm the position of a reconciled Hillary and Bill Clinton, CNN displayed an image of the two of them walking together; Bill Clinton, the reified patriarch of the family, had his arm around Hillary and she was looking upward toward her towering husband. Emphasizing the rightness of this scenario, another woman argued: "I have all the respect for her in the world and whatever she decides, I'm behind her." The broadcast ended with a video of Hillary Clinton introducing her husband. As he stepped to the podium to speak, they embraced one another, cementing a marital reconciliation where all was forgiven.[73]

The correct course of action for Hillary Clinton thus was to accept a marriage filled with infidelity so that the American people too could forgive her husband. Many women, including a journalist, women off the street, and the president of a feminist organization, offered encouragement for Hillary's realization of

Tammy Wynette's song. Such reification of a "stand by your man" sentiment emitted the message that women, including strong women with feminist convictions, ultimately lacked a sense of agency in their marriage. The cheating husband instead was granted greater freedom of action. The pressure to stay with her unfaithful husband and to live out the vestiges of a patriarchal marriage was seemingly even greater for the nation's first lady.

In a broadcast from MSNBC entitled "Investigating the President," Clinton's popularity was again linked to her marital commitment. The MSNBC anchor observed that "Hillary Rodham Clinton is more popular than ever before at least in the public opinion polls." The anchor then asked Judy Markey from WGN radio what was "causing Mrs. Clinton's popularity to soar." Markey responded: "I think people admire . . . not standing by your man so much as standing by your vows . . . she really is in a sense upholding family values . . . I think there are people who admire that." Although Markey acknowledged that others wondered what happened to Clinton's "backbone,"[74] the reference to "family values"—a marker of the 1992 Republican campaign theme[75]—unquestionably reinforced a more traditional and conservative value system of marriage where the gender roles were clearly defined along patriarchal lines of power.

An ABC *Nightline* episode from August 24, 1998, would reinforce similar messages, juxtaposing Clinton as a political powerhouse with Clinton as a jilted wife, noting the uncharacteristic support for the latter. Chris Wallace highlighted the irony: "From the moment she became first lady, she's been a figure of controversy, which is why her current standing is so fascinating, because now, at what may be the low point of her time in the White House, public approval for Mrs. Clinton has never been higher." Wallace attributed much of the rise to a level of "sympathy for someone in pain." The transformation, Wallace suggested, forced "this most untraditional of first ladies" into playing a more "traditional role" as "the wounded wife, and people somehow feel comfortable with that." During the same episode, Chris Bury reinforced the ironic twist of events: "So now Mrs. Clinton, the tough lawyer and savvy strategist, who's helped her husband through so many scandals, finds herself in the awkward position of being treated like a victim in this one. And though her friends insist that is a role she detests, Hillary Rodham Clinton has never been more popular with the American public." The poll that *Nightline* featured showed Clinton's approval ratings topping 70 percent.[76] Such popularity reified the perceived acceptance and preference for a *woman as victim* image, reifying the commonplace that the most exalted women are those who stand quietly by their husbands regardless of their husbands' indiscretions.

Hillary Clinton, in performing the more traditional role of wife and first lady, was now championed for salvaging her husband's presidency. From the same *Nightline* episode cited above, Wallace asked the question that most clearly marked the traditional dimensions of the first lady role: "What does it do to the institution of first lady to have the whole world watching this marital drama?" First lady historian Carl Anthony accentuated how Clinton "upholds this tradition of dignity even in shame," further reifying ritualized practices for first ladies. Referencing the strength of Jackie Kennedy after her husband's assassination or Pat Nixon after Watergate, Anthony stated that "I think the women in the White House have upheld far greater in the long stretch of history than the men have. And I think that that is part of the tradition, that institutional dignity that we've heard about."[77] As the moral compass for the nation, some suggested, First Lady Hillary Clinton would be forced to transcend any personal pain, and shoulder the responsibility for healing the nation, guiding it through the national trauma.

In the process, Clinton was admired and respected in ways that she never could be as one flouting the traditions of authentic womanhood. On *NBC Nightly News* during December 1998, Anna Wintour of *Vogue* magazine talked about Clinton's "dignity" and "courage," which made her a "symbol for American women everywhere."[78] Emphasizing Hillary's role model status, Reverend Gerald Mann of Riverbend Church made the following observation during an NBC News broadcast of September 11, 1998: "And for our first lady, give her the strength to continue to show all of us what grace and courage and mercy look like."[79] Andrea Mitchell would likewise pinpoint Clinton's "grace and courage" during an *NBC Nightly News* broadcast in September 1998, for being "her husband's chief cheerleader at a political event last night."[80] In a subsequent broadcast, Mitchell suggested that Clinton's actions in the face of hardship made her eligible for *Time* magazine's "Person of the Year" Award.[81] Disciplined as an outspoken campaign surrogate, health care task force leader, and ethically suspect lawyer, Hillary Clinton would now be more accepted than ever before as a scorned women standing by her man. *Time* magazine had even contemplated rewarding Clinton with its coveted annual award for facing hardship and humiliation with laudable grace, courage, and strength. The disciplinary process would now be nearly complete.

Yet, for the sake of the president and the Democratic Party in particular, some Democrats seemed to want Hillary Clinton to grovel in her humiliation even further. In a *CBS Evening News* story from September 10, 1998, Bill Plante reported that Clinton expressed forgiveness to her husband through her spokesperson who issued "a short statement." The statement reinforced the message that "the first lady forgave her husband and remained committed to her marriage." Because Hillary Clinton did not voice those words in public herself and because Bill Clinton's poll numbers were slipping, Plante contended that Democrats "want the first lady to say that she forgives him."[82] *NBC Nightly News* made a similar point in a September 11, 1998, story: "The president's aides even want her to give a speech defending him."[83] In this instance, Hillary Clinton was pushed back into the limelight, to be "front and center" in her expressions of support and forgiveness for her husband. Clinton did eventually break her silence and did eventually come forward to defend her husband publicly. As reported on NBC's *Dateline* episode from September 12, 1998, Clinton stated that she was "very proud of the person I'm privileged to introduce. I'm proud of his leadership, I'm proud of his commitment, I'm proud of what he gives our country . . . and I'm proud to introduce my husband and our president, Bill Clinton." Hillary Clinton, the scorned woman, standing front and center before the cameras, exuded a sense of pride in her husband—the one who humiliated her publicly and broke their vows of marriage privately. Pointing to the ironic situation that Clinton faced, Jane Pauley framed Clinton's loyalty as one of her most poignant moments: "What may turn out to be the most enduring image of her political career and most ironic—standing by her man."[84] For these public shows of support and perseverance, Hillary Clinton was called an "amazing trooper" by Evan Thomas on CBS's *Inside Washington* because she took to the "battle station." Nina Totenberg of NPR added that Clinton supported and defended her husband because that's "her nature."[85]

That Hillary Clinton was pressured into publicly and outspokenly standing by her man seemingly helped right the patriarchal deficiencies of the Clinton marriage in the messages that circulated in the press. After all, Clinton had overstepped the boundaries of first lady comportment during the health care debate. These gender transgressions though appeared corrected with the new image of Hillary Clinton as a scorned woman standing by her man. This purification derived from performing the expectations of authentic womanhood for the betterment of the nation-state. As Julie Mostov contends, an "image of the allegorical mother," reflective of gendered nationalism, is "celebrated" for "their pain, suffering and sacrifices . . . as part of the nation's sacrifice."[86]

Part of the disciplining meant that President Bill Clinton's marital power had been reaffirmed during the Clinton-Lewinsky scandal. William Kristol, on ABC's *Nightline* from August 24, 1998, reinforced the problems with Hillary Clinton being too out front on health care. To Kristol, Bill Clinton appeared to be "hiding behind his wife a little bit when he put her in charge of health care. It's hard to criticize the first lady. No one wants to be mean spirited."[87] Although Bill Clinton was certainly condemned for his sexual liaison with a twenty-one-year-old intern, his sexual indiscretions would assume a greater level of normalcy through the language and visual imagery used to depict the affair. These reifications externalized Bill Clinton's responsibility in his own sexual exploits, framing his actions as the epitome of authentic manhood in ways that demonstrated he was no longer hiding behind his wife. Instead, he finally seemed more able to exert his manhood in this complex marital relationship.[88]

Presidents Will Be Presidents

An underlying theme in the coverage of Bill Clinton's affair with Monica Lewinsky, implicitly and explicitly, exonerated him from responsibility in acting out sexually with a young White House intern. Some reports naturalized the conflation of politics and heterosexual sex. In other cases, Clinton was portrayed as unsuspectingly preyed on by a stalking intern, which positioned him as more understandably compliant toward her sexual advancements. The seductress role that Lewinsky played in the news drama not only jeopardized the presidential marriage but also threatened to do irreparable damage to the presidency. Also implicated were Hillary Clinton's many trips abroad, which left Bill Clinton alone far too often. And, Hillary Clinton's own rationalization for her husband's indiscretions seemed to burden her husband's mother and grandmother with failing to protect him from family feuds. These portrayals authenticated Bill Clinton's manhood in ways that reified traditional conceptions of hegemonic masculinity.[89]

Contextualizing Bill Clinton's affair in the history of political (hetero)sexual activity seemed to normalize Clinton's extramarital exploits. Addressing the issue of politics and sex more generally, ABC News interviewed people from Britain. As Mike Lee reported, many Brits worried "that an American president might be brought down." Expressing a sense of exasperation, the first woman interviewed asked: "For what? Loving someone? For a sexual relationship? Where's the problem?" The second British woman normalized the sexual trysts, arguing that "there just seems to be something about politicians and sex." Lee also talked to people in France, Italy, and South Africa, garnering similar responses. "In France," Lee continued, "many shrug off allegations against President Clinton." Reflecting the gendering of such issues in Italy, an unidentified male argued that "Italian males would admire [Clinton], and Italian women would condemn him." The biggest concern overall, Lee contended, was that this issue "could shove important world issues to the background."[90] In the process of normalizing sexual transgressions and male politicians, the broadcast also suggested that private issues represented a distraction from important global and national exigencies. Certainly, a president engaged in an affair with a White House intern would not meet the threshold of political significance.

In turning to the fallout over the presidential drama at home, CNN further typified Clinton's actions by aligning them with past presidential indiscretions.

In a story about the "private lives" of presidents in August 1998, Bruce Morton surveyed sexual scandals involving presidents and presidential candidates, including Gary Hart's affair with Donna Rice during the 1988 presidential campaign that resulted in his withdrawal from the race. Delving more deeply into President John F. Kennedy's sexual encounters, CNN interviewed former Kennedy staffer Hugh Sidey, who admitted that many were "fully aware of John Kennedy's relations with various girls." Yet, Sidey argued that the sexual liaisons "never . . . got in the way of Kennedy being president and so we just kind of shoved it aside." This logic connoted that what happened in the privacy of the president's personal life was inconsequential to a president's performance of his job. Bill Kovach of Harvard's Nieman Fellowship Program made the argument most clearly: "During the Cold War period, even when the Gary Hart thing was going early on, there was still this organizing principle that there was something important in the world that people had to know." And, "they looked to journalists to bring" important topics "to them." Ultimately, the public's obsession with matters of sex was blamed on the celebritization of the presidency and the need for news to be "entertaining," resulting in far too much attention placed on personal issues (e.g., Bill Clinton's underwear). Jan Schaffer of the Pew Center for Civic Journalism concluded in the same CNN broadcast that "there is no prioritizing of what's important anymore because any nanosecond you need to have something new."[91]

Others, particularly male friends and associates of the president, would articulate similar assumptions about male political leaders and their propensity for heterosexual escapades. Clinton's chief campaign strategist from 1992, James Carville, argued on CNN's *Larry King Live* in the summer of 1998 that "this is hardly the first powerful brilliant man that has made an . . . error in judgment when it comes to a woman." As the always colorful Carville concluded, that "we are trying to criminalize this stuff . . . is absolutely ludicrous." In the same news discussion, Leon Panetta, Bill Clinton's chief of staff from 1994 through 1997, emphasized Clinton's "strengths" and "weaknesses," concluding that "presidents are human beings."[92] Panetta's construction in particular stripped the presidency of power involving private sexual matters, even those taking place in the official spaces of presidential authority and performance.

Certainly, there were plenty of people who did not let Clinton off the hook in terms of his own responsibility and abuse of power in his affair with Lewinsky. Democratic Senator Joseph Lieberman of Connecticut engaged in a very public rebuke of the president's actions, calling them "immoral" and "harmful." Republicans were much less likely to forgive; and they were much more likely to make the abuse of power case in their steadfast attempts to remove Clinton from office. William Kristol's statement in the *Washington Post* was featured on the television monitor during NBC's September 12, 1998, *Dateline* special: "Republicans have old-fashioned extramarital affairs with other adults. Those really are moral lapses that are private and more easily forgiven and very different from taking advantage of a young person who works for you when you're president."[93] Kristol's statement, while making an abuse of power case—an argument mired in partisan politics—still normalized the conflation of politics and heterosexual sex. After all, Republicans and Democrats alike were drawn into such sexual interludes. And although Clinton took responsibility for his actions, many ultimately concluded that his actions were just not that big of a deal.

For many in the United States, the affair with Lewinsky assumed a level of trivialization compared to the nation's most important business, attributable more to Starr's out-of-bounds prosecution than to Clinton's misdeeds. Joe Klein claimed on a March 1999 *Nightline* episode that "the ferocity" of Clinton's "prosecutions" would likely "be remembered" far more "than the severity" of the "crimes."[94] Some in the press reinforced a message similar to those voiced internationally—a presidential affair was much ado about nothing. Once Jeanne Meserve of CNN discussed the impeachment criteria of high crimes and misdemeanors in September 1998, she pondered whether a "peccadillo with an intern" qualified as an "impeachable offense." The use of the term *peccadillo*—epitomizing the trivial or the petty—suggested it did not. The coverage overall implied that when it came to the president's sex life, the personal was not political, even when involving presidential sexual encounters in the Oval Office—a worksite of unmatched power—with a young White House volunteer lacking in standing and maturity. Ellen Goodman of the *Boston Globe* offered an opinion that bucked many of the prevailing press assumptions in an MSNBC story entitled "The Female Factor" from September 1998. Goodman argued that politics is indeed personal for the president: "For public offices, especially for the president who is sworn in to uphold the law and the Constitution, there is no room for sex is personal."[95]

MEDIATING MONICA LEWINSKY

Journalists of course also devoted considerable airtime to the object of the president's affection. The idea that Lewinsky represented the responsible party for the affair was advanced by the reductionist naming of the scandal. The affair was often referred to simply as the "Lewinsky scandal" or the "Monica Lewinsky case," removing Bill Clinton's name entirely from such references.[96] And stereotypically, Lewinsky was portrayed as wielding sexual control over a vulnerable president who naturally succumbed to her provocative advancements. Epitomizing the debate over Lewinsky's role in the affair, Bob Faw of *NBC Nightly News* questioned in September 1998 whether she "was predator, prey, or both."[97] A preyed-on Bill Clinton represented a linguistic frame used by several journalists. During an August 17, 1998, broadcast, CNN's Larry King asked his panelists "why" the president "would . . . fall prey to something" like this. None of the discussants, even those who knew Clinton, could produce a satisfying answer, framing the question as a most perplexing issue. Bob Woodward of the *Washington Post* argued that it would be "easier to describe the creation of the universe. You have to leave that to the psychiatrists." Dee Dee Myers, former Clinton press secretary, similarly responded: "Larry, if you could figure that out, you know you have keys to the universe."[98] Questions of power and domination did not factor into these responses. What the responses confirmed, however, was that men will be men and presidents will be presidents. When preyed on, they were seemingly helpless in controlling their sexual urges, even in a work-site that contained the memories of presidents from James Monroe to Abraham Lincoln and beyond.

ABC's *Nightline* episode of March 3, 1999, likewise portrayed Lewinsky as the sexual instigator in a story that revisited Barbara Walter's one-on-one interview with Lewinsky. After watching the interview, Ted Koppel emphasized Lewinsky's show of power, which was reduced to her sexual empowerment mixed with expressions of vulnerability: "A little more complex, perhaps, than we had expected. Flirtatious, manipulative, very expressive eyes, disingenuous, always an undercurrent of sadness."[99] For those who blamed Lewinsky for the affair, NBC's Faw observed, she epitomized a "harlot." And Carmen Pate of Concerned Women for America argued that "Monica Lewinsky's behavior was unacceptable . . . there were no excuses."[100] Reflecting the logic of patriarchy, where authentic women were to imbue the nation's culture and political process with a sense of morality, Monica Lewinsky rather than Bill Clinton stood convicted, at least by some, as the primary guilty party. That another woman (Carmen Pate) would stand in judgment of Lewinsky reflected what Nira Yuval-Davis discusses as the role of women to "rule on what is 'appropriate' behaviour and appearance" and to "exert control over other women who might be constructed as 'deviants.'"[101]

Images of Lewinsky as a stalker seductress were common themes in other press accounts of the relationship. NBC, in their *Dateline* special on September 12, 1998, devoted two hours to discussing the Starr report and the various re-actions to it. Brian Williams, over the course of multiple segments, read large chunks of the report to the viewing audience. Lewinsky was portrayed as laying in wait for the president, using the "government shutdown" as her opportunity "for greater interaction with the object of her affection, the president of the United States."[102] In one of the more incendiary lines, Williams talked of how Lewinsky lifted "up her jacket" and showed the president "her thong."[103] Leon Panetta's take on the affair would reinforce this notion of Lewinsky as a stalker, when he disclosed that we "found her hanging around the Oval Office . . . it was good enough reason to get her out of the White House."[104] The situation apparently became bad enough, Williams reported, that "one officer even suggested putting Lewinsky's name on a list of people who would be refused admission to the White House, but that didn't happen." This image of Lewinsky as a presidential stalker was reinforced by her own testimony. As Clinton began to turn away from her, Lewinsky told of becoming more bitter and angry. In a letter Lewinsky wrote to Clinton, which Williams read on air, Lewinsky complained that "'any normal person would have walked away from this and said he doesn't call me, he doesn't want to see me, screw it, it doesn't matter.' But she went on, 'I can't let go of you. I want to be a source of pleasure, and laughter, and energy to you.'"[105] That Monica Lewinsky was an active agent in the affair should never be denied. Yet, what was most revealing about these depictions was that the coverage imbued Lewinsky with immense levels of power. Consequently, the president of the United States, one of the most empowered leaders on the national and international stage, surrounded by an army of Secret Service and a huge staff of gatekeepers, was seemingly incapable of rebuffing Lewinsky's sexual advancements.

Clinton was implicitly rendered more helpless in this situation because of Lewinsky's sexual magnetism. Lewinsky's mesmeric powers were predictably reduced to her physicality, particularly her provocative smile, eyes, and breasts—parts of the female body that seemingly render men powerless over acts of female seduction. As previously argued, the female smile connoted a sense of authentic womanhood for Hillary Clinton traveling around the world, where a woman was seen but not heard. Her smile also, though, became a mask, in the press vernacular, of Hillary's true emotions as she faced the pain and humiliation of her husband's affair. Lewinsky's smile, her eyes, and her breasts, conversely, represented primary sources of sexual enticement. The camera angles in particular brought viewers in for a close-up view of Lewinsky's seductress body, simulating Bill Clinton's vision.

As Williams continued to read from the Starr report on the *Dateline* episode, the stock footage of Bill Clinton and Lewinsky together in public was shown. Lewinsky was smiling broadly and looking directly toward the president's face as he talked to people around her with his hand on her shoulder. This image was visible as Williams described when the sexual relationship between Clinton and Lewinsky began: "And so just four months after arriving at the White House, when she got a chance to be alone with the president, she told him of her crush. He asked if he could kiss her and their sexual relationship was soon underway. Like any infatuation, the report says in this one, there were emotional highs and lows." As Williams uttered the word *infatuation*, NBC inserted a portrait image of Lewinsky. It was of a facial shot where she smiled broadly toward the camera. By zooming in on the photograph, NBC invited a closer look into the face of the seductress, flaunting her sexuality and promiscuity before the whole world with her broad smile and brazen eye contact with the camera. This vantage point allowed viewers to see the closer details of her face as Bill Clinton would have experienced them in their many close encounters—her bright red lip stick and open-mouthed smile punctuated her sexual availability. The mouth represented the focal point in the photograph, and like Hillary Clinton, Lewinsky was silenced in much of the coverage featuring her smile. Her mouth also served as a key dimension of the Starr report and Williams's narration, with both emphasizing how Lewinsky performed "oral sex" on the president.[106] The female mouth in such coverage of the presidential affair symbolized not a means of verbal expression and exchange (Hillary's outspokenness) but rather as an instrument of male provocation and sexual satisfaction (Monica's sensuality).

This same smiling portrait was used in a separate NBC broadcast in September 1998. Lisa Myers noted how the report revealed that the president "touched [Lewinsky] in very intimate ways, including one episode involving a cigar." Myers continued to explain that the two "were having sex while the president was on the phone with three different members of Congress." As Myers's words were heard, three NBC monitors displayed the same glamorous portrait of Lewinsky, directing a wide smile toward the camera.[107] The smile thus served as a major source of heterosexual provocation, nonverbally reinforcing the underlying assumption that Clinton, even as the most powerful man in the country, was rendered nearly powerless when faced with Lewinsky's premeditated and calculating ploys.

Viewing Lewinsky through the eyes of the president was furthered through the use of imagery and camera angles when Myers discussed Lewinsky's breasts. In recounting Clinton's defense in the Starr report, Myers relayed that the president claimed to have "never touched Lewinsky's breasts or other intimate parts of her body, and therefore had not perjured himself." When Myers made this last statement, we first see the stock footage of Bill Clinton and Lewinsky interacting in a rope line as he shook the hands of supporters. After zooming in for a close-up image of the smiling Lewinsky—mimicking the closeness of Clinton to the seductress—NBC inserted a video of Lewinsky in a tight brown dress. This time the camera zoomed in for a tighter shot on Lewinsky from the waist up, offering a greater view of Lewinsky's breasts that were accentuated by the snugness of her dress.[108] The perspective of the camera, especially through NBC's zoomed-in images, brought the twenty-something intern into full view as Clinton would have experienced her visually. Such experiential observations, when coupled with the assumptions that political men are incapable of controlling their sexualized urges, conveyed the commonplace that Monica

Lewinsky and not Bill Clinton shouldered the primary responsibility for their sexual interludes.

That Lewinsky's body represented the source of sexual power became a threat not just to the president's family but to the nation as a whole. In elevating the significance of the scandal, *Nightline* host Ted Koppel quipped: "So this is the young woman who nearly toppled a president."[109] Brian Williams talked similarly of the Clinton-Lewinsky affair, when he asked Tim Russert if "there [was] a real danger that America will seem like a weakened superpower because of this president's problems." Even though Lewinsky represented a significant threat to the nation—as someone who nearly "toppled the president"—Russert offered reassuring responses to Williams's question. The conclusion reached was that the American system of government could withstand the president's entanglements with a twenty-one-year-old White House intern and his subsequent attempts to deny it: "Ultimately, this democracy is going to work," Russert assured. Tom Brokaw ended the broadcast on another note of reassurance: "This country, its people, and its system of government and politics, have all faced far greater tests and prevailed . . . there's no reason to believe that we'll fail now."[110] That the country could survive Lewinsky's sexual escapades harkened back to the problems of women's entrance into politics in the first place. Lewinsky ultimately would be no match for the strength and power of the male political preserves, especially as other men and women came to Bill Clinton's defense.

THE OTHER WOMEN OF BLAME IN BILL CLINTON'S AFFAIR

Monica Lewinsky would not be the only woman in Bill Clinton's life to help carry the burden of an extramarital affair with worldwide reverberations. Hillary's absence during her diplomatic trips left her husband alone and seemingly more vulnerable to Lewinsky's sexual advancements. As Brian Williams told the story of the Clinton-Lewinsky affair, he would note that most of the "phone sex" between the two "took place when Mrs. Clinton was out of town." Later in the same episode, Jane Pauley would draw similar inferences. In recounting the number of times Clinton and Lewinsky met, Pauley noted "thirteen intimate encounters, often taking place when . . . [Hillary] was out of town—March 29th, Greece; March 31st, Ireland."[111] Alluding to Bill Clinton's propensity to engage in sexual interludes during her absence, Carol Simpson of ABC News asked Hillary Clinton whether or not her marriage could withstand the travel associated with her U.S. Senate bid in August 1999. The first lady responded tersely: "The president is responsible for his own behavior, whether I'm there or one hundred miles away."[112]

This interview suggested that Hillary Clinton unquestionably viewed Bill Clinton as a responsible party in his personal affairs. Yet, in other interviews,

Clinton implied that her husband's childhood was at least partially to blame—
explanations offered during the partisan political context of her own senatorial
campaign. In August 1999, Hillary Clinton gave an exclusive interview to *Talk*
magazine, detailing her own explanation for Bill Clinton's comportment with
Monica Lewinsky. In the interview, which was recounted in multiple television
newscasts, Hillary talked of her husband's "weakness" brought on by "childhood abuse" at a young age. An excerpt of the interview was shown on *ABC
World News Tonight* in August 1999. Clinton reasoned: "He was so young, barely
four, when he was scarred by abuse . . . There was terrible conflict between his
mother and grandmother," leaving toddler Bill Clinton "torn between the two"
most important women in his life. ABC concurrently pictured Bill Clinton's prin-
cipal "weakness" for the audience, re-airing the video of Bill Clinton hugging
a smiling Monica Lewinsky in a rope line. Although Hillary Clinton acknowledged that she experienced considerable "pain, enormous anger," she reportedly stayed with her husband because "I have been with him half my life, and
he's a very, very good man."[113] During a *CBS Evening News* story, Sharyl Attkisson
paraphrased Hillary Clinton's words during the *Talk* magazine interview, calling
it "a sin of weakness not malice."[114] Elaborating further on Clinton's interview,
CNN would also demonstrate how Hillary turned her husband's weaknesses
into a sign of his remarkable strength to endure the childhood abuse: "Yes, he
has weaknesses. Yes, he needs to be more disciplined. But it is remarkable,
given his background, that he turned out to be the kind of person he is, capable
of such leadership."[115] Hillary Clinton further normalized Bill Clinton's actions
as she reinforced his sense of "weakness" during a clip that aired on NBC News:
"Everybody has some dysfunction in their families. They have to deal with it.
You don't just walk away if you love someone—you help the person."[116]

While Hillary Clinton's statements were designed to put the issue to rest early
in her senatorial bid, her public rationalizations even worried her own campaign
staff. As John Roberts of CBS News reported, "Sources close to the first lady say
they were blindsided by her candor and that it may hurt her in the New York Senate bid."[117] *ABC World News Tonight* also explored the notion that Clinton's remarks
excused Bill Clinton's actions. In the end, Joe Lockhart, Bill Clinton's press secretary, insisted that Hillary Clinton believed her husband was "responsible for
his own behavior."[118] Clinton biographer David Maraniss read Hillary's remarks
as someone "searching for rationalizations for his behavior" during an interview
with *NBC Nightly News* on August 2, 1999.[119] While Clinton's remarks may well
have exhibited a sense of candor in the midst of a senatorial campaign, they also
diminished Bill Clinton's responsibility for his own weaknesses.

This coverage ultimately revealed how Bill Clinton's sexual prowess was naturalized in the context of the presidency. The average heterosexual male, the cultural logic suggested, would have had a difficult time resisting the advances of a young seductress with a face and body the likes of Lewinsky's. Hillary Clinton's role in this drama volleyed between that of her husband's public defender and of the scorned woman gracefully saving the nation-state from her husband's indiscretions and the threats of the sexual provocateur. That Clinton left her husband alone for her own political interests may well suggest, in such gender logic, that she was also in part responsible for her husband's transgressions. A marriage based in politics, it implied, encouraged the president to go elsewhere for sexual satisfaction.

Hillary Clinton ultimately became the primary solution to the personal and national predicament in this larger news mosaic, resembling the early familial logic of the nation's genesis. As Shirley Samuels explains, the "threat" of "female 'political sexuality'" would be neutralized by "the figure of the mother"—the republican mother.[120] In the press-created biography, Hillary Clinton would withstand the threat of the seductress to her marriage. By saving her marital union, Clinton as first lady would also save the national union. In the process, Hillary Clinton was sufficiently disciplined and humiliated out of the political spotlight. Monica Lewinsky, the ultimate transgressor, fled to London, helping to remove the threat.[121] And Bill Clinton's indiscretions made him part of the political and presidential club of men who cheated on their wives with minimal consequence.

Yet, the competing images of Clinton as a public defender and a scorned and graceful wife would eventually resurrect suspicions over her authenticity. Many came to believe that her decision to stand by her man had more to do with her political ambitions than her selfless love of her husband or her country. Hillary Clinton, like Monica Lewinsky, would once again threaten the idyllic notions of authentic womanhood and the political process more generally.

The Inauthenticity of Hillary Clinton and Her Political Marriage

The theme of Hillary Clinton as an authentic woman saving the country in graceful and selfless ways would be short lived. The entrenched frames of Clinton as a feminist with considerable political ambition would quickly undermine any traditional images of the first lady. As more and more wondered about the anomaly of a feminist standing by her cheating husband, many soon framed such actions less in terms of victimization and more in terms of political ambition. These seemingly incompatible images would challenge Clinton's authenticity once again and further the residual frame of her decidedly political marriage.

Once the dust of the Clinton-Lewinsky affair had settled and the drama transitioned to a focus on Bill Clinton's impeachment, the news media would continue to spend considerable energy in trying to understand the Clinton marriage. Did Hillary's decision to stay with Bill reflect a foundational love between the two? Or, did it simply reinforce the same news frame of the Clinton political partnership, founded on a shared political agenda rather than a loving relationship? In providing a retrospective on the first couple's marriage, the news media would address these questions by returning to the news frames from the early years of the Clinton campaign and administration, pulling such baseline frames into the present.

In part, these frames survived because news organizations recycled past news stories in subsequent broadcasts. Journalistic retrospectives provide an inexpensive way for the news media to fill in time over the course of a twenty-four-hour news cycle. One consequence, intended or not, is the proliferation and normalization of news frames.[122] During the period of the Clinton-Lewinsky scandal, the news media reified the residual frame of the Clinton political marriage, marked by mystery and controversy. In a September 19, 1998, broadcast of *Time & Again*, Jane Pauley framed the entire retrospective around the Clinton political union: "Bill and Hillary Clinton . . . are no ordinary couple. They're a team, a political partnership that goes back more than two decades." The memorial service image of the two walking on the White House lawn visually evidenced their tough times. Pauley re-anchored the image in the Clinton-Lewinsky drama rather than the memorial service by suggesting that "the toughest time of course is now, the Monica Lewinsky scandal."[123] This video footage of the Clintons walking together would reappear as a transitional image between commercial breaks, recycling past news frames and the video used to symbolize them.

Even in the shorter press stories packaged for the nightly news, the Clinton marriage continued to attract considerable interest. Attention focused in particular on Bill and Hillary Clinton's public expressions of commitment during the State of the Union message in January 1999. The coverage framed the state of the Clinton union through a linguistic play on words derived from an occasion designed to take stock of the state of the nation's union. Suspense was building in the lead-up to the address over whether the president would reference his impeachment and acknowledge his aggrieved wife. So when Bill Clinton engaged in a public display of affection toward his wife, all eyes turned to Hillary Clinton's response as the true assessment of the Clinton marriage. Elizabeth Kaledin of CBS News framed the suspense surrounding the moment all had been waiting for: "It came at the very end of a long speech. Perhaps the one subject many Americans were willing to stay up late to hear the president address—his wife." CBS then featured the passage in the speech where the president confessed his gratitude to Hillary Clinton: "For all she has done in her historic role to serve our nation and our best ideals, at home and abroad, I honor her." The camera then framed a smiling Hillary Clinton who stood and waved to the audience, mouthing the words "thank you." With continued focus on the nonverbal and verbal exchange between the president and first lady, Kaledin observed: "In the thick of an impeachment trial brought on by a sex scandal, in this most public of forums, President Clinton saluted the first lady and, under his breath, said, 'I love you.'"[124]

Kaledin and others would interrogate the authenticity of Clinton's smile and her show of gratitude to her husband. Not surprisingly, the news media depicted the Clinton union as yet another political performance. For the news media, Clinton's smile—a key feature of face politics—once again obscured her true emotions. Kaledin concluded that "as they watched her smile and wave, those who know her admit that it was an excruciating moment." As the camera pulled in for a tighter shot of Clinton's face, others would be brought in to conduct a physiognomic reading of Clinton's face as an indicator of her true emotions. Ann Douglas of *Vogue* magazine drew such conclusions by examining Hillary's face on smaller television monitors in the CBS studio: "She looks quite tired. Her face is drawn in some ways, and this is someone, I would say, under a great deal of strain." Kaledin ended the broadcast by referring to Hillary Clinton's response as a "performance," which offered minimal sentiment that the marriage was about anything other than politics: "But being in the glare of a spotlight with her marriage on display during the State of the Union address is not the type of performance that Hillary Rodham Clinton likes to give."[125] That such a marital exchange would be viewed as public performance in the midst of a constitutionally required presidential ritual was hardly surprising. Journalists nevertheless took on the role of armchair psychologists through repeated and rudimentary readings of Clinton's face and smile.[126]

NBC News also conflated the coverage of the State of the Union address with the state of the Clinton marriage. Andrea Mitchell began the report with the question: "Tonight, the question, 'What is the state of their union?'" That question took on new meaning, Mitchell suggested, after long-term Clinton friend Senator Dale Bumpers (D-AR) relayed that "a relationship between husband and wife, father and child, has been incredibly strained, if not destroyed. There's been nothing but sleepless nights." A disconnect between Bumpers's private insight and the public display of affection on the night of the State of the

Union message led Mitchell to ask: "So which is it? The family all but destroyed by infidelity? Or the public display of affection?" Mitchell ultimately answered her own question by emphasizing the inauthenticity of the Clinton marriage: "People close to Hillary Clinton suggest some of this is for show—political damage control, especially during the impeachment trial." To emphasize the true iciness between the two, NBC aired a video clip, devoid of context, of Bill Clinton trying to grasp Hillary Clinton's hand as she pulled it away. Author Kati Marton furthered the view that the marital exchange was a "performance" when suggesting that "when a camera is on you twenty-four hours a day . . . you have to perform."[127]

In light of this disconnect between the public performance of marital stability and the private indicators of marital strain, the news media would ultimately reassess the authenticity of Hillary Clinton's public image. Was she the graceful, loving wife, recommitting herself to her marriage, or the cold, public defender of her husband eager to return the focus to her own political agenda? Predictably, the press would come down on the side of Hillary Clinton as the political operative, reifying the frames from the 1992 political campaign and the 1993–95 health care debate. Reaffirming Clinton's public performance, Douglas of *Vogue* magazine emphasized Clinton's commitment to her public life and her steadfast political convictions by analyzing Clinton's nonverbal reactions during the State of the Union address: "Clinton's reaction, in this most glaring of spotlights, is not the face of denial but the face of conviction." Again ascribing sentiments to her face, Douglas spoke as if she were giving voice to Clinton's convictions: "Instead of assuming that she's pretending it hasn't happened, we might read what she's doing as 'I know exactly what's going on and here is my response.' I'm saying 'the invasion of the private stops here.' I'm saying 'that public life goes on.' She's a terrific public performer."[128]

Confusion over the real Hillary Clinton would again become a point of news mystery during this newest conflict. Chris Wallace expressed his bafflement over the true Hillary Clinton during an ABC *Nightline* episode in August 1998: "It seems we've never quite known what to make of Hillary Clinton." Wallace elaborated further on the perplexity of Clinton's image that had been a visible part of her news biography from 1992 forward: "[This] brings us back to the confusion about Hillary Clinton. She's clearly both a wife and a key advisor but where does one stop and the other start?"[129] Jeffery Toobin, in a separate *Nightline* broadcast from January 2000, referenced Hillary Clinton's 1998 appearance on the *Today* show with Matt Lauer. A behind-the-scenes White House incident during this period, Toobin observed, shed light on the hotly debated question as to the real Hillary Clinton: "Mrs. Clinton decided that she was going to attack the attackers, and that's where the phrase 'vast right-wing conspiracy' came from. And she was exultant, she was as happy, as motivated as people have ever seen her . . . upon her return to the White House. And she said in a phrase that was memorable for those who heard it, 'I guess that ought to teach them to "F" with us.'" And that was, in many respects, Hillary Clinton at her most real.[130]

This question of the real Hillary Clinton was thus one that occupied a significant amount of journalistic speculation throughout her time on the national political stage. The real Hillary, as defined during the 1992 campaign and the 1993–95 health care debate, was hard-edged, politically calculating, and cold—residual frames cemented with the lapse of time. Any attempt to move away from this image—one depicting a softer or vulnerable image—would eventually be overpowered by the enduring legacy of Hillary Clinton the feminist and political activist. And these frames were still readily apparent when Hillary Clinton did opt to pursue the presidency. This chapter thus ends where it began, with the 2008 presidential campaign.

Conclusion

The question over the real Hillary Clinton of course was a key news frame that permeated a lot of the television news media coverage during her 2008 presidential bid. Ironically, the press coverage of an affair between a president and a White House intern would also contribute to Hillary Clinton's perceived lack of authenticity. In talking about the impact of the Clinton-Lewinsky scandal on Hillary Clinton, Richard Wolffe, appearing on MSNBC in March 2008, noted that when Clinton's White House records were released, "one of the first things they looked for was what was she doing on the day of one of the trips with Lewinsky." Returning to the idea that Hillary Clinton's absence was somehow connected to Bill Clinton's indiscretions, Wolffe concluded: "So this story is always going to be there. It's part, for worse not better, [of] the Clinton brand. That does impact on the question of honesty and authenticity."[131] Most curiously, Bill Clinton's affair with Monica Lewinsky had now become a test of *Hillary's* "honesty and authenticity" during her own presidential bid.

On the same March 2008 evening, Chris Matthews and his guests on MSNBC's *Hardball* would likewise talk about Hillary Clinton's authenticity problems. In discussing the need to "let Hillary be Hillary," Matthews pondered: "It's one thing to say let Hillary be Hillary. We've never really been sure what that is, unvarnished, hair down, one of the boys, one of the girls, nobody is running for anything, just what she's like as a person because she's been in public life since she has been about twenty-eight or something." Although the other major political contenders of the 2008 presidential race, specifically Barack Obama and John McCain, had been in public life for a large majority of their careers, Hillary Clinton would be the one that appeared to struggle most with authenticity problems. Matthews offered the following authenticity judgments of all three presidential contenders: "Barack does very well with people on that issue of authenticity, so does John McCain, Hillary doesn't."[132] Such arguments, I contend, reflect more on political authenticity assumptions than they do on the "real" Barack Obama, John McCain, or Hillary Clinton. Such statements suggest that men are still more likely to be viewed as possessing greater political authenticity than women at the turn of the twenty-first century.

This coverage consequently offered a clear glimpse into notions of authentic womanhood and manhood at the end of the 1990s. An authentic woman demonstrated grace and courage by remaining loyal to her husband in spite of his very public and humiliating affair. She not only stood by his side—more silent and smiling—but she also championed him as someone she most admired. An authentic man, particularly a political one, was understandably drawn to flings with young White House interns because that was what men do and because presidents are preyed on by seductresses with provocative smiles, eyes, and breasts. That both Clintons received high approval ratings during this period of controversy showed at least some level of approval for performing more traditional gender roles.

Once disciplined out of the political spaces of domestic politics during the health care debate, Clinton took her agenda to the international political arenas. The press only marginally followed. Hillary Clinton accordingly gained valuable experiences that helped prepare her to pursue the U.S. Senate. I turn next to the coverage of Hillary Clinton's 2000 U.S. Senate race and the continued controversy over the first lady's authenticity challenges.

CHAPTER 4

Hillary Clinton as Political Candidate

U.S. Senate Campaign—1999–2001

A fter months in the thicket of the 2008 presidential campaign, Hillary Clinton would go public with her complaints about sexist treatment in the press. A May 25, 2008, broadcast of CNN's *Reliable Sources* aired Clinton's stinging critique:

> It's been deeply offensive to millions of women. The manifestation of some of the sexism that has gone on in this campaign is somehow more respectable, or at least more accepted. And I think there should be equal rejection of the sexism and the racism when and if it ever raises its ugly head. But it does seem as though the press, at least, is not as bothered by the incredible vitriol that has been engendered by the comments and the actions of people who are nothing but misogynists.[1]

These objections, which were issued by Clinton and her supporters, led certain news organizations to pose the question: "Was there an element . . . of sexism that hurt her in this race?"[2]

For some members of the press, the answer was decidedly yes. These journalists pinpointed signs at Clinton rallies that read "Iron My Shirts" or played off of the "nutcracker" jokes commonly told at Clinton's expense. Other journalists mentioned Jane Fonda's acerbic quip that Clinton was merely a "patriarch with a vagina." Pictures of a haggard-looking Clinton also circulated on the Internet with Rush Limbaugh accused of saying that "the country isn't ready to look at an old woman."[3] Journalists also turned a scrutinizing glance toward the campaign comportment of Clinton's rivals. When an unidentified woman asked John Mc-Cain, "How do we beat the bitch," Ed Henry of CNN's Election Center charged that McCain "laughed it off, instead of slamming it for being demeaning." Barack Obama would likewise be condemned for his jest that Hillary Clinton was "likable enough" after a moderator from a New Hampshire debate asked Clinton "why some voters seem to like Obama more." Henry framed Obama's words in the following way: "Sexist? Not really. But condescending? Big-time."[4]

The critique was elaborated on the same *Reliable Sources* broadcast. Syndicated columnist Marie Cocco argued the press should shoulder at least some of the blame for the sexism: "Sometimes you put on cable television and you feel like you're in the middle of a locker room." She turned to Tucker Carlson's utterance on MSNBC as evidence of this locker room mentality. Calling Clinton "scary," Carlson jibed that "every time she comes on TV, I instinctively cross my legs." Cocco also referenced Chris Matthews's sentiments that "prominent male politicians, governors, senators who were endorsing Senator Clinton last fall were 'castrados in the eunuch chorus.'"[5] A strong woman running for elected office revealingly centralized these men's attention on their male body parts, symbolizing the sexual threat that Clinton's candidacy posed to the political process and the men who occupied these male preserves.

Others in the press, however, offered a different perspective, asserting that even if these sexist allegations were true, Hillary Clinton needed to buck up and quit complaining. Arguing that Clinton was "whining about sexism," Tucker Carlson concluded in November 2007 that "it's so revealing that their first instinct was, they're being mean to the girl, woe is her."[6] Keli Goff of Black Entertainment Television spoke to the unproductiveness of issuing these sexist charges during a CNN broadcast from 2008. She observed "that Barack Obama has been very smart about his not crying racism." Goff concluded that even if the sexist allegations were true, "I think it's a lose-lose whenever you start blaming the media."[7] And, Charles Krauthammer, a conservative syndicated columnist, made a startling observation on Fox News in May 2008, naturalizing the state of ageism, racism, and sexism in campaign politics: "Barack Obama is losing a lot of votes entirely on the basis of his race. McCain is being savaged every night by the late night comics because of his age. [Clinton], of course, suffers to some degree as a result of sexism. But take it like a man, and I'm using it as a gender-neutral way. That's grown-up politics."[8] What Krauthammer truly meant by the statement, "take it like a man," is certainly open to interpretation. While some women are hyper-sexualized in the spaces of politics, others are defined as men or lesbians, or stripped of sexuality altogether ("gender-neutral" ways).

The takeaway was that Hillary needed to toughen up and grow up if she wanted to enter this masculine world of politics.

As Clinton entered this masculine political arena as a candidate in her own right, a rhetoric of violence would reappear in much the same way as it did during the health care debate. Reflecting the normalized conflation of violence and campaign talk, Tucker Carlson simply noted in November 2007 that Hillary Clinton "took a beating at this week's Democratic campaign debate." And Krauthammer observed how Clinton was "being pushed out of the race" in May 2008. Chapter 2 showed that this kind of language represented a normalized way to talk about politics—reflecting the violence associated with sports and war. What happens though when a rhetoric of violence is targeted toward women situated within the traditionally masculine spaces of a political campaign?

One consequence in the coverage of Clinton at least, was the emergence of a rhetoric of *domestic* violence that is an embedded feature of our political language and our cognitive processing. That violence, linguistically derived from the private spaces of the home, was now transferred to the public spaces of the gendered nation. Even in stories about the sexism of the 2008 campaign, a gendering of linguistic violence existed. In May 2008, CNN's Howard Kurtz introduced a video segment that showed the visible sexism in the presidential coverage of Clinton. Kurtz explained that Hillary supporters "are angry at a campaign that has sometimes seemed to focus on Hillary's clothing, cleavage, and cackle." The accompanying video provided a montage of questionable references to Hillary Clinton as the "scolding mother," "nagging" wife, or "first wife standing outside of probate court." In response to the press treatment, Kurtz posed the following question to the women on the panel: "When you see a candidate who happens to be a woman like Hillary Clinton getting slapped around like this, does it bother you personally?"[9] The coupling of such images of Hillary Clinton as a nagging wife being "slapped around" reflected a language of domestic violence. That Hillary Clinton would be "beaten" by a gang of men in a debate, "pushed" out of the political arena by other political leaders, or "slapped" for being a nagging wife suggested the rhetorical violence at work in the 2008 presidential discourse. Such a rhetoric has become so normalized that it easily filters through our consciousness undetected. These linguistic structures, Roger Fowler maintains, are "highly constructive mediator[s]" in the formation of societal "ideas" and ideologies[10]—ideological structures that can function at both conscious and unconscious levels.

The animosity toward Clinton in 2008, some argued, had less to do with sexism and more to do with Hillary Clinton herself and her route to political power. These rationalizations often drew on news frames generated from her years as first lady that were recycled to reveal the "real" Hillary Clinton. In the aftermath of the Clinton-Lewinsky scandal, however, some began to even question the authenticity of her feminism. *New York Times* columnist Maureen Dowd raised questions about Clinton's personality and comportment on NBC's *Meet the Press* in May 2008. Dowd condemned Clinton's sexism complaints, arguing that "Hillary hurts feminism when she uses it as opportunism, and she has a history of covering up her own mistakes behind sexism." Health care was the example that Dowd turned to as Clinton allegedly blamed its failure on sexism rather than admitting "that she was abrasive or mismanaged it or blew off good advice or was too secretive." In the end, Dowd charged that Clinton's leadership reminded "many men . . . of a female boss they didn't like,"[11] emphasizing the baseline framing of Clinton's personality problems and her likeability limitations.

Others complained that Clinton's accomplishments derived from her opportunistic marriage rather than her own credentials, further eroding her feminist commitments and her political authenticity. Ruth Marcus of the *Washington Post* challenged Clinton's authenticity on the same *Meet the Press* broadcast as she linked her accomplishments to her political marriage. Referring to Clinton's "route to power" as "derivative," Marcus dubbed Clinton's career as "the Adam's rib outgrowth of her husband's career." Admitting that Clinton had been elected to the Senate for two terms, Marcus nevertheless relied on baseline frames in her assertion that Clinton's "road to the White House involves standing by her man no matter how badly he behaved," transforming Clinton into "a flawed vessel for the feminist cause."[12] Clinton's political ambition was also a popular subject during her presidential bid, marking her ambition as somehow more contemptuous than the political ambition of her rivals. During an April 1, 2008, broadcast of *Hannity & Colmes,* Fox contributor Kate Obenshain maintained that "there is something a little off about the Clintons' ambition. It has more to do about personal gain, as opposed to the good of our wonderful country."[13] Collectively, these comments chipped away at Clinton's political authenticity and her presidential preparedness. Clinton came to be construed as disingenuous politically with her alleged turn against feminism standing as a poignant marker of political fakery.

Questions over the sexist treatment of Clinton during the 2008 presidential contest of course cannot be considered without stepping back in time to see the myriad of ways in which sexism was readily apparent in press coverage of her 2000 candidacy for the U.S. Senate. This chapter accordingly examines constancies and changes in the news frames of Hillary Clinton as she stepped into the arena of electoral politics as a candidate in her own right. From the outset, the press raised questions about Clinton's political authenticity, portraying itself as "salivating" over the opportunity to cover Hillary Clinton—a precedent-setting first lady who flirtatiously teased the media over her entrance into the masculine political arena. The challenges reified the news frames from 1992 through 1998, including a return to face politics. Clinton's run for office proved for some in the press that the Clinton marriage was in fact driven by political ambition. Her comportment as first lady was routinely raised as a means by which to accent her ongoing violation of authentic woman ideals.

Yet, new authenticity obstacles emerged within the 2000 campaign, particularly Clinton's carpetbagging attempts to seek election in a state where she never lived or worked. Hillary Clinton's attempts to brandish a New York Yankees ball cap symbolized for some her most egregious act of political forgery. She would also be portrayed as an untrustworthy flip-flopper on issues and as one using her celebrity to ascend to the Senate and ultimately the presidency. Although the true Hillary Clinton was still painted as a power-hungry and personality-challenged feminist, reminders that she opted to stand by her cheating husband undermined this authenticity marker as well.

Out of such coverage emerged a rhetoric of violence that framed Clinton's entrance into the masculine spaces of politics. A campaign constructed as a boxing match or war linguistically caught Hillary Clinton in the political cross-hairs. By the end, the vitriol of such language reflected the rhetorical tenets of domestic violence and the traces of rape, which served the ultimate in disciplinary efforts. This misogynist logic implied that should Hillary Clinton dare to step into such masculine spaces of politics, she justifiably received her due, even if that meant being bruised, battered, or raped for doing so. As already shown, the rhetorical traces of domestic violence remained visible throughout the 2008 presidential race. The gender logic suggested that a woman who flouted the ideals of authentic womanhood should be disciplined for her defiant behavior, reifying the inhospitable image of the nation-state for feminist political leaders.

To show the challenges to Clinton's political authenticity, this chapter chronicles the evolution of television news coverage from the first whispers of Clinton's interest in the Senate race to her transition into political office as a precedent-setting first lady turned U.S. senator. How would the frames from 1992–98 continue to influence her coverage? Ultimately, Clinton would be dubbed as one of the most unlikely and unlikeable of senatorial candidates riding the wave of her celebrity and political opportunism to victory.

Will She or Won't She?

On January 3, 1999, only days before Bill Clinton's impeachment trial commenced, Tim Russert of NBC's *Meet the Press* uttered the nearly unthinkable—Hillary Clinton was considering a run for the U.S. Senate from New York. Resorting to the familiar language of war, Russert gossiped: "Here's a little mini bombshell. Senator Robert Torricelli of New Jersey, who heads the Senate Campaign Committee, told me before the program that if he had to guess, he believes that Hillary Rodham Clinton will run for the United States Senate seat from New York."[14] As the news grew from a whisper to a full-blown conversation by February 1999, certain Democrats expressed elation at the thought. Democratic Congressman Charles Rangel of New York called Clinton "a winner."[15] Harry Reid (D-NV) said Clinton would "be one of the best senators of all time," and Daniel Patrick Moynihan, the Democratic senator from New York whose departure created the opening, assured that "she'd be welcome and she'd win."[16]

Republicans also seemed giddy over a possible Clinton run. To some, a Clinton candidacy portended a certain victory for Republicans. John McCain's (R-AZ) amusement over a potential race between Hillary Clinton and Mayor Rudy Giuliani from New York was on full display in a statement before ABC News in February 1999. With a broad grin and a chuckle, McCain called the potential matchup an "incredible race," perhaps "one of the great races in history." Within the same ABC News broadcast, Ralph Reed, a Republican consultant, indicated he "would be willing to pay her filing fee" because he wanted "to see a Republican win the Senate seat in New York."[17] As Chris Hansen from *NBC Nightly News* observed by the summer of 1999, "It's difficult to say who's more excited, her supporters or her opponents."[18]

Some among the press corps acknowledged the momentousness of a first lady seeking office. In a January 27, 2000, episode of *Time & Again*, David Gregory acknowledged the many precedents that Hillary Clinton had already set: "Hillary Rodham Clinton, the most famous woman in the world . . . She's broken the traditional mold of first lady. The first working woman in the White House. The first to lead a major cabinet-level policy committee. And now, the first to run for public office."[19] The following month, Jim Wooten of ABC News recognized the historical nature of her campaign: "Whatever happens next November . . . will be a bit of history."[20]

Yet, the threats posed by these precedent-setting actions foreshadowed what many in the news saw as the inevitable controversies yet to come. Even Democratic supporters like New York senator Charles Schumer told CBS News that "favorites don't always win and . . . it would be a rough, even nasty, battle against her likely opponent, New York City mayor Rudy Giuliani."[21] Gwen Ifill of NBC News paraphrased Julia Reed, a political writer for *Vogue*, who showed a sense of doubt, suggesting that "a Hillary Clinton candidacy may sound better in theory than reality." To evidence the point, NBC aired a statement from Ralph Reed, prophesying that even though Clinton was "riding this wave" right now, he believed things would change quickly "once she gets to New York and starts getting into dirty New York politics."[22] As to the roughness of the campaign, Andrea Mitchell of *NBC Nightly News* warned that if Clinton ran, she wouldn't be able to do so from the "controlled settings that she enjoys as first lady, refusing to answer any questions from reporters."[23]

Members of the press could hardly stand the anticipation of getting Hillary Clinton into the political arena. The excitement ultimately produced some rather bizarre metaphors. Chris Bury from *Nightline* used "catnip" references to mark the buildup to a Clinton-Giuliani race: "A matchup between Mrs. Clinton and New York Mayor Giuliani is pure catnip for politicians and pundits desperate for a post-impeachment fix."[24] Resorting to salivation language, Chris Wallace of ABC's *Nightline* noted that the New York press was "already salivating over the prospect" of a Clinton campaign.[25] Also staying with a food motif, James Carville, appearing on *NBC Nightly News*, talked of how the New York press was "licking their chops" for such a dream campaign.[26] The most hyperbolic reference came in the form of a sexualized (and masculine) metaphor used by Jack Newfield of the *New York Post*, when he suggested on *Nightline* that Clinton's entrance into the Senate race "would be Viagra for the media."[27]

These linguistic references associated with an impending campaign of a political woman ranged from insatiable sensations of hunger and pharmaceutically induced sexual arousal to plant-induced stimulations in cats. These metaphors alone showed the confusion journalists faced in comprehending Clinton's senatorial run. The reference to Viagra in particular reinforced the ongoing masculinization and sexualization of the political sphere for women.

Sexualizing the political spaces that Clinton prepared to enter re-emerged in other ways. The news media portrayed Clinton's precandidacy exploration as "teasing" the press and the American people with her ego-boosting campaign. Aaron Brown of ABC News noted that during a March 1999 Democratic fundraiser, "the first lady only teased" when addressing questions about her future political plans.[28] Chris Bury of ABC's *Nightline* would use the same linguistic construct after airing a video segment about the first lady. He posed the question, is Clinton "serious . . . or . . . just teasing?"[29] Teasing the press was part of Clinton's dating ritual, some suggested, as Peter Jennings of ABC News spoke of Clinton's "very carefully planned courtship."[30] An inquiring press would expand on this courtship theme as Richard Roth of CBS News spoke of questions Clinton received on her trip to Egypt in March 1999: "An Egyptian reporter popped the question first thing this morning: 'What are your future plans?'"[31] The news language had consequently progressed from connotations of Clinton's sexual flirtation with the public and the press to a marriage proposal from a journalist with questions about Clinton's political plans.

Part of the linguistic courting ritual was a kind of dance that Clinton allegedly displayed before watchful journalists, eager for any clues into her political future. NBC would use a headline that showcased Hillary Clinton as a socialite, "Out on the Town," in the aftermath of the Clinton-Lewinsky nightmare. Andrea Mitchell extended the social flirtation metaphor with references to "the first lady's candidate dance."[32] The underlying messages of the press suggested that after struggling for months through the tumultuous news coverage of her husband's affair, the first lady was in need of flattery. As Bill Plante of CBS News concluded in February 1999, "At the very least, all the attention has to be flattering. And even if she doesn't run, she will at least have helped to change the subject."[33]

Clinton's smile as she stepped to the edge of the political arena would now be imbued by the press with more sexual innuendos, a far cry from the deceptive smile of backroom political and financial deals, the vacuous authentic womanhood smile, or the scorned smile of marital agony. Clinton was now portrayed as someone eager to have the entire spotlight directed toward her. As Bill Plante of CBS talked of Hillary Clinton's enjoyment of such flattery in the story referenced above, the news cameras featured images of the Clintons' visit to Mexico in February 1999. In these shots, Bill and Hillary were shown alongside the first couple of Mexico. One image embedded in the broadcast zoomed in on a smiling Hillary Clinton interacting with a grinning Mexican president—Ernesto Zedillo. Bill Clinton was featured on the margins of what was framed as a more intimate exchange between the first lady and the Mexican president, whose wife was totally cut out of the zoomed-in shot. Hillary's smile in this scene connoted a sense of flirtation with another male who gazed adoringly at the first lady. These images corroborated the insinuation that Clinton was enjoying the attention she received from a doting male of stature and significance as she contemplated a senatorial run. ABC's *Nightline* would exhibit a similar tone in its coverage of Hillary Clinton and the president of the Russian Federation, Boris Yeltsin. Noting that Hillary "played on the world stage," Chris Wallace of *Nightline* wondered how she "will play in New York." Framing the exchange as one that involved two world leaders "playing" together before a global audience, ABC News showed footage of Hillary Clinton greeting and kissing Yeltsin on his cheeks. Both were smiling broadly at one another.[34] This suggestive framing implied that Clinton's smile revealed her enjoyment of the sexual flirtation with men of power, especially in the aftermath of the publicity over her husband's affair. The framing of Clinton's smile showed the ongoing ways in which women's participation in politics continued to be sexualized.[35]

As winter turned to spring in 1999, Clinton began canvassing the state of New York, looking very much like a political candidate. The tenor of the news conversation gradually shifted from a rhetoric of teasing to one of authenticity assessment. In July 1999, Clinton finally announced that she had formed an exploratory committee for the U.S. Senate. In November, she confirmed that she was in the Senate race even though she would not make the official announcement until early 2000. By May, Clinton had clinched the Democratic nomination but her likely political opponent was in doubt. While Rudy Giuliani seemed like the inevitable challenger throughout much of 1999 and well into 2000, he eventually dropped out of the race in May, citing health issues and other personal matters. Hillary Clinton's opponent would ultimately be Rick Lazio, a former congressman from the state of New York. Whether being compared to either Giuliani or Lazio, Clinton would inevitably be dubbed as the less authentic candidate. Unlike her challengers, she had never worked, lived, or gone to school in the state she sought to represent. Clinton's authenticity, as it had been since she entered the national spotlight in 1992, would be challenged in a variety of old and new ways.

The Inauthentic Political Candidate

Once the press became convinced that Hillary Clinton was seriously pursuing elected office, the surveillance of her campaign activities ramped up in very noticeable ways. ABC's Sam Donaldson evidenced the media frenzy over a potential Clinton candidacy in February 1999: "Perhaps never before has a routine announcement of disaster relief aid been made in such a highly publicized, star-driven fashion or covered by such an overflow crowd of reporters and cameras. But then, never before has a first lady considered running for the Senate from New York."[36]

In making sense of this precedent-setting case, the news media would rely on familiar Clinton frames from her earliest days on the campaign trail with her husband and the drama surrounding his presidential affair. The political marriage of Hillary and Bill Clinton continued to attract considerable attention. Yet, several new frames debuted during the 2000 campaign, some of which would pull through to her presidential candidacy in 2008. The new frames related to what some in the press portrayed as her lack of genuine motive for seeking office as she embarked on a "carpetbagging" campaign in New York. Her carpetbagging actions were made all the more ludicrous, some claimed, by her pledged allegiance to the New York Yankees baseball team. In the end, these frames fueled the underlying theme of Hillary Clinton as a political opportunist and celebrity, using her husband's coattails to pursue a vanity campaign in a state where she had no roots or association. And even though Clinton had often been depicted as the political brains and steely force behind her husband's political successes, she was now framed as a flip-flopping candidate who was unelectable because of her political ineptitudes. All of these press frames furthered the underlying assumptions of Clinton's political inauthenticity. Attempting to reconcile the image of a first lady with that of a U.S. senator seemed nearly incomprehensible; viewing an avowed feminist as an effective mainstream political candidate seemed downright preposterous. How could Hillary Clinton appear as anything other than inauthentic?

MAKING SENSE OF HILLARY CLINTON'S POLITICAL CANDIDACY

In the beginning of Clinton's senatorial campaign, journalists expended considerable time trying to identify Clinton's true motives for even thinking about elected office. Capturing the oddity of the thought, Chris Wallace of ABC's *Nightline* gave voice to journalist Joe Klein's vision of a Clinton candidacy, calling it "astonishing . . . and deeply weird."[37] Getting further into the psychology of Hillary's motives, Peter Jennings of ABC News summarized the prevailing hypotheses posited by the press and the public. Some thought the idea was a "practical joke being played on the press" and others suggested that the rumors represented Clinton's "way of no longer being seen as a victim" in the postimpeachment days.[38] Bob Schieffer of CBS News also made connections to the impeachment tribulations, surmising that many saw the rumors as a "trial balloon" and "a diversion to draw attention away from the impeachment scandal."[39] A variation on this theme was relayed by Tony Snow of Fox News, who wondered if Clinton was seeking "redemption" after the controversy over her husband's affair abated.[40]

Many ultimately came down on the side of Clinton's political ambition as her primary political motive, with the Senate serving as a stepping stone to the presidency. Dan Rather of CBS News interjected this sentiment into his newscast in February 1999 when he noted that "those urging her to run" for the Senate argued it would "position" her "to run for president later." Rather then pondered, "Is she thinking about running for president or vice president in 2000 instead of . . . the Senate?" In answering the much sought after question, Rather explained that "no one in a position to know will say."[41] NBC's Tom Brokaw took the question straight to the first lady-turned-Senate candidate herself: "When your opposition begins to whisper that she only wants to get to the Senate so she can run for president of the United States, doesn't that hurt you some in New York?" Clinton responded, "I've said I'm going to fill my full six-year term." When Brokaw pursued the question further, Clinton emphasized that "right now for me the most important job we face is electing Al Gore and Joe Lieberman."[42]

Well before Clinton would make her candidacy official, she would have to convince New Yorkers that she deserved to represent them even though she had never called New York her home prior to testing the congressional waters there. The constant drumbeat of carpetbagging complaints throughout Clinton's 2000 campaign demonstrated the importance of geographical or spatial politics to one's authenticity and legitimacy for elected office.

HILLARY CLINTON AS CARPETBAGGER

The metaphor of a carpetbagger dates back to the U.S. Civil War. It represented a derogatory label created by the South to apply to those northerners who moved to the South during and after the Civil War and supported the Republican Party platform. From its inception, carpetbagging pertained to party politics and involved controversies over geographical spaces.[43] Because Hillary Clinton was born in Illinois, was educated in Massachusetts and Connecticut, and had lived her adult life in Arkansas, her decision to seek the U.S. Senate seat from New York seemed to be more about political opportunism than a clear investment in the citizens of New York.

Early on, carpetbagging was used as a dominant linguistic frame to define Clinton's pursuit of electoral office. Andrea Mitchell of *NBC Nightly News* characterized these geographical issues accordingly in May 1999: "Her chief problem? Persuading New Yorkers she's not a carpetbagger." Mitchell then invited viewers to "listen closely to how this Illinois-born, longtime Arkansas resident tries to sound like a native New Yorker." NBC subsequently displayed a video clip of Hillary Clinton offering the following rationalization: "New York is truly a microcosm of America, everything from our biggest, most dynamic, diverse city to rural areas."[44] Despite this rationalization, the complaints would persist. As Clinton announced her exploratory committee in July 1999, CBS News aired a story that featured protesters at a Clinton rally waving signs that read, "Carpetbagger" and "Go Home, Hillary"[45]—slogans often chanted during Hillary rallies. One woman from the crowd spoke openly about the level of animosity some New Yorkers felt toward Clinton's intrusion into New York politics. After Diana Olick noted that "some residents . . . were hostile toward their potential new neighbor," CBS inserted a clip of an unidentified woman referring to Hillary's candidacy as "ridiculous," sounding more like "a joke" than a legitimate run for office.[46]

The issue of carpetbagging was central to Clinton's opposition, made up of Republicans and Democrats. Jesse Ventura, newly elected Republican governor of Minnesota, uttered the following statement on NBC's *Meet the Press*—a statement re-aired on *CNN World View* from February 21, 1999: "I think you should live in the state and be a resident of the state to run for the Senate, not play hopscotch across the country."[47] Rudy Giuliani, Clinton's one-time political rival, linked these geographical issues with authenticity directly when his views were aired on an April 1999 episode of MSNBC's *Hardball*: "That's how you do it. You do it based on reality and authenticity . . . I do have a record and . . . I've been running New York City." Giuliani then compared his candidacy to Clinton's, implying the genuineness of his image and the counterfeit identity that Clinton was attempting to forge: "This is the difference between reality and perception, between authenticity and . . . political slogans."[48] Even some New York Democrats bothered by Clinton's attempts to cross over the state's political boundaries denounced her audacious display of carpetbagging. In November 1999, state senator Carl Kruger (D-NY) charged that "when someone comes to New York once every couple of weeks and creates a traffic jam" and then "buys . . . a million-dollar home in West Chester, and wants to call herself a New Yorker, it's a wake-up call for all of us." Andrea Mitchell of NBC News summed up Clinton's image problems in this way: "But her number one problem—many New Yorkers don't see her as one of them."[49]

The backlash to Clinton's candidacy revealed most vividly the role of geographical location in authenticating a person's political identity. Being "one of them" was equated with spatial propriety and the sharing of land marked as the state's official territory. Linda McDowell talks of the "rules" associated with "power relations" that help "define boundaries" and create "mechanisms of inclusion and exclusion."[50] For the skeptical press and her political opponents, Hillary Clinton's feigned allegiance with the New York Yankees would prove most decidedly that she was indeed a political opportunist and a carpetbagger to the nth degree.

HILLARY CLINTON AS NEW YORK YANKEES FAN?

The debate over Hillary Clinton as a fan of the New York Yankees began in June 1999. Clinton had appeared on the *Today* show and disclosed her support for the team that many loved to hate[51]—a team that would visit the White House later in the day to celebrate their 1998 World Series victory. Katie Couric, co-host of NBC's *Today* show, asked Hillary Clinton about the Yankees during a June 10, 1999, interview because of their impending presidential visit. At that moment, Clinton declared: "I've always been a Yankees fan." When Couric expressed surprise, Clinton explained that even though she was decidedly a Chicago Cubs fan, she "became . . . enamored of the Yankees" as "a young girl." Clinton grounded such support in her youthful desire to cheer for an American League team; she chose the Yankees because a Chicagoan could not easily back both the Cubs and the White Sox.[52] Once the team visit actually took place later in the day, the television cameras captured Hillary Clinton receiving a baseball cap from Yankees' manager Joe Torre. A smiling Clinton excitedly accepted the cap and placed it on her head during the team photograph. Of the exchange, Ted Koppel offered the following summary on *ABC World News Tonight*: "And here in Washington today, the White House unveiled the planet's newest Yankee fan—first lady Hillary Clinton." Koppel framed the Yankee ball cap incident as a "photo opportunity" for Clinton since she was "mulling a possible run for Senate in New York." Koppel's concluding remarks foreshadowed the controversy yet to come over the baseball cap caper: "It should be noted that Mrs. Clinton grew up in Chicago as a Cubs fan."[53]

From the moment that Hillary declared her enthusiasm for the Yankees and donned the Yankee cap, her words and her nonverbal expressions of support came to symbolize the carpetbagging label for the press and her opposition. As NBC's Andrea Mitchell contended on July 3, 1999, "Her biggest liability is her carpetbagger label." The accompanying video would zoom in on Clinton wearing the Yankee hat during the team photograph at the White House as she stood next to Yankee owner George Steinbrenner.[54] Jim Wooten of ABC News detailed the uphill battle Clinton faced in becoming a New York Yankees fan. Because Clinton had only lived in New York for five months, Wooten reasoned, it would be hard for newcomers such as her to navigate the "chaotic" politics of the state, "much less be accepted" as one of the hordes of "real Yankee fans."[55] Frank Buckley of CNN would explicitly tie Hillary's claims of being a Yankee fan to her lack of genuineness. He argued in October 2000 that when "First Lady Hillary Clinton donned a New York Yankees cap, declared herself a fan . . . [c]ritics declared her, fair or not, a fake."[56] Giuliani would make political hay out of the incident early on in the campaign when he appeared on David Letterman in an Arkansas Razorback jersey and proclaimed: "I'm going to get off the airplane in Little Rock and I'm going to say, 'I've never lived here. I've never worked here. I ain't never been here. But I think it would be cool to be your senator.'"[57]

Throughout the campaign, the Yankee cap moment would be construed as a political gaffe, symbolizing Clinton's political missteps and political naiveté. During an MSNBC program entitled *Hotwire* from July 6, 1999, the show's narrator, Gregg Jarrett, would use the Yankees cap to mock Clinton's political chances. After airing her statement on the *Today* show, Jarrett laughingly asked the all-men's group gathered for the discussion whether "she [was] politically smart and savvy enough to be a senator and to win this race." Before turning to his panelists for a response, Jarrett quipped, "Was that moment as uncomfortable for you as it was for me?" One panelist, newspaper journalist Tom Squitieri, answered Jarrett's disparaging question in the affirmative: "That was a pretty interesting political plumber's nightmare."[58]

A more extended example from ABC's *Nightline* of September 13, 1999, offered further insight into how Clinton's professed Yankee allegiance was used as a marker of her political inauthenticity. Placing the focus on Clinton's political miscalculations, Chris Bury offered the following perspective: "For Hillary Clinton, the first stumble may have been that cap. The sight of this Illinois native, longtime Arkansan, and current Washingtonian in a Yankees cap annoyed even some of those New Yorkers who support her candidacy." *Nightline* then turned to a series of testimonies that pinpointed the level of animosity directed toward Clinton over the cap and her campaign. Ed Koch, former long-term Democratic mayor of New York, offered a stinging rebuke: "I do think putting on the Yankee cap was ridiculous . . . You don't become a Yankee fan by putting on a Yankee cap when you've been supporting other teams over the years." *Nightline* then aired the insights of Jack Newfield, columnist for the *New York Post*. When introducing Newfield's statements, Bury asserted that Newfield "calls himself a Bobby Kennedy Democrat but he could not abide that cap." Elaborating, Newfield stated: "That's okay to be a Cubs fan . . . [but to] put on the hat and then say I've always been a Yankees fan and now when I come to New York I'm going to root for the Yankees. It was bogus." Bury next explained that Clinton admitted she blundered on the issue but had yet to apologize. Clinton's words and actions on the baseball front ultimately led journalist Adam Nagourney of *The New York Times* to label her a "novice candidate," committing "a basic beginner's kind of mistake."[59]

The controversy over Hillary Clinton's Yankee cap offers insight into the gendering of political authenticity. In this context, sports represented an important dimension of geography, which in turn served as a key authenticity marker for Hillary Clinton and her candidacy. As Varda Burstyn argues, national commitments to sports represent deep-seated "allegiances" engrained in our "psyches" and consequently our "language and culture," producing "rules, rituals, and ideals of sport." Clinton's sporting of a Yankee cap arguably violated such rules on two fronts. First, she portended what many viewed as a false allegiance to a team whose proximity was far removed from where she resided. And, second, at least symbolically, she crossed over into a decidedly masculine space of sports; her wearing of a baseball cap most visibly showcased that sense of spatial and perhaps even gender impropriety. One only need observe the group picture of Clinton with the Yankee players to see which person stood out. As a woman professing interest in a men's sport, she contaminated the sanctity of masculinity. After all, sports developed in the nineteenth century as an "antifeminine" activity designed for young boys to enhance their masculinity by distancing themselves from their homes and their mothers.[60] As she had done during the health care debate, Clinton had once again crashed what was construed as an all-men's party, appearing as an out of place imposter pretending to be a baseball enthusiast. By extension, Clinton's masquerade as a Yankee fan symbolized her masquerade as a U.S. Senate candidate given the incongruent image between a first lady (expected to be the embodiment of authentic womanhood) and a U.S. senator (more aligned with authentic manhood than womanhood). Male journalists and political opponents especially would cry foul over Clinton's brazen audacity. Clinton's handling of the Yankees fiasco demonstrated, as several observed, that she lacked the political savvy needed to run a successful senatorial bid.

HILLARY CLINTON AS POLITICAL NOVICE

As shown in chapter 1, Hillary Clinton was often portrayed as the true politician of the Clinton partnership during her husband's presidential campaigns. Yet, when she became a political candidate in her own right, the news media and Republican opponents now constructed Hillary as a campaign novice. Apart from the Yankees controversy, the issue that tended to attract the most critical scrutiny involved Clinton's trip to the Middle East. While there she offended Israelis and their sympathizers when slow to critique offensive remarks voiced by Suha Arafat—wife of Palestinian president Yasser Arafat. This example, as with the incident surrounding the Yankees ball club, demonstrated for some that Clinton lacked the political savvy necessary to win a U.S. Senate seat.

As part of her role as first lady, Clinton traveled to the Middle East in November 1999. While in the West Bank, Clinton listened through interpreter headphones as Suha Arafat accused the Israelis of using poisonous gas on the Palestinians. At the end of the speech, several of the networks showed video of Hillary Clinton embracing Suha Arafat—a gesture that attracted the scorn of many domestically and internationally. Compounding the issue, Clinton was slow to condemn Arafat's remarks, fostering a debate over her comportment as first lady and U.S. Senate candidate, suggesting a deep division between the two roles.

The attacks from Clinton's opposition were swift and targeted; the news media quickly responded as well. Giuliani stated publicly that "I don't think I would have even been there," and "I certainly wouldn't have embraced the person who said it, hugged them, and kissed them."[61] Both CNN and NBC featured Giuliani's statements as a means to frame the controversy over the story. CNN titled one of its segments as a "Lesson in Politics" that put Hillary Clinton in the "political hot seat." Walter Rodgers of CNN explained the incident in this way: "Mrs. Clinton . . . was caught off guard by the wife of Palestinian president Yasser Arafat" who delivered "a withering attack on Israel in Arabic."[62] NBC's Andrea Mitchell framed the details of what many characterized as Clinton's political misstep: "Mrs. Clinton's trip to Israel backfired politically. Yasser Arafat's wife accused Israel of using poison gas on Palestinians. The first lady listens politely, waited a full day to respond." Of the situation as a whole, Mitchell reported that it "turned into a diplomatic incident."[63]

The international incident demonstrated for her Republican opposition and some journalists that Hillary Clinton was not ready for primetime politics. Over the next couple of weeks, the dominant message was that Hillary Clinton was prone to political mistakes, weakening her campaign chances. On November 22, 1999, Dan Rather of *CBS Evening News* introduced the story, indicating that "fair or unfair, another whispering campaign is underway in New York, aimed at First Lady Hillary Clinton and her hopes of winning a Senate seat." The resounding words whispered about her campaign by "Republicans . . . and some Democrats" were "'ineffective' and 'blunders,'" leading some to speculate that she was "considering pulling out of the race."[64] The following evening, Andrea Mitchell of NBC News would emphasize similar themes by posing and then answering her own question: "So what's gone wrong after a promising start? Observers say a series of missteps." Mitchell transitioned next to the Arafat incident as NBC showed a newspaper headline that read, "Shame on Hillary: First Lady Silent in Face of 'blood libel' on Israel." Mitchell referred to the image from an unidentified newspaper as a "tabloid nightmare."[65] George Stephanopoulos on *ABC World News Tonight* echoed the same message on the same evening, concluding that "her campaign was floundering."[66]

Such "whisper campaigns" led to Clinton's public announcement that she intended "to run" for the U.S. Senate, with plans to make the announcement official in February 2000. In responding to the Arafat issue, Aaron Brown of ABC News summarized Clinton's defense of her silence on the grounds that she was "there as first lady." In voicing her own explanation, Clinton argued back: "I think there were people who believed that I should have caused an international incident over whatever it is she said." To avoid future conflicts of interest, Clinton announced she would be scaling back her "duties as first lady."[67]

Clinton's announcement gave the press the opening needed to comment on her attempts to navigate two seemingly very distinct roles—first lady and

Senate candidate. Once again, the press reified a sense of great danger associated with Clinton seeking to navigate the divide between a role marked by ceremony and a role marked by politics. These themes reinforced the treacherous navigation that Clinton tracked during the health care debate in particular. In a story entitled "Balancing Act" from *NBC Nightly News* on November 1999, pollster John Zogby argued that "it's a highly risky endeavor. And her problem is trying to somehow balance her position as first lady . . . with her needs . . . as a candidate."[68] The risk that Dan Rather emphasized was attributed more to Clinton backers who were "urging her to move to New York immediately, stop trying to be . . . first lady, and be more of a fighting candidate."[69] CNN would emphasize the same difficulties in trying to serve in two roles concomitantly. As Walter Rodgers explained, "Her difficulty—she came to the Middle East both as a prospective candidate for the Senate from New York and as wife of the president." Emphasizing the danger of the role traversal and the accompanying political complexities, Rodgers argued that Clinton worked hard to "avoid the trip wires of Middle East politics," recognizing that "there's no such thing as a safe political trip to the Middle East." "Now," Rodgers concluded, "she's paying a political price."[70]

As Clinton weathered the storm over the Arafat incident, some in the news would continue to imply that Clinton was a weak candidate. This time, the focus centered on her flip-flopping tendencies—a signature marker for any candidate's political authenticity. By the summer of 2000, Hillary Clinton would be accused of flip-flopping over the location of a U.S. embassy in the Middle East. For some this move represented an obvious attempt to regain favor with Jewish voters upset by her response to Arafat's anti-Israeli comments. As Kelly Wallace of CNN explained, Clinton called for moving the U.S. embassy from Tel Aviv to Jerusalem, a move supported by the Israelis, yet one she previously opposed. Clinton made the point publicly: "I'd like to see that move be made before the end of the year." Even though Israelis would be happy with the move, Palestinians would not. In response, Wallace explained, unnamed "political observers say the first lady's comments, politically motivated or not, will help with Jewish voters" who were upset by her "embrace of . . . Arafat's wife late last year." Hinting that a political motive underlay the switch in positions, Wallace concluded that "Mrs. Clinton has had a bumpy ride trying to court Jewish voters in New York."[71]

Even after she officially entered the Senate race in February 2000 and seemingly stepped into the political arena with both feet, the image of a politically inexperienced candidate continued to reverberate. NBC News, for example, made political fodder out of the fact that Hillary Clinton left a diner in New York without leaving a tip for a waitress whom Andrea Mitchell defined as a "single mom with no benefits." Mitchell framed Clinton as a "neophyte" and a "rookie politician."[72] Even as Hillary Clinton's poll numbers began to improve, the credit for such gains would not be given to Clinton's strength as a candidate but to her opponent's miscues. Jim Axelrod of *CBS Evening News* argued on April 6, 2000, that "Mrs. Clinton may not be the mayor's toughest opponent." Representative Peter King (R-NY) then concluded, "In many ways, this is not Rudy against Hillary, this is Rudy against Rudy, and right now Rudy is losing."[73] Mitchell would emphasize the same point, undercutting Clinton's contributions to her own campaign advancements: "Hillary takes the lead for the first time in a year, largely, say pollsters, because of self-inflicted wounds by her opponent."[74]

Although many of the news frames from the 1992 campaign demonstrated greater consistency over time, one such memory frame would exhibit considerable transformation. Hillary Clinton would no longer be portrayed as the strategically savvy and shrewd political advisor. When serving as a behind-the-scenes advisor for her husband—as a strong woman standing behind the public man—Clinton's persona was one of political intelligence and calculation. Once out from behind her husband's political shadow, she was subsequently portrayed as a political novice, reifying a sense of her political inauthenticity. Associated more with ceremony than politics, the first lady position was not construed as a political one, even though Clinton worked on two presidential campaigns, organized a health care task force, promoted policies designed to advance the lives of women and children, and traveled extensively across multiple continents addressing human rights issues, world health crises, Middle East peace negotiations, and a host of other matters. The role's association with the ideologies of authentic womanhood overshadowed Clinton's performance of the role, contributing to the mindset that she was politically unqualified to be a U.S. senator. Clinton's marriage to the president of the United States would further undermine her political candidacy in very familiar ways.

THE INAUTHENTICITY OF THE CLINTON MARRIAGE

The Clinton marriage would once again become a topic of conversation during Hillary Clinton's Senate campaign. With the impeachment hearings and thus the Clinton-Lewinsky affair still fresh in the minds of Americans, many among the press and the U.S. public continued to wonder why a feminist like Hillary Clinton opted to stay with her unfaithful husband. The frames from 1998 and the controversy over the affair would continue to haunt Hillary Clinton; the residual frame of political partnership would become another way in which to inauthenticate Hillary Clinton and her Senate candidacy.

As in 1992, the Clinton marriage during Hillary's own election cycle was seen through a political prism. For a May 17, 2000, story, NBC News used the headline "Power Couple" to frame their news segment. First, NBC aired Hillary Clinton's statement where she thanked her husband for being by her side during the campaign: "I am delighted that the president is here this evening, and I am so grateful . . . for his support. I would not be standing here tonight were it not for Bill, and were it not for all he has done for me." Transitioning from Clinton's statement of support, Andrea Mitchell sarcastically asked, "The same Bill Clinton who was impeached after scandalizing the nation and his wife?" To remind the audience of such scandalous times, NBC showed footage of Bill Clinton denying his relationship with Monica Lewinsky—"those allegations are false"—followed by the postmemorial footage of the Clintons walking together on the White House lawn, holding hands but clearly psychologically distanced from one another. Mitchell then wondered aloud: "How did they go from this less than two years ago, to this?" Reaffirming the notion of a political partnership, Mitchell disclosed that "even longtime political associates concede it is an amazing story of political reinvention—the ultimate power couple."[75] The inauthenticity of a marriage grounded in a political partnership was buttressed by a rhetoric of "reinvention," with NBC emphasizing Hillary Clinton's transformation from first lady to spousal victim to political candidate. As a candidate with a distinct identity apart from her husband, the press would take note of what some observed was a marriage between two people living worlds apart. As Peter Jennings of *ABC World News Tonight* observed in November 1999, "The president and the first lady in two different places, conducting separate political lives."[76]

While continuing to punctuate the Clintons' political partnership, the press also called attention to a political reversal in this marriage that defied easy explanation. After all, Hillary Clinton had moved from the political margins to the political spotlight, leaving Bill Clinton to lurk in the shadows as Hillary's political advisor. Such a turnabout resulted in an unusual series of events, many reasoned, even for this political marriage. Andrea Mitchell accentuated the role reversal while implying that Clinton's run for the Senate might simply be a vanity campaign about self-empowerment: "Critics may call it a power trip, but the bottom line, friends say, is that this couple has banded together once again, politically and emotionally. It's her turn, the president believes, and he's helping with every decision."[77] This role reversal meant that Bill Clinton was no longer in the political spotlight, which many believed would be a difficult challenge for him. As CNN's Donna Kelley commented: "For President Clinton, his wife's candidacy is a role reversal of sorts that might take a little getting used to." The evidence of the role reversal was shown, Kelly Wallace suggested, when "the president and Chelsea picked up coffee for her" as "Mrs. Clinton prepared for her Senate announcement."[78] That a presidential husband would step back to allow his Senate candidate wife to stand alone on the political stage, front and center, reinforced the oddity of the Clintons' marital rearrangement.

Clinton's campaign would go to great strides, however, to assure voters that the Clinton marriage was genuine. They did so by poking fun at the role reversal and by producing a video that depicted what life would look like for the couple once Bill left the White House and Hillary entered the Senate. Before airing the video, Andrea Mitchell first indicated that "the president jokes . . . about Hillary's career taking off while he's left behind." NBC then aired a clip from the video spoof, showing Hillary getting in the car as Bill bolted out of the house with her lunch yelling, "Hillary, wait, wait, you forgot your lunch."[79] That such humor was needed to blunt the audacity and ideological anomaly of the spousal reversal demonstrated the entrenched gendered assumptions about marriages. A husband, particularly the president of the United States, willing to take a backseat to his wife's candidacy seemed so unnatural that all one could really do was laugh. This sense of marital transformation in politics would further erode Clinton's authenticity as a political candidate. How could anyone take a woman seriously who moved from a role defined by her marriage to one defined by political access and legitimate power?

In answering this question, some suggested that Hillary Clinton really was incapable of forging such independence—her political viability was forever tethered to her political husband. During a June 7, 2000, episode of *Hardball*, MSNBC's Chris Matthews compared Hillary Clinton to a hermit crab:

> That's the crab that finds its protection and its identity by hiding under a shell . . . Is that what [Hillary Clinton] is, a hermit crab, somebody who doesn't have a separate identity or doesn't have the sense of self-confidence to lead their own careers, but has found this crab, this shell, Bill Clinton . . . that she's chosen to hide behind for thirty years as kind of protection and identity?

In response to Matthews's psychological assessment, Laura Ingraham, author of *The Hillary Trap*, defined Hillary Clinton's marital comportment as a behind-the-scenes power grab: "Hillary has siphoned off her power the old-fashioned way, by sticking with a man who could give her social status, social prominence, and at the end of the day, a large, large slice of political power pie and that's what Hillary has gotten out of this."[80]

That Hillary Clinton's political identity was tied to her husband's led some to challenge the legitimacy of her campaign. They contended that her fame derived from her husband's career rather than her own achievements. Conservative radio host Oliver North, on the MSNBC show, *Feedback*, argued most unabashedly in April 2000 that Hillary Clinton's "never done anything. She's accomplished nothing."[81] In discussing views about Clinton's marriage and career, NBC News discussed a poll among women voters from June 2000, where more than 50 percent of the respondents viewed Clinton more negatively. Historian Doris Kearns Goodwin gave voice to some of the complaints from career women especially, suggesting a level of "resentment" linked to "the fact that they have to climb the ladder step by step to get where they are. And there's a sense that Hillary has catapulted over the top of everyone else in New York to run for office, in part, on the basis of her marriage and her celebrity as opposed to simply her accomplishments."[82] First Lady Hillary Clinton thus would forever be known as Bill Clinton's wife in the Clinton partnership, disavowing the possibility of a credible role reversal within a logic steeped in patriarchy. This news coverage reinforced once again the entrenchment of gender roles and news frames in the nation-state.

Other complaints stemmed from Hillary's response to her husband's affair. That she stayed with Bill Clinton was part of this critique. As Dan Harris of *ABC World News Tonight* suggested in October 2000, some voters questioned her character because she opted to stay married to Bill Clinton: "Her character issues surfaced again from viewers who submitted questions about why Mrs. Clinton stayed with her husband after the Lewinsky affair."[83] Yet, likewise important for the press at least was Hillary Clinton's refusal to offer a full accounting of what happened in the privacy of the Clinton household once the news went public about Clinton's affair with Lewinsky (see chapter 3 for Clinton's previous explanations). According to some in the press, she would not be cleared for office until she persuasively dealt with these inquiring questions. Foreshadowing a need for greater transparency, Andrea Mitchell noted that Clinton "ducked questions about Monica Lewinsky and Whitewater. But aides know she'll have to deal with that before she can make her case for becoming a senator."[84] Author Gail Sheehy predicted on *ABC World News Tonight* in late 2000 that once Hillary Clinton published her memoirs, we would learn little about "what really went down between her and Bill Clinton and the answer to the big question that everybody always asks, 'why did she stay with him?'"[85]

Initially, Clinton defiantly refused to answer such questions during a separate interview with ABC News in August 2000: "I think my business and my family is really to be kept private." Yet, Clinton would ultimately address the matter. Linking Clinton's decision to stay with her husband to the viability of her campaign, Peter Jennings asked her "if it disappoints you particularly that . . . some of the young women . . . for whom you would really advocate independent thinking resent you because you didn't leave your husband." Defending her feminist credentials, Clinton responded that "for my entire adult life, [I] argued and fought for and worked for the right of women to make their own decisions, make their own choices in their lives. That's what I've done, and that's what I would hope for any young woman."[86]

The last exchange pointed to what some in the press suggested was Hillary Clinton trying to have it both ways—to position herself as both a strong woman *and* a scorned wife—and attempting to take advantage of contradictory images. Laura Ingraham would appear on another episode of *Hardball* in April 2000 to promote her book. In this appearance, she condemned Clinton's double standard: "She can't have it both ways. She can't hold herself up as a feminist role model for strong women and, on the other hand, play the first victim when it's convenient for her." Elaborating on the same theme later on in the show, Ingraham implied that Clinton had a flip-flopping image problem: "You can't be first victim one day and strong first lady the next and Senate candidate a week later."[87] This last illustration in particular reified just how separate and noninteractive these positions actually were perceived to be in the public vernacular. Warranting particular notation was the marked division between a "strong first lady" and "Senate candidate"—seemingly irreconcilable positions.

These sentiments suggested that Hillary Clinton had gone through too many image makeovers to be viewed as an authentic political candidate. The change from a gendered role as first lady to an implied gendered role as Senate candidate furthered the political incongruity. From her lack of genuine motive in seeking office to her carpetbagger status to her opportunistic political marriage, the news media would find a myriad of ways in which to frame Hillary Clinton as an inauthentic person and an inauthentic political candidate. The image makeovers merely reinforced the perception of Clinton as a candidate lacking in genuine qualifications and convictions. For politics, questions of authenticity have been a chief character concern from the nation's formation. The ultimate goal was to sniff out and remove from contention those political figures whose character epitomized "duplicity" over "authenticity."[88] The news media, as the fourth estate, came to serve as self-anointed authenticity evaluators; journalists had long ago dubbed Hillary Clinton as an inauthentic individual in her press biography. By 2000, authenticity questions undermined her political viability and became one of the bigger summits for Clinton to conquer. Andrea Mitchell exemplified Clinton's authenticity obstacles in her question as the 2000 campaign came to a close: "What about her authenticity as a New Yorker? Are people still reluctant to accept her as a New Yorker and accept her in this new role?"[89]

THE INAUTHENTICITY OF HILLARY CLINTON'S CELEBRITY CANDIDACY

That Clinton's candidacy was arguably based on her celebrity rather than her achievements represented a significant attack against her authenticity as a political candidate. As P. David Marshall contends, one undercurrent of celebrity is its "antipathetic" quality, where "success" is achieved "without the requisite association with work."[90] From the moment rumors spread that Hillary Clinton was thinking about a political run, linguistic frames of her stardom emerged. Notions of her "star power" and "rock star" status were prominent as she took "center stage" on the campaign trail.[91] Aaron Brown on *ABC World News Tonight* concluded in March 1999 that with a Clinton campaign, "politics has met celebrity and has become news."[92] Once Clinton achieved the nomination, some in the news media linked her success to her celebrity. In May 2000, Pat Dawson on NBC's *Today* show claimed that the Democratic nomination ceremony in New York "was an artful use of political theater. A clear attempt to take advantage of the Clinton celebrity."[93] Referring back to Robert Kennedy's Senate bid from New York, George Stephanopoulos on ABC's *This Week* observed in May of the same year that New York had always liked "big celebrities to run" in their elections.[94] In the end, Clinton's celebrity ultimately led some to charge that she exhibited a sense "of entitlement," while others argued that the Democrats held "a coronation of sorts for Hillary Rodham Clinton" in her acceptance of the Democratic nomination.[95]

The vacuous nature of Clinton's celebrity led to a focus on her political opportunism; a candidate willing to ride the winds of her celebrity into office was seemingly willing to do whatever it took to secure election, even if that meant violating her true convictions. Once Clinton lessened her responsibilities as first lady, Diana Olick of *CBS Evening News* asked the following question in December 1999: "Will shedding the house, the role, and her husband's policies make Mrs. Clinton a better candidate or just another politician who'll do anything to win?"[96] Many came down on the side of the latter—Hillary Clinton would do just about anything to assure her victory in November. On *NBC Nightly News* in early 2000, *Vanity Fair*'s Annette Bening was quoted as saying: "She always appears to be doing what's politically expedient in the most transparent way."[97] Matt Lauer of NBC's *Today* show offered a specific instance when Clinton appeared to be working against her political convictions, revealing the politically contradictive Clinton. During a funeral for a Catholic cardinal, Lauer pointed out that Hillary Clinton stood with others who gave a standing ovation when the speaker mentioned the cardinal's antiabortion stance. Lauer wondered: "standing for something that is in opposition to what you believe. And I'm curious what was going through your mind at that point?" Clinton defended her action as a "sign of respect." Accentuating what appeared as a lack of true conviction, Lauer concluded: "But you'd already shown your respect by attending the funeral . . . and didn't it lend to the image that politicians will stand in almost any group that is politically beneficial and march in any parade?"[98]

In taking an aerial view of Clinton's coverage during the 2000 campaign, one can see the ways in which past news frames converged to reinforce the commonplace that Hillary Clinton lacked political authenticity. The Yankees cap issue only strengthened the mountain of opposition as Clinton stepped firmly into a masculine space of sports. Hillary Clinton, as a trespasser in New York politics and sports, violated both geographical and gender boundaries. The Clinton marriage represented another key marker of her inauthenticity as the coverage reinforced the image of an ambitious political partnership with designs on a second Clinton in the White House. That Clinton opted to stay with her husband after the affair reaffirmed the cynicism of journalists. Hillary Clinton's political ambition even seemed to trump her convictions, many in the press suggested, with her willingness to do whatever it took to win a U.S. Senate seat.

The implication throughout was that Hillary Clinton was untrustworthy. Rick Lazio's campaign continuously emphasized the message: "Hillary Clinton. You just can't trust her."[99] This assertion reflected the themes that emerged from the coverage over health care (secretive), Whitewater (lies), and her husband's affairs (she was part of the cover-up). A person who could not be trusted, the logic implied, lacked the character to serve as an elected official; honesty, after all, was a key marker of one's character.

Even though the news media expended considerable energy spotlighting the inauthentic qualities of Hillary Clinton, journalists also continued to mark those qualities that they believed most captured the real Hillary Clinton. These frames would borrow from the themes of the past, showcasing the first lady-turned-Senate candidate as the same cold, untrustworthy, and divisive individual many in the press had come to know and loathe since 1992.

The Authentic Hillary Clinton of 2000

In authenticating the "real" Hillary Clinton, the press would emphasize Clinton's love of power and control—an image grounded in the memory frames from the health care debate. Also recycled was the sentiment that Clinton represented a polarizing force as epitomized by the "lightning rod" metaphor and the belief that as a strong woman, she faced likeability issues—frames that were visible from 1992 onward in the news coverage of her. As a political candidate, an "anti-Hillary" frame emerged, functioning as a linguistic frame that stood in for all of the negative attributes applied to her. When combining the authentic and inauthentic frames of Hillary Clinton, the takeaway message from many journalists was that Hillary Clinton was simply unelectable.

Once Rick Lazio became Clinton's Senate opponent, his campaign worked hard to define Hillary Clinton as one bent on pursuing political power and doing whatever she could to achieve such ends, even if that meant lying to the American people. Dan Rather and Ed Bradley of CBS News raised this theme when interviewing Clinton during the Democratic Convention in August 2000: "Your opponent in New York says . . . 'She covets power and control and thinks that she should be dictating how other people run their lives.'" Hillary Clinton initially tried to laugh off the question by saying, "He said that? Oh, my goodness." Yet Bradley persisted in the questioning. In his follow-up response, the *60 Minutes* journalist implied that the complaint was one shared by more than simply her Senate opponent: "If there is that perception of you that some have in New York, how do you counter that perception?" This time, Clinton took the question seriously and responded, "By letting people get to know me."[100]

The issues over Clinton's questionable character reinforced the sentiment that she was a polarizing figure who divided voters. Jeff Greenfield of CNN made the following observation in the lead-up to the Democratic National Convention: "Monday night, it's not just Bill Clinton speaking. He's preceded by Hillary Rodham Clinton. And if Bill Clinton is a polarizer to some people . . . Hillary Clinton is even more so."[101] Kevin Newman of ABC's *Nightline* would make the same point, calling Clinton a "polarizing political figure," which led former New York City mayor Ed Koch to point out that Clinton was "not universally liked."[102] One key frame that captured the sentiment of her polarization was that of the lightning rod—another linguistic frame from 1992. As Tish Durkin of the *New York Observer* noted on ABC News on October 8, 2000: "This woman creates some profound animosity in some quarters," leading to the epitaph that "she is a human lightning rod."[103]

The idea of Clinton as a polarizing lightning rod accentuated what appeared to be Clinton's personality problems. These personality problems sounded a lot like the frames that circulated in 1992 when Clinton was featured as a cold and calculating feminist. Andrea Mitchell argued on September 13, 2000, that many Democrats were upset during the convention because "rather than being charming and being supportive of Al Gore, that it was all about her. It was very pedantic, didactic, hard edged."[104] The idea of a hard-edged feminist was popularized in 1992 as was the sense of Clinton as a radical political figure. On NBC's *Meet the Press* in May 2000, Republican operative Mary Matalin cautioned Clinton against attacking Lazio. "If she does this," Matalin predicted, "it will only reinforce her worst negatives." Matalin concluded that the only way Clinton could beat Lazio was "if she stays the nice little lady, the unthreatening lady. As soon as she opens her mouth," it "says, 'extremist, radical, risky.'"[105] Hillary Clinton's outspokenness would once again underlie the stereotype of her extremism (e.g., her feminism)—key attributes of her alleged personality problems. That Hillary Clinton was seemingly more polarizing than her impeached husband revealed much about the news coverage of Clinton's bid for political office. These negative attributes ultimately helped authenticate the real Hillary Clinton as too polarizing, too unlikable, and too incendiary for New York voters.

Because of all of her many negatives, the press stressed, a large percentage of the American people did not much like Hillary Clinton. Chuck Todd on MSNBC's *The Mitchell Report* summarized a new poll taken in May 2000: "Of the people who support Lazio, 50 percent say they do it because they dislike Hillary Rodham Clinton . . . his strength is her."[106] The theme that Hillary Clinton was her own worst opponent was reinforced on CNN's *Inside Politics* in July of the same year. Judy Woodruff referred to a report from Frank Buckley that showed that "many people, after listening to her, say they still don't like the first lady, wouldn't vote for her."[107]

These negative attributes would lead to a general "anti-Hillary" frame that captured the totality of all that was wrong with Hillary Clinton as a person and a political candidate. Once Lazio became Clinton's primary opponent, the "anti-Hillary" linguistic frame began to resonate more routinely in news coverage. On CNN's *Inside Politics* from June 23, 2000, Tish Durkin of the *New York Observer* offered an updated assessment of the horse race between Clinton and Lazio, maintaining that "a very substantial anti-Hillary vote . . . now has her in a dead heat with a Republican in a state that has got 2 million more Democrats than Republicans."[108] Also from a discussion on *Inside Politics* less than a month later, Margaret Carlson of *Time* magazine talked about how "the anti-Hillary" vote was not a guaranteed voting bloc for Giuliani but that it would certainly "go to Rick Lazio."[109] The frame of the "anti-Hillary vote" would catch on as a key reference point for pollsters. Lee Miringoff of the Marist Institute for Public Opinion mentioned Lazio's negatives in September 2000, concluding that the "anti-Hillary vote gets him into the 40s, but he's going to have to do more . . . to get into the 50s."[110] The size of this "anti-Hillary" contingent was used to frame Clinton's electability problems and to demonstrate a "discontent with her candidacy."[111]

The emergence of the "anti-Hillary" frame was reminiscent of the "Hillary Factor" frame from the 1992 and 1996 presidential campaigns. Both represented a shortcut means by which to totalize all of Clinton's negative features accentuated in the world of television news. Given that all of her aggravating attributes would be too numerous to mention in each broadcast, this two-word catchphrase would be an efficient means for the press to express the electorate's dislike of this woman. On its face the "Hillary Factor" was more ambiguously negative. Yet, the 2000 version of this linguistic shortcut—the "anti-Hillary" frame—more boldly cast the negative reception Clinton encountered in New York.

This persistent negative framing helped explain the level of animosity still directed toward Clinton. By the end of the campaign, the "anti-Hillary" press frame had evolved into a *hating Hillary* drumbeat. During an interview with CBS News in May 2000, Craig Crawford of *Hotline* offered advice to Rick Lazio as he entered the race: "The first thing he needs to do is harness the contributors Giuliani found, which are the people who hate Clinton all over the country."[112] Even Hillary Clinton would have to explain why people felt so much "antipathy" toward her. Bryant Gumbel on CBS's *Early Show* posed the following question to Clinton in June 2000: "A whopping 53 percent of his supporters say they are dead set opposed to Hillary Clinton. How do you explain that kind of antipathy?"[113] As Hillary Clinton prepared to be sworn in, the press would reinforce the level of hatred that Clinton attracted. Clinton author Gail Sheehy emphasized on CNN's *The Spin Room* that even though women did come out in support of Clinton, a "secret . . . focus group" commissioned by her campaign exposed "why . . . women hate Hillary." What surfaced, Sheehy suggested, was that "she thinks she's better than we are. She thinks she's entitled, and what she did then was come down from her perch as sort of queen and go to the malls, go to the shopping centers, go to the diners, learn how to leave a tip, make . . . common cause with upstate women."[114] To demonstrate a level of genuineness as a political candidate, Hillary Clinton thus needed to show that she loved shopping, eating, and tipping—the credentials required for this political woman to attract votes. Such a transformation was required before women would stop hating her.

The depths of the animosity directed toward Clinton would expectedly exacerbate the level of rhetorical violence that made its way into the news frames of Clinton. The following section examines the implications of defining a controversial political woman through an aggressive rhetoric of sports, war, and violence, particularly a woman framed as an outspoken feminist.

The Rhetoric of Domestic Violence and Rape in the 2000 New York Senate Race

As addressed in chapter 2, politics is commonly processed through a rhetoric of sports, war, and violence. Press constructions of New York politics would turn up the ferocity of this incendiary rhetoric. Don Imus of MSNBC framed Clinton's candidacy with a question that implied the brutality of New York politics during a February 17, 1999, episode of *Nightline*: "Is she nuts?" Chris Wallace repeated Imus's question and asked: "After all she's been through, why in the world would Hillary Clinton sign up for what promises to be a brutal campaign?" On the same broadcast, former Republican senator from New York Alfonse D'Amato made the case that the "New York press corps is one of the toughest" in the country.[115]

To capture the toughness of New York politics, the press routinely construed the 2000 political contest as a street brawl, a boxing match, or a war zone that normalized the rhetoric of violence. Journalists, portrayed as salivating over such a campaign, seemed to relish the anticipated abuse that Clinton would likely endure in the campaign. These frames evolved into a strand of brutality that reflected the linguistic tenets of domestic violence or rape, demonstrating a new form of disciplinary rhetoric that portended the consequences of a strong woman's entrance into the zones of political masculinity. Once in the zone, she would have to prove an ability to endure the intense competition like a man. In spite of Clinton's audacious intrusions into a political campaign as a first lady, she nevertheless persevered and prevailed, overcoming what many suggested were steep odds in her unprecedented victory. The news media would once again have to recalibrate their frames to keep pace with this precedent-setting political woman.

THE RHETORICAL VIOLENCE OF ELECTORAL POLITICS

A chorus of television news voices helped heighten a sense of threat that Hillary Clinton would encounter in a campaign for the Senate, leaving some to wonder if she was really up to the challenge of electoral politics—New York style. During a *CBS Evening News* broadcast of July 27, 1999, John McLaughlin—a Republican pollster—suggested that Giuliani was "going to be in her face and he's going to be the one who sets the agenda for this election, not her."[116] New York as an in-your-face kind of political climate was not for the faint of heart. As Gloria Borger of CBS News asserted in May 1999, even Clinton's friends wondered if she could "really take the heat" given that she had been "sheltered from the press" as first lady.[117] The Lazio campaign implied that Clinton in fact was not prepared for the intensity of the campaign or the job as senator. Mike Murphy, Lazio's campaign manager, made the following claim about Lazio's debate performance on ABC's *This Week* in September 2000: "We think Rick really broke through as somebody who's tough, able to deliver for New York. I mean this isn't high tea. This is a New York Senate race, it's about who's going to be a tough, effective advocate for the state."[118] The implication of course was that the raucous world of politics was no place for a ceremonial first lady, hostess extraordinaire, and server of tea. Hillary Clinton, who in 1992 was portrayed as hostile to baking cookies and holding teas, was now seemingly accustomed to the "high tea" of royalty.

The language used to depict the roughness of New York politics further emphasized Clinton's lack of political preparedness. A typical representation construed the campaign as a street brawl known for dirty fighting. In characterizing the "fight" between Clinton and Giuliani in July 1999, Diana Olick of *CBS Evening News* noted: "And so the street fighting begins, curiously with neither candidate anywhere near the streets of New York and neither one even officially declaring to be in the fight."[119] The grittiness of the fighting was captured by Jim Dwyer of the *New York Daily Press*, who argued on CBS News in March 1999 that "the news people are dying for it. It would be the most vicious fight in the history of New York politics, not a single punch thrown above the belt, we hope."[120] The below the belt insinuations implied groin punches—the epitome of dirty fighting among men trying to win a fight through any means necessary. As a woman, would Hillary Clinton be prepared for such dirty fighting? As a woman, would she even be able to follow through on hits below the belt? These dirty boxing metaphors would reinforce Clinton's lack of battle readiness—a central theme of Lazio and his staffers. After all, what first lady would really be prepared for "a blood fight against evil"[121]—prose used by Lazio's campaign manager.

The news media responded in kind, with an elevated rhetoric of violence. As journalist and author of *The Money Men* Jeff Birnbaum suggested on Fox News in May 2000, Lazio had "a smile and a knife . . . out for Mrs. Clinton but delivering it in a very affable way and it's really been working."[122] The idea of stabbing Clinton with a smile reinforced the sadistic nature of these rhetorically violent attacks with Lazio exhibiting minimal remorse. The male press corps were also portrayed as out for Clinton, reifying the decidedly masculine nature of politics. Chris Bury of ABC's *Nightline* offered a masculine political portrait in February 1999 as he envisioned "thirty guys . . . yelling at her to explain the $100,000 profit she made in the commodity trade in Arkansas in 1979." This context stood in sharp contrast to what Bury depicted as the first lady's "media exposure," which he charged had "been carefully choreographed for the most positive and often glowing results." To further this sense of disconnect between a New York political race and Hillary Clinton's aspirations to enter, ABC aired an image of Clinton dressed in a dark suit, adorned with pearls. How could such a woman, used to pearls, high tea, and kid glove treatment, ever enter, let alone succeed, in a "blood fight" involving knives and groin punches?[123]

Boxing metaphors and analogies would buttress the intensity of the New York campaign that made the first lady appear even less equipped for such a robust fight. Tom Brokaw of NBC News referred to Rudy Giuliani as a "Republican heavyweight" in February 1999,[124] while Frank Buckley of CNN's *Inside Politics* suggested that both campaigns were "downplaying expectations of a K.O. in the ring."[125] Most strikingly, Jerry Nachman, editor of the *New York Post*, depicted the matchup between Clinton and Giuliani as an "Ali-Frazier fight," calling it "one of the great bouts of all time."[126] The idea of substituting Hillary Clinton in for either Ali or Frazier would further the inauthenticity of her candidacy. How could she stand up to a "heavyweight" boxer, particularly in one of the greatest bouts of all time, with a sport that represented an avenue for male aggression? Could she ever rise to the appearance of one physically equipped to knock out her heavyweight opponent? And if she did, what would be the gendered consequences on her political image? Just as Clinton seemed like an imposter Yankee fan—as a non–New Yorker and a woman—she also would be out of place in a gritty street brawl or boxing match for the ages.

Clinton's lack of authenticity would be furthered through a rhetoric of war that naturalized the aura of the campaign's aggressiveness. Andrea Mitchell called Lazio's style of campaigning more of a "stealth campaign" with a "low profile,"[127] as she made mention of Clinton's "war chest" in a separate NBC broadcast.[128] Enhancing the rhetorical vitriol of the campaign discourse, Dan Rather portrayed Clinton's life as one "under political siege" as he attempted to discover whether she was truly seeking the Senate seat.[129] ABC News also characterized Hillary Clinton as opening "a new front in her political battle" against Giuliani.[130] And former Senator D'Amato conflated the rhetoric of boxing and war in 2000, suggesting that "there's every minefield that you can just think about . . . It would be a slug fest."[131]

Linguistic traces of domestic violence and rape also emerged in the news coverage of Clinton's campaign. Whether intentional or not, the conflation of violence and politics produced a gendered timbre associated with violence against women. Jerry Nachman made the following observation on *Nightline* in early 1999, when he talked about the level of excitement and implicit threat surrounding Clinton's entrance into the campaign: "I'm not sure she has the belly for what the press is now doing jumping jacks waiting to do to her."[132] In unpacking this one sentence, Nachman reinforced the message that Clinton likely could not stomach the combative nature of New York politics. His reference to "jumping jacks" could also be construed as someone preparing for a political fight, limbering up in anticipation of an impending sporting event. Most revealing were the latter words of the sentence—"waiting to do to her." The use of this language implied a level of sexual violence directed toward Clinton by the New York press should she enter the race. Even if not reading this passage for its sexually violent implications, "jumping jacks" combined with the "waiting to do to her" implied the press was pumping up as they prepared to take such physical aggression to this audacious political woman.

The underlying assumption was that if Clinton had the nerve to step into the political arena, she opened herself up for whatever actions followed. Historically, women have often been seen as provoking sexual attacks through their provocative clothing or presence in seamy environments that incited sexual violence. Given the longtime sexualization of politics for women, this language depicted Clinton as a sexual provocateur, inviting the violence because of her spatial intrusions where she did not belong and was not welcome.[133]

Another example exhibited the violent implications associated with war in the framing of Clinton's political candidacy. During a *Nightline* episode on June 23, 1999, Joe Klein of *The New Yorker* made the following observation when discussing just how aggressive Rudy Giuliani could be against Hillary Clinton during the campaign: "If he treats her like another candidate, that'll be okay. If he treats her the way the Serbs treated the Kosovars ... which is ... his natural impulse, he might be in some trouble."[134] This analogy minimally suggested that Giuliani's "natural impulse" was to go to war against Clinton. Yet, that particular war carried additional implications of violence. Within the debate over the U.S. intervention into this European conflict, allegations of war crimes, genocide, and rape were commonplace. One justification for U.S. intervention into this complex war was that Serbian officials condoned the raping of Kosovar women as a means to increase the number of Serbian children born to the women of Kosovo.[135]

What Klein meant by such a comparison may not be known to even Klein himself. Yet, the undercurrent of war crimes, genocide, and rape offered a particularly violent characterization of the kind of treatment that Giuliani would most *naturally* wish to enact against Clinton. We need to at least consider what these analogies say about the ideological commonplaces of women, politics, and violence—particularly sexual violence. What does the phrasing suggest about the U.S. political system when contemplating how a male political candidate would naturally wish to act out against a female political candidate? Were these representations linked to Clinton's gender, and would they still have surfaced were Giuliani running against a male candidate? Though these questions are impossible to answer, they still are in need of critical consideration.

Arguably, images of women and rape represent one potential outcome when perceiving politics as a war zone—a war between Democrats and Republicans. These discursive constructs draw on similar imagery of violence associated with war. While men may be killed, beaten, or taken as political prisoners during wartime, women (and sometimes men) can also become the victims of rape. These acts are decidedly ones of extreme gender violence and expressions of masculine gender power and control. In the process, women are constituted as powerless victims in need of protection. Even in wartime, women can experience a "social stigma," Elissa Helms argues, because of perceived morality lapses and loss of respectability associated with rape victims. Women can be marginalized and shunned in a nationalism context for bringing on the violence against themselves, further humiliating the nation-state.[136] This example demonstrates most vividly that the warlike construct of political campaigns creates a language reminiscent of enemy combatants. Women are portrayed as powerless victims rather than strong leaders in the masculine images of the nation-state. Klein's words suggested that Hillary Clinton would receive a level of sympathy once again as a victim of male aggression.

Another example that reflected the language of domestic violence originated from MSNBC's *Hardball* and involved an exchange between host Chris Matthews and guest Peggy Noonan—former Reagan speechwriter and author of *The Case against Hillary*. The extended exchange unfolded as follows:

NOONAN: Hillary and Rudy is going to be like Marie Antoinette, the sort of princess person, versus Jake LaMotta the Raging Bull. God knows what's going to happen. It ought to be very exciting. Mrs. Clinton has never taken it full in the face before . . . She's always arranged her life so that she's never face to face with anyone who means to harm her . . . She does the harm from far away with a twelve-foot cordon around her. It's going to be wonderful to see them in the same room looking at each other just like us and going like this to each other . . .

MATTHEWS: What happens when people see Jimmy Cagney putting that grapefruit half in the face of Mae Clarke, in this case Hillary Rodham Clinton? . . . Do you think that what you've just described is going to sell well to the average woman voter out there? Some tough guy putting a half grapefruit in the face of Hillary Clinton? . . .

NOONAN [LAUGHINGLY RESPONDED]: It is actually very delicate but I have a feeling Giuliani's going to handle it . . . You know, the first guy to face this was George Bush Sr. versus a new girl in town named Gerri Ferraro . . . I think in the case of Hillary Clinton, full aggression will probably be in order from the guy and Mrs. Clinton will be hard pressed to say, "I can't believe he hit me . . ."

MATTHEWS: So you would advise if you were in his corner with a towel over your shoulder . . . "Jake, get in there and punch, right, not be nice?"

NOONAN: Yeah. I'd be playing the Rocky music and saying spit out the water, get in there.[137]

This extended example showcased the ways in which a rhetoric of violence—of domestic violence—seeped into the language of political actors. The language reflected the gendered imagery of politics and the underlying threats to women should they dare to enter the political arena. The boxing metaphors and being punched in the face reflect the violent sports metaphors that typify political discourse. Yet, the references to Marie Antoinette helped sexualize the violence. Antoinette, a woman who suffered the ultimate in violent deaths on the grounds of political and alleged sexual misconduct, reified the potential consequences for women in politics. Clinton was also pitted against the "Raging Bull" and "Rocky," who assumed more positive, acceptable, and decidedly masculine images in popular culture. Clinton, conversely, was featured as a "princess" and both Clinton and Ferraro were called "girls" who really could not handle the violent political contexts. Matthews's reference to James Cagney and Mae Clark most vividly furthered the symbolism of domestic violence. Matthews's comparison was to a 1931 film, *The Public Enemy*, where Cagney, an evil gangster, famously and violently smashed a grapefruit into his girlfriend's face because she questioned him about his drinking over breakfast—depicting what we now would understand as an act of domestic violence. Once Cagney's character performed the act of violence, Clarke's character sat quietly and cried. This reference drew on an analogy of domestic violence and suggested that Hillary Clinton would likely sit by quietly and passively as Giuliani engaged in aggressive attacks against her. Also revealing was Matthews's assumption that the violence against Clinton or Mae Clarke would only matter to women; men seemingly would be unphased by the violence against women.

This imagery functioned as a level of perceived threat to women interested in political office. If women opted to enter the spaces of masculine violence, they did so at their own risk and seemingly consented to the abuse just by entering the contest. A sense of aggression toward Clinton played out during her debate with Lazio—an act of aggression that ultimately backfired. More than anything, it demonstrated how a campaign predicated on a show of linguistic aggression toward Hillary Clinton created an environment where a male political candidate would opt to leave his debate podium and violate Clinton's personal space in a show of nonverbal aggression.

During the first Clinton-Lazio debate in September 2000 (Buffalo, New York), Lazio asked Clinton to sign a pledge against the use of soft money in the campaign. Toward the end of the discussion, Lazio removed the pledge from his pocket and asked Clinton to sign it on the spot. In the process of delivering the pledge to Clinton, Lazio left his debate podium, walked toward Clinton, and entered her personal space, stating, "I want you to sign it." He then stood over Clinton, gestured toward her with his hand, and lingered in her space as he continued to issue his demands. Clinton initially took a step toward Lazio but stepped back as he came closer to her and pushed the pledge toward her.[138]

Of Lazio's political act of aggression toward Clinton, Dan Rather of *CBS Evening News* commented: "Even for a New York audience accustomed to in-your-face politics, it was a memorable spectacle that's been part of the most closely watched Senate race in American history."[139] Of the same debate moment, Sam Donaldson on ABC's *This Week* asserted that "some people say, 'Well, it was halting and she was shocked by it.' Others say, 'Well, that will actually help her.'" Cokie Roberts tagged on to Donaldson's observation, arguing that the move "does help her" because Clinton's "favorability ratings went way up when she was the wounded woman during . . . the Clinton scandal . . . And it's when she comes across as brittle and school marmish . . . that the people don't like her . . . When she . . . is looking pained and wounded, it works."[140]

While Lazio's actions were challenged by voters and journalists, the stunt nevertheless revealed a political climate where an act of spatial aggression occurred during a debate between a former congressman and a sitting first lady. A vitriolic campaign now included a more physically intimidating act of spatial confrontation as Lazio came within inches of Clinton while making demands of her. Cokie Roberts's response was particularly illustrative as she portrayed any jump in Clinton's poll numbers not to her overall debate performance but to the actions of her opponent. These depictions prompted the use of a memory frame that accentuated Hillary Clinton's status as a scorned wife and thus a disempowered victim. Roberts's comment also reinforced the message that Clinton was unlikeable unless she was the object of spousal infidelity or bullying behavior by a man. This reasoning implied that only under conditions where Clinton lacked agency in her marriage or was the recipient of male aggression would she ever be likeable enough for voters to pull the lever in her favor.

THE RHETORICAL RE-DISCIPLINING OF HILLARY CLINTON

Recalling the memory frame of Clinton as a scorned wife would function as another means for the news media to discipline Clinton by having her relive the private humiliation as a wife of a cheating husband in very public settings. The rhetoric of violence would continue to resonate in the news coverage that challenged Clinton's marital choices.

A CBS News broadcast from January 19, 2000, used a language of violence ("battered") with Clinton's private role as a woman scorned. In introducing the story, Dan Rather charged: "but on the campaign trail, [Clinton's] now getting battered . . . about her personal life." Reporter Bob Schieffer then explained that during the Buffalo debate, Clinton "was blindsided by a TV reporter who asked: 'Are you planning to leave your husband when his presidency is over?'" Schieffer then noted that Clinton was asked in a radio interview about her own marital fidelity, sexualizing the discussion of Clinton's political candidacy. CBS featured the radio interviewer's question: "You were on television last night talking about your relationship with the president Bill Clinton. Have you ever been sexually unfaithful to him and specifically the stories about you and Vince Foster? Any truth in those?" Clinton would respond in indignant ways, affirming her marital stability and charging that the infidelity questions were "out of bounds." CBS then aired a statement from Howard Kurtz of the *Washington Post* who argued "I think it's fair game to ask the first lady whether she plans to stay married to her husband. These questions about infidelity . . . are completely salacious, appalling and shouldn't be part of what we call journalism." That CBS would feature a denouncement of such lines of questioning was significant. Schieffer closed the segment by stating that "today even some veteran reporters are shaking their heads and wondering, 'What will someone ask next?'"[141]

Yet, within the story, the depiction of Clinton as a "battered" (and "blindsided") political candidate in the context of her personal life implied the linguistic consequences when conflating women, marriage, and political campaigns. Dan Rather used the word *battered* when referring to Clinton's personal life during a political contest—a common reference in the context of domestic violence ("battered wife"). Portraying Clinton as the object of linguistic abuse ("battered" and "blindsided") in her public and personal life illustrated the subtle and likely unconscious implications of a rhetoric of violence that framed Hillary Clinton's political actions. In another reference by CBS News in May 2000, Clinton was compared to Tina Turner because of their shared celebrity; yet, Tina Turner was also a well-known victim of spousal abuse.[142] The television news referee, Howard Kurtz of CNN, who found the questions of her marital future appropriate, suggested that Hillary Clinton made herself and her marriage "fair game," a reference containing multiple implications, including ones marked with sexual innuendoes.

Further disciplinary acts seeped into the news coverage, making Hillary Clinton, rather than her husband, answer for his extramarital affair. During the same Buffalo debate, Tim Russert of NBC News played the segment from the January 1998 *Today* show interview where Clinton stated definitively that the allegations about her husband's affair with Monica Lewinsky were baseless. Russert then asked: "Do you regret misleading the American people?" Suggesting that Hillary Clinton rather than Bill Clinton was responsible for the deceit put her on the defensive for her husband's actions. Acknowledging the level of pain that she experienced, Clinton responded: "Tim, that was a very, a very painful time for me, for my family, and for our country. Obviously, I didn't mislead anyone. I didn't know the truth."[143]

These would not be the only times that Clinton would have to relive those "painful" moments and account for her own actions in response to her husband's affair. After the second debate between Clinton and Lazio, Andrea Mitchell explained on NBC News that "perhaps the toughest moment for the first lady, a question from the moderator: 'Why didn't she leave her husband?'" NBC then aired Clinton's response as she looked directly into the camera: "The choices that I have made in my life are right for me. I can't talk about anybody else's choice. I can only say that mine are rooted in my religious faith, in my strong sense of family, and in what I believe is right and important."[144] Even as Clinton embarked on her own political campaign, she would still be held accountable for her personal actions in response to her husband's affair. Being reminded of such a painful and undoubtedly humiliating time would further the public disciplining of Clinton, who faced a rhetoric of violence and a series of humiliating questions. These questions served as a reminder that she was, and always would be, a scorned woman, even as she pursued her own political career.

In certain ways, the rhetoric of domestic violence and public disciplining that Clinton faced in her news coverage reflected the patterns of domestic abuse in the home. The typical cycle of violence in the family setting often begins with a level of near normalcy, where the couple does not experience conflict until stressors present themselves, elevating the level of tension in the relationship. Once a triggering moment occurs, tensions soar, resulting in some kind of explosive response with verbal and/or physical consequences that injure one or both parties and damages the relationship. The victim, in response, feels a level of "fear, humiliation, confusion, and disrespect—along with pain," often undermining that person's self-respect and leading to changes in behavior in order to lessen the future threat of abuse. A honeymoon period likely follows, where the abuser feels a level of regret until another triggering event occurs and the cycle begins again.[145]

The disciplinary rhetoric that framed Clinton from 1992 to 2000 showed similar linguistic patterns, culminating in an intensifying rhetoric of violence. Clinton would first face gender disciplining in 1992 after she appeared too front and center in the campaign. The campaign reacted by reducing her public visibility and outspokenness. The rhetoric of violence appeared more consistently in response to her leadership role on health care and her alleged misconduct in Whitewater. Within this heated context, a linguistic violence culminated in death threats and Clinton's image being burned in effigy. This linguistic violence was targeted to an individual who functioned as a cultural scapegoat—or in Burkean terms—"the principle of the discord."[146] At that point, Clinton again retreated from the legislative arena and stepped increasingly into more international spaces, far removed from the glare of the national news cameras. The disciplinary rhetoric would take a different shape during the Clinton-Lewinsky saga; Hillary Clinton was reduced to the aggrieved wife lacking agency when her husband lied to her and the American people and violated their marriage vows. This humiliation would become a popular memory frame, following Clinton into the 2000 political race. This stamp as a scorned woman seemed permanently etched in the memory of Hillary Clinton's public identity and her political biography, serving to right the patriarchal power of the Clinton relationship and the presidential marriage.

By 2000, when Clinton engaged in another precedent-setting act of vying for public office, the rhetoric of violence would exhibit new levels of aggression and misogyny, culminating in a rhetoric of domestic violence, tinged with accompanying rape imagery. Journalists salivated over Clinton's entrance into the political ring, which made her fair game for whatever treatment followed. The disciplinary actions took place through a rhetoric that battered, blindsided, punched, knifed, and also smashed grapefruits in Clinton's face. Increasingly, a rhetoric of violence achieved a more feverish pitch in order for the news media to capture the intensity of the political drama.

The disciplinary cycle, however, did not end with Clinton's Senate victory in 2000. The legacy of a rhetoric of domestic violence reappeared in the coverage of her presidential campaign in 2008. The following example represented the pinnacle of rhetorical vitriol and domestic disciplining. On February 25, 2008, Fox News introduced a segment on how the Democratic Party might best encourage Hillary Clinton to bow out of the Democratic presidential primary. Sean Hannity insisted that Hillary Clinton was "desperately trying to cheat . . . and seat delegates when she agreed not to from Michigan and in Florida." He then pondered whether someone would have "to go to Hillary Clinton and say get out of this thing?" In response, Republican strategist Pete Snyder argued: "Someone's going to have to go out there and take her behind the barn. I grew up in Lancaster, Pennsylvania, and that's kind of the term they use for that."[147] The notions of "take her behind the barn" reinforced a sense of violence—seemingly domestic violence—given the focus on the family barn. Clinton, thus, needed to be disciplined for overstepping, once again, the bounds of power in the politics of the nation-state. As the 2008 primary campaign came to a close, increasing talk centered on "pushing" Clinton out of such political spaces to pave the way for Barack Obama's presidential bid.[148] Unlike the Senate race in 2000, however, Clinton, as a candidate in the 2008 presidential contest, would be compelled to retreat from the presidential campaign because she failed to win enough delegates in the primary process. The language throughout suggested that even when Clinton succeeded as she did in 2000, she still needed to be warned against overstepping such entrenched boundaries.

With a Win and a Warning

As shown throughout this chapter, the press accentuated the many ways in which Hillary Clinton represented an inauthentic political candidate—a carpetbagger, political opportunist, political novice, and political celebrity with a questionable marriage. In the latter few months of the campaign, the tone of the coverage began to shift once it became clearer that Clinton was remaining in the campaign, was a dogged campaigner and debater, and was ticking up in the polls. Chuck Todd of NBC News acknowledged that "to her credit, she's run a very good campaign." In response, even Andrea Mitchell, one who often exuded a tenor of negativity and cynicism, admitted that Clinton gets "tremendous marks" on her role as first lady.[149] By October 2000, Lee Miringoff of the "Marist Poll" observed on NBC's *Today* show that "Hillary Clinton has become a little bit more likeable, a little bit more experienced as a candidate than I'd say she was six months ago."[150]

In the end, of course, Hillary Clinton did prevail, defeating her opponent by more than 10 percentage points and topping 55 percent of the popular vote—an accomplishment that early polling suggested was not achievable with the "anti-Hillary" vote.[151] In the process, Clinton achieved what no other woman had even attempted, which was to transition from the nation's first lady position to an elected post in the U.S. Senate. Peter Jennings, anchor of *ABC World Tonight*, made this point during his November 8, 2000, broadcast: "And in the highest-profile Senate event of the night, Hillary Clinton won the New York Senate seat. She is the first first lady to run, much less win."[152] On the same evening, Lisa Myers of NBC News recognized the accomplishment and noted an irony of the moment, ensuring that the viewers didn't forget the impeachment of her husband: "The first first lady ever elected to public office, Hillary Clinton will become an instant celebrity in the Senate, serving alongside Republicans who tried to convict her husband during impeachment."[153] In this one sentence, Myers coupled Clinton's electoral achievements with her celebrity and the memory of another distinction that marred her husband's legacy and forever tarnished her own.

Much of the post-2000 election was wrapped up in the drama over who would ultimately win the presidency in the Bush versus Gore battle. Even so, Clinton continued to attract media attention, especially as she prepared to enter office. Senator-elect Clinton's accomplishments would be tinged with words of wisdom and warning. Her celebrity status was woven into such stories, implicitly accounting for her victory in the lead-up to her swearing-in-ceremony. The day following her victory, the Republican Majority Leader, Trent Lott from Mississippi, offered some advice to Senator-elect Clinton: "I think it would be wise for her to take a little time to maybe just observe things and get used to the process and . . . not try to assert . . . too aggressively her obvious celebrity status."[154] Diana Olick of *CBS Evening News* also made the case that Clinton needed to know her proper place, attributing the following statement to unnamed sources: "But her colleagues seem, at least publicly, to want her to feel at home in the Senate—as long as she knows her place, that is."[155] These statements reinforced three common memory frames attached to Clinton. First, Clinton was prone to aggressive behavior. Second, Clinton's victory was dependent on her celebrity rather than her own political skill. And third, Clinton was known for violating spatial protocol and needed constant disciplinary reminders to tamp down such incendiary activity.

In the process of accentuating her celebrity, Linda Douglass, now of ABC News, would also demote Clinton from her status as a "dignitary" to that of a political novice. Douglass observed that Clinton was "whisked into the Capitol like a visiting dignitary, but in the United States Senate, Hillary Clinton is a beginner." Commenting on how Clinton was handling the attention and the demotion, Douglass concluded that "the president's wife is struggling to appear humble in her new world where power comes from seniority, not celebrity." This rhetoric further substantiated the sentiment that Clinton needed to know her rightful place in this new role. By labeling Clinton a "beginner" and calling her the "president's wife" rather than "senator-elect," Douglass undermined her political identity as a U.S. senator. Her celebrity status and her poor acting job as a humbled Senate newcomer accentuated the idea of an imposter politician.[156] As Clinton prepared to enter the U.S. Senate, her disciplinary frames would accompany her. Those around her, including some in the press, wanted to make sure she conformed to the expectations of the position—practices that Clinton seemingly ignored as an activist first lady, warranting repeat reminders.

A similar theme foreshadowed an impending conflict for the new U.S. senator, who many predicted would not fit in well with her new colleagues. These themes stemmed from memories of Clinton's likeability problems. Her alleged personality issues—tied to the hard-edged feminist frames of 1992— continued to function as authenticity markers for Clinton as she basked in her campaign victory. In introducing Greta Van Susteren's CNN broadcast on January 3, 2001, the narrator asked, "Will New York's junior senator fit in with her colleagues and constituents?"[157] ABC also emphasized the possibility of political infighting among the women in the U.S. Senate, as some worried that Clinton would not demonstrate her proper place as a junior senator. One unidentified woman senator warned that "she had better not see herself as first among equals."[158] The sentiment that Clinton was a difficult and haughty woman led some to question her ability to fit into a position that relied on backroom and backslapping deals and required one to be liked by the people who sent her to Congress. These frames reinforced age-old stereotypes that strong women often exhibit personality problems that make them standoffish and incapable of collegiality. Her personality and seemingly her gender, correspondingly, did not fit the profile of a successful political leader, restricting her ability to "fit in."

Conclusion

Although Clinton won the campaign battle and her place in the U.S. Senate, what were the larger implications of her victory for women and politics? In many ways, Clinton's political life showcased a woman of great determination. When faced with significant political and personal obstacles, she refortified herself and refused to be sidelined for too long. She bounced back from a turbulent campaign in 1992 and took on a leadership role in health care reform. She rebounded from her marginalization on health care and the Whitewater charges to develop her political credentials as a U.S. emissary, fighting on behalf of human rights initiatives. And, after being humiliated by a cheating husband, she forged her own path and emerged victorious in a hard-fought political campaign for the U.S. Senate. Hillary Clinton thus persisted and ultimately prevailed against significant political odds in a complicated electoral process. That Hillary Clinton proved victorious in this Senate campaign indeed represented an important milestone in U.S. politics, particularly as one of the most controversial political women in U.S. history moved from a more traditional and nonelected role of first lady to a coveted position of U.S. senator. Such a transition would have been unimaginable for much of the nation's history. Clinton's ability to overcome these political and linguistic hurdles demonstrates, as I discussed in chapter 1, that press frames are, at times, forced to keep pace with the political actions of political women, demonstrating the agency of political women and the limits of press control.

Yet, such press coverage of Hillary Clinton's bold actions also revealed that many voices in the news, including political pundits, had a hard time envisioning that leap from what many saw as a feminine position of social power to a masculine position of political power. Clinton's attempts to cross the chasm fueled perceptions of her inauthenticity as a political candidate. They also showed the mountainous hurdles that Clinton had to surmount in order to achieve victory. In the process, she would have to enter and prevail in a discursively violent contest portrayed as a "blood sport" and a war where she endured punches below the belt, knife attacks, and potential knockouts. Hillary Clinton's chances of success were certainly enhanced by her financial advantages, political connections, and career experiences afforded very few. She was also advantaged by her whiteness and her heterosexuality. In the long term, even as Clinton prevailed because of her own tenacity and the political advantages she enjoyed, the residue of these news frames suggested that if women did enter the spaces of authentic manhood, they needed to prepare for the rhetorical violence that could follow. These frames accordingly sounded a word of warning for all women who contemplated a step into the patriarchal spaces of politics. I next turn to the legacies of these news frames by reflecting further on Clinton's candidacy in the 2008 presidential campaign, her time as U.S. secretary of state, and the treatment of other political women in the press, particularly the first ladies who trailed Clinton into the White House.

Conclusion

Hillary Clinton in the News: Lessons Learned

I n a May 17, 2008, episode of *The Beltway Boys*, Fox News addressed the thorny subject of how Hillary Clinton would drop out of the Democratic presidential primary. Co-host Fred Barnes turned to a familiar sports metaphor to comprehend the closeness of the Democratic race, expressing his excitement over the possibility of an "overtime" in the presidential primary that mimicked a too close to call "basketball" game. The other "Beltway Boy" co-host, Mort Kondracke, mentioned the growing "rumors" that Clinton was "forcing her way onto the Democratic ticket" in a way, he charged, that others dubbed her "testicular fortitude." Barnes defined the situation as a "huge problem for Obama," warning that if he "knuckles under" and ultimately selected Clinton as his "running mate," it would show a "sign of weakness."[1] When Hillary Clinton finally announced she was exiting the presidential race in June 2008, CNN's Jeanne Moos lamented, more tongue in cheek, her departure's impact on late night comedians. Moos pondered, "Where, oh, where, are we going to get laughs?" In offering a caricature of the candidate, Moos defined Clinton as "a woman" with . . . Yet, before Moos could finish her sentence, CNN spliced in a response from the president of the steelworkers union (Paul Gibson), who simply uttered: "testicular fortitude."[2]

When Hillary Clinton entered the ultimate of masculine spaces—a presidential contest no women had successfully traversed before—certain news frames shifted from a focus on Clinton's feminism to her alleged masculinity, with explicit references to male body parts. Journalist Joe Klein furthered these testicular themes in a November 2009 *Time* magazine article. Klein suggested that by appointing Clinton as secretary of state instead of his running mate, many believed Obama had "succeeded in neutering her." With this framing, Hillary Clinton had gone from exhibiting a sense of "testicular fortitude" to being neutered, reinforcing once again the masculine disciplining of women candidates. When Clinton was framed as too empowered, whether as a presidential surrogate, legislative task force leader, or political candidate, the news coverage exhibited a linguistic disciplining. With the exception of Clinton's U.S. Senate races, this disciplining accompanied an exodus from the most contentious spaces of electoral or legislative politics. A language of violence—sometimes symbolizing sexual or domestic violence—became part of the disciplinary discourse. Yet, even as Clinton was known to step out of the political spotlight, the news media often anticipated her return to power and the bright glare of the television cameras. As Klein acknowledged after Clinton's presidential defeat, "This is Hillary Clinton we're talking about," leading him to anticipate her next bold move: "How will Clinton choose to use her power?"[3]

In this concluding chapter, I assess what the verbal and visual news coverage of Hillary Clinton tells us about the gendered nation, political authenticity and character, and news framing of U.S. political women at the turn of the twenty-first century. The assumption of this project is that news narratives in combination with other political discourses contribute to the national imaginary.[4] Those who become routine fixtures in news stories can function as didactic character models to be admired and emulated, chastised and even despised. Journalists (along with the aid of news writers and news producers) serve as some of the nation's most powerful biographers, contributing stories and pictures that make up the chapters of a political leader's life. Persistent news frames contribute to biographical thematics that accompany political leaders over the course of their political lives. These news frames are reliant on the ideologies of the nation-state (e.g., nationalism, gender, character, authenticity) just as they simultaneously contribute to the ideological renderings of the nation. Conceptions of authentic womanhood and authentic manhood in particular bring together ideological forces that can empower yet also bind the nation's political leaders, offering a gender baseline that fuses with other markers of political authenticity to define an individual leader.

Political authenticity judgments and character evaluations become most visible when tracing the evolving coverage of Hillary Clinton over the span of some sixteen years as she engaged in precedent-setting activities as first lady, legislative task force leader, and political candidate. In the process, Clinton confronted allegations of illegal wrongdoing over a land deal gone bad, traveled far and wide as a U.S. emissary, faced humiliating details of marital infidelity, and pursued political office, first as a victorious Senate candidate and then as a failed presidential contender. The news media would be forced to keep pace with a woman who defied gender stereotypes, often resorting to press frames steeped in tradition to do so.

Specifically, this final chapter features five implications derived from the examination of the television news coverage of Hillary Clinton from 1992 to 2008:

1. The press corps serve as didactic biographers and political authenticity judges for the nation-state.
2. The news media engage in problematic meaning-making practices in their use of video and photographs.
3. The news frames can rely on a rhetoric of violence in targeting political women that reflect the traces of domestic violence and rape and the lingering fears over feminism.
4. News frames can function as rhetorics of deterrence and constraint for political women.
5. The political agency that women political leaders enjoy comes at considerable personal and cultural costs.

In discussing these implications, I show how news frames of Hillary Clinton circulated in popular culture throughout 2008 and beyond, moving from news screens to other media contexts.

The Press as Didactic Biographers and Political Authenticity Judges for the Nation-State

As the introduction of this book showed, sorting the authentic from the inauthentic has been a preoccupation among Western cultures from antiquity onward. In the United States, the founding generation in particular was preoccupied with selecting leaders of sound character to help nurture idyllic virtues within the new American citizenry—a citizenry conceived as deficient in decorum, enticed by corruption, and prone to mob behavior.[5] Messages about character—the character of presidents and the people—have been a persistent source of challenge and critique. From the moment U.S. political biographers began to publish life histories of political candidates in the early nineteenth century, their stories became the object of interrogation and deliberation. Scott E. Casper characterizes early campaign biographies as "partisan" publications that "drew partisan responses."[6] From the outset, the character of the nation's leaders was politicizing, inviting support and suspicion, votes and vitriol.

Authenticity judgments take center stage in the character disputes that biographies incite. In news biographies especially, political authenticity serves as the raison d'être of the image-making struggle. As relatively unknown political leaders enter the spaces of politics and become the subject of media attention, a competition arises. Political leaders strategically unfold their life stories before the public in an attempt to fashion their own political images. Journalists in turn (with the help of oppositional voices) work to tell the back story—the one that leaders ostensibly leave out. The seeming omniscient ability of journalists to penetrate the image façade, especially with their cameras, is reified as they exert considerable energy in contesting the public image or unraveling the private mysteries.

A key mission of this book is to show how judgments of Hillary Clinton's political authenticity were integral components of her press frames that helped inflame the controversies over her political leadership. In framing Clinton early on as a more outspoken and out front feminist, the press and her opposition portrayed a woman with personality flaws—too cold, hard-edged, and unlikeable to serve as an admirable first lady or a viable elected official. Clinton's true personality, many journalists implied, explained why the American public found her so polarizing and unappealing—a personality at odds with traditional prescriptions of authentic womanhood and expectations of a successful political leader. She was concurrently framed as deceitful, secretive, and evasive by the press during the debates over health care and Whitewater, and her Republican opposition insisted that she was inspired by unbridled political ambition. When taken together, these negative features formed the foundation of her political *authenticity* (polarizing feminist and political activist) as well as her *inauthenticity* (dubious and opportunistic celebrity politician).

In the end, the image of Clinton in the press portended a paradoxical person of mystery whose self-portrait confounded any version of the "real" that many expect from a first lady, senator, or presidential candidate. Even her authenticating commitment to feminism was questioned in the press by the time she sought the presidency. So marred with character flaws, the press surmised, Clinton and her handlers strove to keep the real Hillary hidden from public view. Clinton's biographical portrait was not only unflattering, it also exposed a potentially devious and deceitful person who warranted constant media surveillance in order to capture the true Hillary Clinton and her true political motives. Unlike other political leaders whose biographies have been used to inspire and teach, Clinton failed to achieve the threshold as a national role model throughout much of her political career. Instead, Clinton's legacy, at least in part, represented an object lesson for discouraging others, particularly women, from defying authentic womanhood ideals and engaging in acts of political advancement.

Absent from Clinton's press biography is a reflexive accounting of the news media's contributions to a troubling and contradictory political image. Once the press creates a portrait of political authenticity, any deviation from the defining sketch, however limited, however exaggerated, is branded as *inauthentic*. Journalists become the authenticity deputies in this process, identifying behaviors that correspond and contradict the original character portrait. Political leaders of course do seek to control the message and encourage positive coverage just as they express contradictory ideas and engage in politically motivated behaviors. Yet, the press's own assumptions—their own biases—are often contradictory and paradoxical—especially noticeable in the framing of gender politics. Clinton's progressiveness was at once celebrated and condemned. Clinton's political precedents were the subject of admiration and the object of derision. She was chided for seeking the political spotlight and admonished for hiding from it. She was condemned for her celebrity by a press that helped create it. And she was reprimanded for her authenticity as a feminist and political activist yet treated with suspicion and doubt when following the expectations of authentic womanhood.

First and foremost, this book tells us as much if not more about press practices than it does about Hillary Clinton's political authenticity. The need for breaking news, for scandalous intrigue, for enhanced ratings, and for twenty-four-hour broadcasting feeds the dogged pursuit of the politically (in)authentic. A snapshot of the news frames portrays a press deeply distrusting and cynically conspiratorial, expecting to be hoodwinked by political leaders without genuine political motivation beyond self-gain. Too many political leaders may well fit this profile, but the press would have us believe that most leaders do, compounding the cynical feel of U.S. politics. Yet, is it the case that Hillary Clinton is so inauthentic and mysterious, or is it more that the press has persisted in telling us so for so often and so long?

This book in particular reflects the authenticity dilemmas that women in politics often experience. Clinton addressed this predicament in her own autobiography: "People who wanted me to fit into a certain box, traditionalist or feminist, would never be entirely satisfied with me as me." Clinton went further in recognizing the ways in which she defied convention, serving in many "different, and sometimes paradoxical, roles."[7] Because of the still underlying masculine nature of the public sphere, women's intrusion into such spaces may still appear as a violation of national propriety and authentic womanhood. Minimally, women's entrance into these spaces is not as normalized for women as it is for men.

An authenticity quandary results, where the image of the public-political woman assumes the appearance of contrivance regardless of how that image is punctuated by the press, by the opposition, or by the political leaders themselves (except for those moments when women are portrayed as exceptionally strident or personally scorned—both of which contain decidedly more negative implications than positive ones). In the process, women are chastised for being too much of a feminist, being too much like a man, being too shrill in their public performances, or for being too emotional and dependent on men.

Most assuredly, male candidates routinely encounter their own authenticity demons. Both male and female candidates are evaluated on matters of political motive, issue consistency, geographical ties, and a willingness to take unpopular stances on contentious issues. Democratic presidential candidate John Kerry was forever known as the flip-flopping politician in 2004, and Republican presidential candidate Mitt Romney was repeatedly challenged in 2008 and 2012 for adapting to the political winds of the moment.[8] Columnist Joel Achenbach paradoxically defined "Romney's inauthenticity" as the "core" of his "authenticity" during the 2012 presidential election—the ultimate consequence for one whose authenticity is routinely in doubt.[9] Even a revered political figure like Abraham Lincoln was forced to justify his shift in policy positions, once defending himself before a critic: "I don't think much of a man who is not wiser to-day than he was yesterday."[10]

Women arguably face added layers of authenticity challenges because of the conscious and unconscious assumption that politics persists as a masculine profession taking place in decidedly masculine spaces. Before being taken seriously as a political candidate or a legislative leader, a woman must first overcome a sense of her imposter status in her news biography, persistently struggling to prove herself as a strong woman and a credible political leader in ways that often contradict the long-held expectations of authentic womanhood.

Overall, we must ask ourselves whether authenticity should be the privileged benchmark for electability that it has become. Can we ever really know the "genuine" candidate—can we ever "know" the real behind the so-called image? The unfortunate result of authenticity disputes is that these fixations enhance the cynicism about politics as we come to believe no one is genuine and the political process is inherently flawed, perpetuating a sense of anxiety and uncertainty about our leaders and the U.S. political process in general.[11] And in the search for the "real," news organizations engage in deceptive practices of their own that further erode public trust and enhance political cynicism.

A Case of Visual Manipulation and Meaning Creation

Importantly, news organizations manufacture meaning in ways that many journalists find disingenuous and deplorable when used by political leaders and
their surrogates. The use of face politics reveals the practice of *creating* narrative
contexts for decontextualized news film and photography. When the locations of
Clinton's images were indiscernible, news organizations assumed considerable
power in framing and defining the visual images to fit their larger news stories
about her mysteries, her private actions or thoughts, or her authentic self. The
irony of course is that as the news media are eager to expose political leaders
who create misleading, deceptive, and fake images, members of the press also
participate in acts of political trickery, decontextualizing and recontextualizing
visual images into whatever story they seek to tell.

The NBC News practice of mining the August 1998 U.S. memorial service
for images of a Hillary Clinton in private turmoil and a Clinton marriage on
the rocks demonstrates most vividly the ways in which such decontextualized/
recontextualized practices create new meaning for floating visual signifiers.[12]
Close-up images of the face are particularly vulnerable to redefinition because
the clues that help define the original context are often obscured. While some
news professionals may well defend the recontextualization practice,[13] the bottom line is that when doing so, they engage in acts of visual manipulation and
even fabrication. As Paul Messaris and Linus Abraham contend, visual images can provide "documentary evidence" that help create a "commonsensical"
impression of "nature (. . . factual representations) to subtly camouflage the
constructed, historical, and social roots of ideology."[14] Imagery, arguably, should
remain tethered to its contextual origin just as we expect the written and spoken
word to be cemented in context.

Decontextualized facial shots in particular lend an emotional tenor to the
news narrative in ways that explain their utility. The face becomes all important
to the news story because of the long-held physiognomic presumption that a
person's character is most visible in one's facial contours. In the process, the
facial shots reinforce the news slant of the story, add a level of intrigue and appearance of subterfuge, and/or suggest a contradiction between a leader's words
and her true political ambitions. The coverage of Hillary Clinton's evolutionary
smiles captured the range of decontextualized portraits. A seemingly smug
smile during her controversial battles on health care connoted a woman with
clear political ambition, eager to hoodwink the American people in more malevolent ways. A smiling facial portrait posted behind the news anchor during
Whitewater showed Clinton arrogantly casting off such somber matters. Her

broad smile reinforced moments of authentic womanhood when positioned in international spaces of ceremony. And her seemingly forced smile during the Clinton-Lewinsky scandal represented a means by which to mask her pain, clinging to some sense of strained normalcy in the wake of devastating and humiliating marital discord. What is crucial to understand in all of these instances is that news organizations made choices. In some cases, the chosen film coincided with the actual story being told (Clinton traveling in Pakistan). In other cases, the visual context was indiscernible to the viewing public, widening the vaults of video footage and photography available to news writers. That news teams detach video images from their original context awards them full license to use the decontextualized film and photographs in limitless ways and with minimal threat of consequence.

This practice of *face politics* and its relationship to political authenticity is also visible in newspaper reports. A case in point related to a March 25, 1999, story in the *Washington Post* that addressed Clinton's U.S. Senate campaign. Within the story, the article's author, Michael Powell, questioned Clinton's authenticity directly: "How did this self-described feminist, who helped stage manage her husband's presidential career and battled for health care reform, emerge as an icon of persevering womanhood?" Powell ultimately concluded that "even Democrats who admire and cheer her find the image inversions vertigo-inducing." A close-up profile image of Clinton's face appeared above the fold, covering a significant portion of the news space. What little background appeared in the photo was dark, eliding any contextual clues. The image, taken by *Washington Post* photographer Nancy Andrews, was not atypical because of its zoomed-in proximity to Clinton's face. The angle though was atypically positioned below Clinton so that the reader was gazing up toward her facial profile in extreme close-up fashion. The decontextualized face shot ostensibly functioned as a means to help answer the pressing question Powell raised in the article's title: "What Are We to Make of Her?" The caption below the photo suggested that Clinton's face functioned as a political Rorschach test: "For the moment at least, Hillary Rodham Clinton is whatever New York politicians seem to want to make of her."[15] Putting pop psychology into practice, the message implied that the real Hillary was unknowable—part of the ongoing mystery that aligned with a suspicion of Clinton's dodginess. The combined verbal and visual messages implied that while the true Hillary Clinton was perhaps far too elusive to ever truly know, she could be whatever anyone wished to make of her—including the inquiring news media.

In a different example of face politics, the *Washington Post* featured another close-up facial photograph in an August 23, 2009, story on Clinton's role as

U.S. secretary of state. This colorized photograph also appeared above the fold and took up a large space at the top of the page. In this instance, Clinton was staring straight into the camera of Kevin Lamarque of Reuters and Corbis. The image was so close up that her whole face filled the frame. Her chin and the top of her head were cut off, the lines on her face were vividly distinguishable, and her eyes drew the attention of the reader. Overall, the story challenged the sexism of Clinton's news coverage as secretary of state; yet the focal point was on how Clinton was *"quietly* revolutionizing American foreign policy." Again, such close-up photographs seemingly offered a vantage point by which to peer into Clinton's soul physiognomically,[16] exposing the mystery surrounding the true Hillary Clinton or the secretary of state's "quiet revolution." The story's title deepened the mystery, relying on a theme from a Clinton presidential primary ad about Barack Obama—"It's 3 a.m. Do you Know Where Hillary Clinton Is?"[17] The news media, ironically, used these decontextualized images to stand in as meaningful clues into the "real" Hillary while simultaneously stripping the "true" Hillary of any satisfying essence. The press would turn to disingenuous means by which to suggest the disingenuousness of Clinton's character, expos-ing the authenticity hypocrisy of such press practices.

While Clinton was repeatedly called on to defend her actions, her words, and her private decisions, journalists or news organizations would not be called out for their editing tactics, preserving their role as the "authoritative interpretative community."[18] Therein, they exuded an appearance of objectivity as if they were standing outside the contested spaces of political image making rather than playing a leading role in the creation and the (in)authentication of the political image. It would be Hillary Clinton instead who would pay the biggest price for the alleged authenticity defects.

Framing Political Feminists with a Rhetoric of Violence

As soon as Hillary Clinton uttered the famous words about Tammy Wynette in January 1992, the news spotlight shone brightly on her. That spotlight would grow even brighter and wider over the span of the next nine years and beyond. When Clinton was confirmed as a U.S. senator on January 3, 2001, she was swarmed by television news cameras that made it nearly impossible for her to walk as flashes of photography lit the room and captured her every move. When she spoke, news microphones were pushed toward her face and she was hemmed in by journalists and camera crews encircling her.[19] Hillary Clinton's world, from 1992 onward, would be a mediated world infused with imagery of no-holds barred sports competitions and brutal wars that anticipated signifi-cant casualties in their wake.

Because she was the subject of intense media surveillance, Hillary Clinton's public words and deeds were tracked, monitored, and scrutinized from early 1992 onward, with moments of retreat occurring after she experienced a public and linguistic disciplining. When Clinton became too outspoken and out front in the 1992 presidential campaign, the incendiary reactions from the news media and the Republican opposition helped convince the Clinton campaign to move her from the political spotlight to the political margins. The baseline frames of Tammy Wynette, cookies and teas, and co-president helped symbolize her overempowerment and authenticate her as a hard-edged feminist. The same pattern of outspokenness and overexposure followed by a rhetorical disciplining would be repeated as Clinton led the task force on health care. As a victimized wife during the Clinton-Lewinsky scandal, she was disciplined through constant reminders that regardless of her accomplishments, she would always be remembered as a scorned woman. Clinton the feminist had been appropriately silenced, humiliated, and forced to stand in the shadows of her husband's marital indiscretions and forced to retreat off stage as first lady. Once Clinton entered the spaces of electoral politics as a candidate, a rhetoric of violence became all too common in the press coverage, resulting in linguistic traces of domestic violence and rape framing Hillary Clinton's political activities. Although the volatility of this rhetorical violence would ebb and flow, it exuded a visible intensity whenever Clinton became more bold in her political maneuvering. The closer Clinton was aligned with the stereotypes of feminism, the more heated the disciplinary rhetoric became; the more aligned she was with authentic womanhood, the more such disciplinary rhetoric dissipated. This coverage ultimately revealed the ongoing threats that political women—particularly those most aligned with feminism—seemed to the nation-state.

Symbolic violence against Clinton chained out into other mediums of popular culture. A *South Park* episode entitled "The Snuke," which first aired in March 2007, demonstrates the ongoing confluence of rhetoric, rape, and war in depictions of Hillary Clinton as a U.S. senator and a promising presidential contender. Situated in a fictionalized setting of the Fox television drama *24*, we learn that terrorists have "snuck a snuke up" Hillary Clinton's "snizz." Unbeknownst to Clinton, an incendiary device had penetrated and lodged itself in her vagina, requiring a character named Brian to physically remove the "snuke" bomb. For this dangerous procedure, Brian donned a gas mask and a protective suit to perform a gynecological exam on Clinton. Clinton not only consented to the exam, but she was also portrayed as a willing participant, expressing sexual pleasure with the words "Oh my" uttered in a noticeably sexy and southern accent. Throughout the vaginal procedure, Brian expressed his level of disgust, repeatedly coughing, groaning, and muttering, "it's dark," "it's cold." As the intensity of the delicate process approached its climax, an explosion of liquid was emitted from Clinton's vagina. Clinton once again exuded a level of sexual pleasure, repeating the line, "Oh my," as she looked directly into the camera. At the conclusion of the episode, we learn that because Brian "enter[ed] Hillary Clinton's vagina to find the snuke," he ended up "being killed by what lives inside." The tag line on the website read: "Brian is mutilated by Hillary Clinton's vagina."[20]

Two implications derive from the comedic rape of Hillary Clinton. First, the terrorists entered and hid a device in Clinton's vagina, selecting a woman senator as their target of terrorism and using sexual violence as their mode of political expression. Second, the representations portrayed Clinton as both sexually "cold" and sexually excitable, enjoying every moment of the rape. The latter in particular reified the commonplace that women who enter into the political territory of men are complicit in any acts that follow, thereby consenting to the sexual violence, at least implicitly. Clinton's entrance into these contexts of war and politics, seemingly led to her attack, where the violation of a public, political woman symbolized the retaliation against the nation-state by an enemy force.

Lara Logan is a journalist who experienced the actual violence of a gang rape during her coverage of the Egyptian uprising for CBS News in February 2011. Had not a group of Egyptian women protesters and members of the Egyptian army stepped in to save her, she likely would not have survived the brutal attack. Logan fortunately did recover from the attack and returned to CBS as a correspondent for *60 Minutes*. During a conversation between Logan and journalist Marvin Kalb in November 2011, Kalb noted that women journalists have "suffered many forms of sexual violence" when covering war. In response, Logan observed that because "the media's a big boys club . . . it's taken a very long time for women to be taken seriously on the same playing field . . . in war." In order for women to continue making inroads into this male-dominated profession, Logan advised, "you shut up and you take it and you do your job." Normalizing sexist and brutal treatment across professions, Logan insisted that all "women live with a degree of sexual harassment."[21] Logan's commentary of course offered a very dim view about women and politics on both the international and national stages and in the profession of journalism. Disturbingly, a political uprising led to the rape of a female journalist entering the spaces of the revolution; the victim of such violence also made clear that the brutality against women represented a normalized response and something women must endure for the sake of gender progress. Violence against women touches women in wartime and peacetime, reflecting a pressing public matter of significant consequence.[22]

The presence of discursive violence in news frames though can become so naturalized that such rhetorical imagery doesn't rise to a level of social and political concern, reifying the ongoing hegemonic masculinity of politics and the disciplining of political women in the nation-state. Discourse analyst Marian Meyers talks of the need to "read between the lines" for the "implied meanings" that "draw on consensual understanding and stereotypes" in news about "domestic violence."[23] Clinton was visibly pummeled in the press for her gender and political transgressions as a feminist. Too few calls for reform were heard, implicitly legitimating the rhetorical violence against Clinton as an authenticated representative of feminism—a form of political activism still viewed, Mary Douglas Vavrus suggests, as too "extreme," "counterproductive," and disruptive to the political and social harmony of the nation.[24]

This disciplinary rhetoric would quickly recede when Clinton stepped out of the electoral or legislative processes and performed roles more consonant with authentic womanhood (speaking out on behalf of women and children domestically and internationally). A similar pattern reoccurred when Clinton became U.S. secretary of state, likewise removing her from the day-to-day legislative and political processes. The *Washington Post* referenced Secretary of State Clinton's highest approval ratings in a Gallup Poll from March 2011, where she surpassed 66 percent in favorability indicators.[25] Outside of the politicized electoral and legislative spaces and the corresponding scope of news surveillance, the negativity of the press often subsided. Clinton consequently was able to travel the world with diminished press attention and favorable poll numbers in the period after the health care debate and as U.S. secretary of state. Also revealing was how Clinton's favorability scores rose during the Clinton-Lewinsky scandal. Even though the mediated surveillance intensified, her actions were positioned within her private and public role as wife of the president, reliant on more traditional lines of patriarchal power in the family and the nation. Whenever Clinton consequently stepped into the electoral or political arena, the frames of negativity were pronounced; once she stepped out, the surveillance typically dissipated along with the rhetorical vitriol.

Any respite Clinton enjoyed from the news surveillance was often short lived, however. Even though Clinton could escape the intense media coverage involving her international travel as first lady, the negative attention would return at the first hint of controversy. Clinton's 1995 participation in the UN's Fourth World Conference on Women was a clear case in point. When entering a complex foreign policy dispute as first lady, the news surveillance returned along with the critical coverage of her transgressive behavior. In January 2013, Candy Crowley of CNN News explained the shifting poll numbers during speculation over Clinton's 2016 presidential bid. According to Crowley, Clinton's approval ratings as secretary of state were "so high" because she was "not in politics."

All that would likely change, Crowley implied, should she step back into electoral politics. John King then observed that Clinton "took some punches" when she testified in front of congressional committees on the U.S. embassy attack in Benghazi, Libya. The violent rhetoric consequently returned as soon as she stepped back into the halls of Congress,[26] revealing just how incendiary the spaces of electoral and legislative politics can become, especially for a woman framed as the personification of feminism.[27]

Women's controversial presence in these contested spaces suggests that legislative and electoral politics—as it was for suffragists long ago—still isn't a welcoming place for women, particularly outspoken ones. Instead, politics is a place where women need to brace themselves for discursive harassment and vitriol. Whether or not gender was consequential to the shooting of Congresswoman Gabrielle Giffords (D-AZ) can never be known, but the incident reminds us of the political venom that politics can produce, contributing to the tragic deaths of presidents, civil rights activists, and other political leaders. If women opt to enter such promiscuous spaces, the message is clear from the news framing of Hillary Clinton—they do so at their own risk, prepared to suffer whatever consequences may follow.

News Frames as Rhetorics of Deterrence and Constraint

The legacy of Hillary Clinton's disciplinary news frames became most visible by the ways in which her successors were covered as first ladies; they too were warned about stepping too far into the charged political arena. The memory frames of Hillary Clinton would thus serve as another means by which to discipline the women who came after her to the first lady post. In this way, Clinton's news coverage functioned as what Lisa M. Burns calls an "iconic" news frame, where the news media use the memories of past first ladies to characterize the performance of more contemporary first ladies.[28] The news media consequently serve as guardians of the politicized spaces of authentic womanhood, sitting in wait for any sign of gender irregularities.

An "anti-Hillary" linguistic frame, for example, became a very popular means by which to contrast Laura Bush with Hillary Clinton—a frame that first appeared during Clinton's 2000 Senate campaign to label those who opposed Clinton's candidacy. When Clinton was compared to her successors, the linguistic shortcut was more reminiscent of the past "Hillary Factor" and "Hating Hillary" frames, crystallizing the animosity expressed toward Clinton in one easily understood and catchy phrase.[29] Early on in Laura Bush's tenure as first lady, she received high praise for her comportment in the role. Nanette Hansen of CNBC referenced a Pew Research Center poll that showed Bush's approval numbers as topping 64 percent in September 2001. The "editor" of the poll concluded that even though Bush had yet to "make a strong impression on the American people," she had already received "very wide acceptance." The editor concluded that Bush was "almost the anti-Hillary. She's not nearly as divisive; broadly accepted."[30] These constructions resembled the linguistic and residual frames from 1992 to 2008, where Clinton was portrayed as a polarizing force, a political lightning rod, and a radical feminist who attracted debate and inspired animosity. Kelly Wallace used the same "anti-Hillary" construct during a CNN report from September 8, 2001, that reported on Bush's "early childhood development" campaign as she prepared to testify before Congress. Wallace accentuated clear differences between the two women, asserting that "it's almost cliché by now" but "Laura Bush is the anti-Hillary, and observers believe that's just the way the American people want it." CNN then inserted a statement from an unidentified male who characterized ideal first lady comportment—the imbued "essence" of authentic womanhood: "If you don't overdo it, if you have kind of minimal public actions, you can sometimes have maximal public effect and affection."[31] Most of Bush's efforts occurred outside these deliberative spaces and her choice of causes fell within the traditional parameters of the first lady role. Peter Beinart referenced these sentiments with the same "anti-Hillary" frame on CNN in May 2002, noting that the "Bush administration is trying to actually recast the first lady job in this kind of Laura Bush, anti-Hillary Clinton, kind of less political role."[32] These anti-Hillary themes translated into a reverence for a more traditional first lady and applauded the presidential wife who stayed away from the highly charged partisan spaces. In other words, Hillary Clinton personified a feminist first lady; Laura Bush did not.

In furthering the comparisons between Clinton and Bush, the press also resurrected images of Hillary Clinton's personality problems and her intrusions into spaces she purportedly did not belong. *The Chris Matthews Show* from MSNBC devoted a segment to Clinton's future in politics during December 2004. In addressing Clinton's presidential chances, Gloria Borger chuckled and commented, "Well let's say Hillary Rodham Clinton ought to be looking for her softer, gentler side right now." NBC's David Gregory associated Bush's high approval ratings with the sense that "Laura Bush makes no pretense" at being a "policy maker," which stood in stark opposition to Clinton who sought "to run health care" even though "she wasn't elected to anything." Republican strategist Kathleen Parker reinforced Gregory's position, arguing that "the reason Laura is popular is because she understands that she is the wife of the president and not the president."[33]

Praise for reifying authentic womanhood ideals and scorn for leaping over these gender boundaries demonstrate the ways in which news frames can function as rhetorics of deterrence and constraint. Women who violate tradition face public disciplining; women who reinforce the tried and true rituals are met with more noticeable levels of public admiration. And it is through such coverage that the news media contribute to the rhetorical binding of gender performance.

Coverage of Michelle Obama during the 2008 presidential campaign also demonstrated a level of disciplinary warnings that also encouraged more traditional performances of the position. On the campaign trail, Michelle Obama received partisan words of caution from Republican strategists like Dan Schnur, who issued the following edict on NBC Nightly News in September 2007: "People aren't electing a co-president. And they're very wary when they see a wife or a husband overstepping those traditional bounds." These forebodings would intensify from the press, Republicans, and even Democrats once Obama uttered the following in February 2008: "For the first time in my adult lifetime, I'm really proud of my country. And not just because Barack has done well, but because I think people are hungry for change."[34] For the press, Obama's comments represented a potential campaign gaffe. The alarm was sounded by Mark Halperin on Fox News, where he counseled, "She's got to be more careful." While praising Obama for being "normal and nice . . . and . . . a great advocate for her husband," he also pinpointed what he saw as her tendency to "sound a little pessimistic, a little bit harsher, a little bit less explainable than you'd like in a campaign spouse."[35] These cautionary claims sent a clear message to the Obama campaign that Michelle Obama needed to quiet her outspokenness.

Three feminist frames of Hillary Clinton's media biography—co-presidency, Tammy Wynette, and cookies and teas—served as additional words of warning in the coverage of Obama. CNN, for example, featured a discussion between Joe Pagliarulo and Amy Holmes on June 11, 2008. The legacy of Clinton's co-presidency frames was reflected in Holmes's recommendation to Obama that "she has to soften her image considerably. We saw back in 1992 that Bill Clinton and Hillary had this buy one, get one free." Pagliarulo agreed, responding: "The co-presidency. Americans really didn't like that." Holmes also warned Obama that "they're voting for the person on the ticket. The first lady is an unelected office, and when Hillary Clinton tried to do health care for him, that went down in flames."[36]

CNN then merged the co-presidency residual frame with two stock frames from 1992—Tammy Wynette and cookies and teas. Rather than standing beside her man or even out in front of her man as Hillary Clinton had reportedly done in 1992, Holmes put Obama on notice that she's "going to have to stand behind her husband, support him," even as she continued to be "out on the stump."[37] This evidence revealed most vividly that the positioning of the male and female bodies mattered; candidate wives needed to know that they were best placed behind their husbands in the masculine spaces of politics. On June 15, 2008, ABC's *Good Morning America* used the cookies and tea clip to ensure that the memories of Clinton's transgressions were refreshed in the minds of viewers. The clip was replayed once the journalistic voiceover asserted that Obama "has become a favorite target for critics, drawing many to compare her rival on the national stage to that of another . . . first lady."[38] Hillary Clinton's baseline frames consequently helped constrain the political behavior of Clinton as well as a new generation of candidate wives and first ladies.

Others would challenge this logic of tradition. During a June 17, 2008, story, CNN correspondent Roland Martin, a commentator known for his liberal leanings, condemned the practice of compelling political wives to conform to particular gender expectations: "You've got some weak men on the conservative side who, frankly, don't like strong women." He compared the treatment of Obama to that of Hillary Clinton as the Republicans, Martin claimed, were trying to turn Obama into an "angry black woman." Hilary Rosen of *The Huffington Post* attacked the entire electoral process for compelling image makeovers of political wives. Rosen argued, "I think what's going on with Michelle Obama is what goes on with most political spouses, which is you have an identity. You're strong and your husband or wife appreciates you for that identity." Yet, the electoral process results in "your authenticity" getting "beaten out of you," Rosen complained. Consequently, the "spontaneity has to go away, because in essence, you know, it is much more your job to be controlled and be . . . the support role: seen, not heard." Rosen then offered a final prediction: "And I think that, as the general goes on, she's going to . . . fade back into kind of a more supportive role."[39] This broadcast showed an important condemnation of these reactionary practices even as it simultaneously rehearsed the ongoing need to restrict first ladies from the political spotlight (and used a rhetoric of violence directed toward wives to do so). Despite the outcry, the journalists' predictions seemed to come true in terms of an Obama makeover.

In her husband's first term at least, Obama performed the first lady role in more traditional ways, likely a combination of choice and fear over a disciplinary backlash. Michelle Obama chose as her signature issue a healthy eating campaign for children with an important "Let's Move" dimension of fostering increased exercise among children. In addition, she became very active in supporting military families, another activity that takes place primarily outside of the political sphere and the media spotlight. Yet, there remained some evidence

of discord within the Obama administration over just how political Michelle
Obama should become. A *New York Times* piece about Jodi Kantor's book—*The
Obamas*—suggested that even when Michelle Obama asked to be involved in
promoting the health care bill, the Obama administration, "recalling the public resentment of Hillary Rodham Clinton's involvement in health care as first
lady, mostly declined her offer."[40] Overall, Obama seemed relatively successful
in keeping out of the spaces of extreme controversy during the first years in the
first lady role.[41] Yet, fears over the backlash were rumored in a story Kantor wrote
on the eve of President Obama's second inauguration, where she argued that
Michelle Obama "treats the job of first lady like a dangerous country through
which she must navigate safe passage."[42]

Michelle Obama indeed garnered high approval ratings for her more traditional performance of the role. Like the ratings for Hillary Clinton during her
days of international travel and the Clinton-Lewinsky affair, Obama's ratings
hovered in the 60 percentile as first lady. During the campaign of 2008, Gallup
reported her approval ratings at 54 percent; when her husband campaigned
for re-election in 2012, they had risen to 66 percent—a number rivaling the
ratings of Laura Bush.[43] Favorable ratings for assuming more authentic womanhood ideals and negative ratings for participating in partisan and political
debates suggest the negative consequences for first ladies who enter contested
political waters. The warnings sent to both Bush and Obama demonstrate the
ways in which the news media and political pundits can serve as guardians of
such political protocol, helping to preserve the sanctity of the political spaces
for those properly accorded such access. First ladies are often seen as out of
bounds when stepping in front of their husbands during a political campaign
event or entering the legislative arena as first lady with hot button political issues. Some first ladies undoubtedly prefer a low-profile role while others may
not. That neither Bush nor Obama chose to consistently go where Clinton had
traveled evidences the ways in which discursive news framing of Clinton can
function as a rhetoric of deterrence and even constraint.

The consequences of such rhetorics of threat arguably extend beyond politics. When women watch Hillary Clinton being pilloried for violating gender
expectations—that is, stepping outside of the gender lines—it can send words
of warning to all women about the consequences of defying gender stereotypes.
Anyone thinking about living their lives as a feminist is put on notice that the
consequences can be swift and consequential. Some feminist scholars suggest
a level of intensifying opposition to feminism at the turn of the twenty-first
century that, more than anything, represents a crisis of masculinity.[44] In the
process of corralling feminist progress, gender anxieties may be as much about
preventing the perceived erosion of masculine power. The intensity of the dis-

cursive backlash may also shed insight into a nostalgia for traditional notions of patriarchy in the home, the workplace, and the nation-state.

Women's Political Agency—The Costs of Remembering and Forgetting

At times, the news media did demonstrate a commitment to recalibrating notions of tradition and progress, recognizing the precedent-breaking advancements of political women like Hillary Clinton and Elizabeth Dole. Early on in the coverage of a contentious issue like health care and the 2000 Senate race, the news media would also acknowledge and at times celebrate the important inroads Clinton was making to advance gender progress. Journalists seemed to recognize that they were covering a precedent-setting political woman who could change the terrain for women in politics forever. Some seemed eager to document the milestones and to be part of the history-making process. These stories often led to a survey of important advancements that women were making in the world of work. The coverage of Clinton consequently demonstrated that the press is compelled to keep pace with the historic actions of political women like Clinton, helping chip away at the layers of sexism in political life and the stereotypical pull toward binary logic. As Susan Gal notes, "Redefinitions" can be "lasting and coercive."[45]

Yet, Gal also observes that recalibrations can be "momentary and ephemeral."[46] The elasticity of such confines can consequently exhibit the pull of tradition and the preference for snapping back into the safer and more clearly understood positions of tradition. Most vividly, the news media seemed befuddled with how best to track and cover a precedent-setting political woman. From 1992 through 2008, the press predictably returned to the question of Clinton's mysterious and incomprehensible gender actions. These reactions showed just how resilient and reactionary the ideological pull of tradition continues to be in the hands of news organizations—organizations still run predominantly by men,[47] facing the pressure of time, searching for short-cut frames and multipurposed images, and seeking to ensure the satisfaction of sponsors and viewers. Erring on the side of tradition seemingly reaps more benefits than costs, more gains than risks.

Throughout her time in the national political spotlight, Clinton continued to pursue her political goals during the first decade of the new millennium, confronting new challenges and assuming new political roles. She would do so with the support of many in her bid for the presidency as well as in the face of loud opposition eager to re-employ the negative memory frames of the past. As Clinton approached the end of her tenure as U.S. secretary of state, the news coverage of her took a noticeably positive turn, with some in the press routinely championing her as one of the most powerful and popular political leaders in the country.[48] A November 7, 2011, cover story in *Time* magazine served as a representative example—a narrative that more readily accepted power in the hands of a political woman conceived as politically smart and successful. The issue featured what had become known as the Hillary Clinton doctrine of foreign policy, which combined the "hard power of military strength" with the "soft power of U.S. finances and values" to produce a "smart power." That Hillary Clinton as secretary of state was associated with her own military doctrine, a practice typically reserved for presidents, demonstrated just how much political clout she came to enjoy in her cabinet post. As an "embodiment" of her own doctrine, Clinton revealed the ways in which "smart power" integrated "hard" and "soft" forces.[49] As first lady, legislative activist, and political candidate, Clinton was more derisively framed with such words as "hard" and "power"; she was seldom associated with "soft" symbols because of the stereotypes linked to what the press dubbed as her strident and feminist personality. And past coverage typically exhibited an explicit unease with Clinton's accumulation of power and her political drive and ambition. The *Time* magazine story, however, showed a tearing down of the stereotypical binaries, legitimizing power in the hands of Hillary Clinton—a nuanced conception of power that conjoined "hard" and "soft" to produce "smart." Silenced were the past memory frames of illegitimate power. In their wake were new frames of Clinton transforming U.S. foreign policy "in the 21st century." Some in the press would correspondingly show concerted signs of altering the framing of Clinton's political activities in ways that lauded her political agency.

The more positive framing of Clinton's power was reinforced through the discussion of her impressive poll numbers. *Time*'s own polls revealed that should Clinton have entered the 2012 presidential race, she would have more handily defeated the 2012 Republican opponents than President Obama (by some 17 to 26 points). She was most admired for her "endurance" and "punishing 18-plus-hour-a-day schedule on her weeklong swing from Libya to Central and South Asia." Clinton was even praised for her comportment on long trips, as she maintained "an easy and relaxed demeanor, speaking off the cuff and calmly responding to bitter criticism," even "as glazed looks settled over her staff."[50] Positive references to Clinton's comportment and personality represented a perspective seldom seen in past news frames that centered most commonly on her personality flaws and annoyances.

The visual imagery accompanying the stories reinforced evidence of Clinton's "smart power," combining elements of "hard" and "soft." The front cover positioned Clinton in an officious-looking leather chair with a desk full of papers as she performed the official and necessarily hard task of secretary of state. The softness was accentuated in her dress—a dark suit coat, adorned with a white ruffled blouse and pearls wrapped around her neck, with both pearls and diamonds adorning her wrist. As she looked official, pen in hand prepped to sign many official state documents, she also displayed a touch of glamour, with visible lipstick and eye makeup showing through the black-and-white image. Clinton's smile in this image connoted a sense of confident self-satisfaction and accomplishment. The look of malevolent power or unbridled ambition seemed replaced by a look of calm assurance bolstered by her "smart power" as she glanced away from the camera as if unaware of its presence. Although the aging of her face and her tired eyes revealed the passage of time since she first stepped onto the national stage, the look of triumph and satisfaction produced by her slight smile also shone through. The look communicated that she had persevered in spite of a very rocky path, achieving her own goals and uplifting the country in the process. In the end, Hillary Clinton had persevered, the featured photograph suggested. Hillary Clinton had prevailed politically.

These verbal and visual frames connoted that without question Clinton had become a successful political leader in her own right, making important contributions to U.S. foreign policy and U.S. diplomatic relations. Her successes in this role were undoubtedly easier to achieve without the constant glare of the news cameras and the assertion that she was illegitimately engaged in U.S. political practice. It is difficult for any political leader to be perceived in more uniformly positive terms when in the quagmire of electoral politics and legislative debate. Once removed from such spaces, the hunt for the politically authentic seemed less central to the news media mission, allowing for a more unencumbered pursuit of her professional and political mission. Clinton's appointment as secretary of state also gave her a political legitimacy that she arguably lacked in some of her other political power plays. It certainly is rather remarkable that Clinton was able to shed many of the linguistic traces of the negative coverage that defined her pre–secretary of state biography, showing that women political leaders can succeed in spite of strong and enduring opposition. As such, while the news frames contribute to a rhetoric of constraint, they do not rise to the level of rhetorical control. Clinton routinely refused to give up and simply retooled and retried other paths in the pursuit of her political ambitions. Her life story as a white, heterosexual woman of privilege, with political access to power, helped forge that path.

The story also demonstrates most vividly that as watchdogs of political authenticity, journalists provide important judgments that contribute to a political leader's legacy. Journalists would be some of the first to commemorate Clinton's successes once she had passed through the gauntlet of news surveillance and persevered in spite of the insatiable scrutiny. After her testimony on Benghazi in January 2013, Lisa Miller of NYMAG.COM celebrated Clinton's "powerful" show of strength. Yet, she would do so by weaving together many of the memory frames addressed in this book—referencing Clinton's authenticity and feminism with a reliance on a rhetoric of violence. Miller called Clinton an "authentic, authoritative leader," a "post-menopausal woman," and a "feminist." For Miller, Clinton's authenticity meant that she "Finally Has Permission to be a Bitch"—the title of her op-ed. Clinton's ability to stand up to the congressional leaders confirmed for Miller that "*the woman is bulletproof*," able to withstand the violent political world that she encountered.[51] While referring to Clinton as a "bitch" represented a term of endearment for Miller, her comments nevertheless rehearsed the same stereotypical, incendiary, and misogynist coverage that Clinton encountered over her twenty years in the political spotlight by Republican opponents and adversarial journalists.[52] The implication that Clinton was a bitch in earlier contexts was neither flattering nor empowering, typecasting strong political women as nearly inhuman and unfeeling. This coverage naturalized the need for bulletproof vests in order for political women to withstand all of the bullets and arrows that would assuredly be aimed at them. It reinforced the same assumptions posited by CBS's Laura Logan after her sexual assault: "You shut up and you take it and you do your job." In the gendered nation, violent conditions have become far too normalized for women who dare enter the battles of war and street brawls we call politics in the United States. These implications still pulled through even those stories designed to celebrate Clinton's strength and stamina in weathering such brutal conditions.

While much of this book has examined the ways in which Hillary Clinton was framed in the press and consequently remembered, it is also important to reflect on that which will likely be forgotten and dropped out of news memory. That Hillary Clinton will likely go down in U.S. history as one of the most powerful political women to date is without question. That legacy, however, will likely not tell the full tale of the news constraints and political hardships that she endured in her obstacle course from first lady to secretary of state. While she will undoubtedly be remembered as a controversial first lady, the traditional news frames that chastened her for being too publicly visible and outspoken will likely fade from public memory. The depth of animosity that she faced while in the spaces of electoral and legislative politics will also likely fade, especially the recognition that a rhetoric of violence framed her many precedent-setting actions. Such "forgetting," Bradford Vivian argues, helps construe the "past" as "radically adapted to better serve the political and moral needs of the present."[53] Such forgetting shows how the discursive practices of meaning making function at a more invisible level in news memory frames, as if melting away with the passage of time. That Hillary Clinton became a person worthy of national veneration and a gender role model may well be the takeaway message that stands the tests of time. The legacy of the suffragists that emphasized their ultimate sense of victory similarly overwhelms the memory of their years of tireless campaigning, public humiliation, and moments of physical abuse that stood in the way of their citizenship advancements.[54]

The cautionary tale for women interested in politics or other positions of leadership is most pronounced. While words of warning come from multiple sources, the news frames of Clinton showed how pervasive a language of patriarchy and misogyny was in U.S. political culture from 1992 through 2008. While the sexist coverage did attract attention, a wealth of the coverage reified such sexism with visible silence from the journalistic community, the political establishment, and the American public. This book reveals the subtle and not so subtle ways in which politics is still construed as a masculine political world, reinforcing the political legitimacy (and thus authenticity) of men over women in the political arena. Coverage that ultimately produced images of domestic violence and rape suggests just how much work lies ahead before women can enter politics without facing threats for performing outside the boundaries of the gendered nation.

Notes

Introduction

1. John Springer, "Bernstein: Hillary Clinton is Inauthentic," *Today*, June 1, 2007, today.msnbc.msn.com/id/18981558/print/1/displaymode/1098/ (accessed June 1, 2007). See also Bernstein, *A Woman in Charge*.

2. Maureen Dowd, "Liberties: The Boy Can't Help It," *The New York Times*, August 4, 1999, A19. Susan Morrison argues that "authenticity" represented "the buzzword of the 2008 presidential campaign." I agree with Morrison but would also suggest that authenticity has represented a preoccupation for U.S. politics since the nation's genesis. See Morrison, ed., *Thirty Ways of Looking at Hillary*, xi.

3. See, for example, Schwartz, "The Character of Washington," 202–22; Trachtenberg, *Lincoln's Smile*, 32; and Trilling, *Sincerity and Authenticity*.

4. Boorstin, *The Image*, 265.

5. Greenberg, *Nixon's Shadow*, xx.

6. See Etzioni, *The Active Society*, 634, 636; and Edelman, *Constructing the Political Spectacle*, 59.

7. Howard Fineman, "Look Who's Running," *Newsweek*, October 11, 1999, newsweek.com/nw-srv/issue/15_99b/printed/us/na/na0815_1.htm (accessed October 13, 1999).

8. David Brooks, "Those Were the Days: No Wonder Kerry is Running on Vietnam," *Pittsburgh Post-Gazette*, August 25, 2004, 2, online at LexisNexis Academic (accessed July 16, 2006).

9. Ron Fournier, "Analysis: Turning Up the Authenticity," Washingtonpost.com, June 4, 2007, www.washingtonpost.com/wp-dyn/content/article/2007/06/04/A (accessed June 5, 2007).

10. Gould, ed., "Hillary Rodham Clinton (1947-)," 641. See also Winfield, "Introductory Note," 221.

11. This project represents a feminist study designed to hasten the demise of "sexism." As bell hooks argues, "feminism is a movement to end sexism, sexist exploitation, and oppression." hooks supports such a definition because it "implies that all sexist thinking and action is the problem, whether those who perpetuate it are female or male, child or adult. It is also broad enough to include an understanding of systemic institutionalized sexism." See hooks, *Feminism is for Everybody*, viii. I also see feminism as an ideology that seeks to destabilize and overturn the "subordination" of women to men in both public and private settings. The ultimate goal is to disrupt hegemonic masculinity. See Offen, "Defining Feminism," 119–57. Bonnie J. Dow also rightly points to an important concern in that "television's representations of feminism are almost exclusively filtered through white, middle-class, heterosexual, female characters . . . Television programming, therefore, draws from and contributes to the consolidation of a racially, sexually, and economically privileged *version* of feminism, that for the American public, has come to represent feminism in toto." See Dow, *Prime-Time Feminism*, xxiii. I am a feminist scholar concerned with promoting equity in terms of gender, race, sexuality, and class. I am an Anglo-American, upper middle-classed, married, heterosexual, mother of two sons.

12. B. Anderson, *Imagined Communities*, 6.

13. For a more in-depth discussion on the role of nationalism and U.S. political discourse, see T. Parry-Giles and Parry-Giles, *The Prime-Time Presidency*.

14. Bruner, *Strategies of Remembrance*, 1. See also Eberly, ed., "The Quest for America's Character," 3–24.

15. V. B. Beasley, *You the People*, 5.

16. Yarbrough, *American Virtues*, xvii.

17. Schwartz, "The Character of Washington," 213.

18. See Mayer, ed., *Gender Ironies*, 10. Erika Falk argues that questions of "personality and character" have become increasingly important for women involved in political campaigns. See *Women for President*, 67. For the media's role in issuing character judgments, see Neil Verma, *Theater of the Mind: Imagination, Aesthetics, and American Radio Drama* (Chicago: University of Chicago Press, 2012), 76; and S. J. Parry-Giles and Kaufer, "Lincoln Reminiscences," 199–234.

19. See Cardoso, *The Media in the Network Society*, 336; and Gorham, *National Service*, 182.

20. *Plutarch's Lives*, vol. 1, trans. Bernadotte Perrin (London: William Heinemann, Online ed., 1914), Google Books, books.google.com/books?id=UbhLAAAAMAAJ&printsec=frontcover&dq=Plutarch+Parallel+Lives&hl=en&ei=eus3To6eOZSRgQfBofCuAg&sa=X&oi=book_result&ct=result&resnum=3&ved=0CDwQ6AEwAg#v=onepage&q=witticism%20or%20a%20joke&f=false, 4, 191–93 (accessed August 9, 2011).

21. Waldstreicher, *In the Midst of Perpetual Fetes*, 125.

22. Casper, *Constructing American Lives*, 4.

23. Mason (Parson) Locke Weems, *The Life of Washington*, ed. Marcus Cunliffe (Cambridge, MA: Belknap Press of Harvard University Press, 1809/1962).

24. James Boswell, *The Life of Samuel Johnson*, 3rd ed. (London: H. Bald-win and Son, Online ed., 1799), Google Books, books.google.com/books?id=4 _RaAAAAMAAJ&printsec=frontcover&dq=Boswell,+Life+of+Johnson&source=bl &ots=sR9j9v-YRS&sig=dktFCYw3ypNFuGquYLGKIjTM-ZQ&hl=en&ei=vmq7TMD _HYLGlQe_qOXvDQ&sa=X&oi=book_result&ct=result&resnum=6&ved=oCDsQ6 AEwBQ#v=onepage&q&f=false (accessed September 18, 2010). See also Boys-Stones, "Physiognomy," 19–124; and Hartley, *Physiognomy*.

25. Davy Crockett, *An Account of Col. Crockett's Tour to the North and Down East* (Philadelphia: E. L. Carey, Online ed., 1835), Google Books, books.google.com/ books?id=051x5N-FZcoC&printsec=frontcover&dq=David+Crockett,+An+Account +of+Col.+Crockett%27s+Tour+to+the+North+and+down+East&hl=en&ei=h6P -TdLBJJPfgQeP9qTvCg&sa=X&oi=book_result&ct=result&resnum=1&ved=oCC4Q6 AEwAA#v=onepage&q&f=false (accessed November 7, 2011); and Charles S. Todd and Benjamin Drake, *Sketches of the Civil and Military Services of William Henry Harrison* (Cincinnati: U. P. James, Online ed., 1840), Google Books, books.google.com/books?id=N _EEAAAAYAAJ&pg=PR6&dq=.Charles+S.+Todd+and+Benjamin+Drake,+Sketches +of+the+Civil+and+Military+Services+of+William+Henry+Harrison&hl=en&ei =dNk5Ts3ZDpHpgQep3bzPBg&sa=X&oi=book_result&ct=result&resnum=2&ved =oCDYQ6AEwAQ#v=onepage&q=cabin&f=false, v–vi (accessed November 27, 2011).

26. Casper, *Constructing American Lives*, 1–18.

27. See James Parton, *Life of Andrew Jackson*, vol. 3 (New York: Mason Brothers, 1860); and John Locke Scripps, *The First Published Life of Abraham Lincoln* (Detroit: Cranbrook Press, Online ed., 1860/1900), Google Books, books.google.com/books?id=0eknAAAAYAAJ &printsec=frontcover&dq=John+Locke+Scripps&hl=en&ei=cGMOTo7oBcjVgQe At8C7Cw&sa=X&oi=book_result&ct=result&resnum=1&ved=oCC4Q6AEwAA#v =onepage&q&f=true, 16 (accessed December 1, 2011).

28. Casper, *Constructing American Lives*, 225, 237. Casper contends that many biographies of living individuals were published in "newspaper and magazine sketches . . . and campaign biographies."

29. Falk argues that the question of character has become a larger preoccupation in contemporary politics for women in particular as the news attends to their biographical past with greater frequency. While this preoccupation is a more historical phenomenon than Falk acknowledges, she nevertheless persuasively demonstrates that "women received character mentions about 37 times for every 10,000 words, whereas men received such mentions 28 times per 10,000 words." See *Women for President*, 122.

30. "The Obamas," Politics and Prose Bookstore/Sixth and I Historic Synagogue, C-Span Video Library, January 12, 2012, www.c-spanvideo.org/program/303665–1 (accessed January 13, 2012).

31. "The Duty of a Biographer," *The United States Democratic Review* 28 (March 1851): 255–57.

32. "Herndon's Lincoln: A New Biography," *New-York Tribune*, July 7, 1889, 12.

33. Starr, *The Creation of the Media*, 135–36.

34. Casper, *Constructing America Lives*, 106–12.

35. Sidney Lee, *Queen Victoria: A Biography* (London: Smith, Elder & Co., Online ed., 1903), Google Books, books.google.com/books?id=WJANAAAAIAAJ&pg=PA555 &dq=Queen+Elizabeth+Biographies+Nineteenth+Century&hl=en&ei=9kC5Ts7FGJCI twfjx5ShBw&sa=X&oi=book_result&ct=result&resnum=2&ved=0CDEQ6AEwAQ #v=onepage&q&f=false, 555 (accessed November 8, 2011).

36. Casper, *Constructing America Lives*, 106–12; and Connell, *Masculinities*, 68.

37. McDowell, *Gender, Identity, and Place*, 4. McDowell explains the discernments between "space" and "place" by acknowledging the "relational" aspects of space and conceiving of "place" as "location." She further explains that space represents a "set of places, from a home to national territories, with associations and meanings for individuals and groups." I am opting to use the concept of "space" throughout this study because of its close association with matters of citizenship. See McDowell, "Spatializing Feminism," 32, 150; Rose, *Feminism and Geography*, 43; and Gilbert, "Identity, Space, and Politics," 30.

38. Domosh and Seager, *Putting Women in Place*, 7. There are multiple conceptions of public and private. Pat Armstrong talks of "public" in two ways. The first relates to "those services, supports, and regulations established by governments." This conception holds particular relevance in terms of the news media's coverage of Hillary Clinton's legislative work on health care. The second conception of public is the one that reflects the meaning relevant to the discussion at this point, which involves the "world outside the private household." Contrastingly, Armstrong defines "private" as that which "is not done by governments," often linked to nonprofit activities. It can also refer to internal thoughts of an individual unbeknownst to others. The term *private sphere* is often aligned with domestic activities occurring within the familial household. All of these conceptions are relevant to this study. See Armstrong, "Restructuring Public and Private," 37. See also Ryan, "Gender and Public Access," 265–66.

39. Jones, Nast, and Roberts, eds., "Thresholds in Feminist Geography," xxxiii.

40. Palczewski, "The Male Madonna," 374, 376–77. See also Matthews, *The Rise of Public Woman*. For more on some of the derogatory representations of women as lesbians, see Faderman, *Odd Girls and Twilight Lovers*.

41. Mary G. Chandler, *The Elements of Character*, 4th ed. (Boston: Crosby, Nichols, and Company, 1856), 8. See also Kevin Berland, "Inborn Character and Free Will in the History of Physiognomy," in *Physiognomy in Profile: Lavater's Impact on European Culture*, ed. Melissa Percival and Graeme Tytler (Newark: University of Delaware Press, 2005), 31.

42. Palczewski, "The Male Madonna," 374, 376–77. See also Matthews, *The Rise of Public Woman*.

43. Many feminist scholars continue to recognize the powerful force of patriarchy (and racism, classism, homophobia) on the politics of the nation in both historical and contemporary contexts. See Mayer, *Gender Ironies*, 1–2, 6; Smith-Rosenberg, "Political Camp," 275; Enloe, *The Morning After*, 238; and Werbner, "Political Motherhood," 221–22.

44. Laws, "Women's Life Courses," 56.

45. Martha Washington to Fanny Bassett, October 22, 1789, Washington Family Collection, Manuscript Division, Library of Congress, container 3, 1–3.

46. Abigail Adams to William Smith Shaw, December 23, 1798, William Smith Shaw Family Papers, Manuscript Room, Library of Congress, container 1, 1–3.

47. Louisa C. Adams, January 29, 1820, Louisa C. Adams Diary, Adams Family Papers, Manuscript Room, Library of Congress, reel 265. Quotations from the Adams Papers are from the microfilm edition, by permission of the Massachusetts Historical Society.

48. "A Visit to Mrs. James K. Polk," James K. Polk Papers, Manuscript Room, Library of Congress, Series 8, Reel 2.

49. Lucretia Garfield, April 20, 1881, Lucretia Garfield Diary, Lucretia R. Garfield Papers, Manuscript Room, Library of Congress, container 88, 22.

50. Susan Zaeske defines a "promiscuous audience" as one comprising women and men. See Zaeske, "The 'Promiscuous Audience' Controversy," 191–207.

51. Allgor, *Parlor Politics*, 113, 118–19. It is important to note that early on the capital city was called Washington City.

52. See Bess Furman, "Ladies of the White House Series," n.d., Bess Furman Papers, Speech, Article, and Book File, Manuscript Division, Library of Congress, 1–12; Lucretia Garfield, March 1, 1881, Lucretia Garfield Diary, Lucretia R. Garfield Papers, Manuscript Room, Library of Congress, Container 88, 1–3; and Allgor, *Parlor Politics*, 117–18.

53. Hardesty, *Women Called to Witness*, 92. Many of these charities were still controlled by men.

54. See Patricia Brady, "Martha (Dandridge Curtis) Washington," in *American First Ladies: Their Lives and Legacy*, ed. Lewis L. Gould (New York: Garland Publishing, Inc., 1996), 3–15; and Jean H. Baker, "Mary (Ann) Todd Lincoln," in *American First Ladies: Their Lives and Legacy*, ed. Lewis L. Gould (New York: Garland Publishing, Inc., 1996), 174–90. The U.S. Sanitary Commission offered support for wounded soldiers and gave more aristocratic men an opportunity to participate in the war effort who did not go to war. See Giesberg, *Civil War Sisterhood*, 25–30.

55. Dudley Harmon, "What is Mrs. Wilson Doing?: The Part the President's Wife and His Daughters Have in the War," *The Ladies Home Journal*, July 1918, 22, 44.

56. Sims, *The Power of Femininity*, 83.

57. U.S. Congress, House of Representatives, Certain Allies in the District of Columbia, Hearing Before the Committee on the District of Columbia, H.R. 13219, 33 Congress, 2nd session, March 13 and 18, 1914. See also Burns, "Ellen Axson Wilson," 79–102.

58. See Lash, *Eleanor and Franklin*, 400; Donald A. Ritchie, "Congress," in *The Eleanor Roosevelt Encyclopedia*, ed. Maurine Beasley et al. (Westport, CT: Greenwood Press, 2001), 104; and U.S. House of Representatives, "Select Committee Investigating National Defense Migration," *National Defense Migration*, 77th Congress, 2nd session, January 14, 1942. See also Blair, "No Ordinary Time," 203–44; and Blair, "'We Go Ahead Together,'" 62–82.

59. Troy, *Mr. and Mrs. President*, 152–55.

60. "Mrs. LBJ: Saleslady for 'Great Society,'" *U.S. News and World Report*, March 27, 1967, 22.

61. Troy, *Mr. and Mrs. President*, 250–55; and "Interview with the First Lady: Rosalynn Carter Takes on the President's Critics," *U.S. News and World Report*, April 9, 1979, 49–50.

62. Eleanor Roosevelt, "National Conference on Fundamental Problems in the Education of Negroes," May 11, 1934, Anna Eleanor Roosevelt Papers, Speech and Article Files (3029), Franklin D. Roosevelt Presidential Library. See also Blair, "'We Go Ahead Together.'" I also wish to thank Diane Blair for her extensive archival research on Eleanor Roosevelt that contributed to the completion of this book project.

63. "Mrs. Ford Vows to Continue Rights Amendment Campaign," *Washington Star-News*, February 15, 1975, A3.

64. "Interview with the First Lady: Rosalynn Carter Takes on the President's Critics," *U.S. News and World Report*, April 9, 1979, 49–50.

65. Watson, *The Presidents' Wives*, 147–49.

66. John and Abigail Adams were the first presidential couple to live in Washington City and occupy what would become known as the White House. See Green, *Washington*.

67. Ian F. Haney López conceptualizes whiteness as follows: "The existence of Whites depends on the identification of cultures and societies, particular human traits, groups and individuals as non-White . . . Whiteness is the source and maintaining force of the systems of meaning that position some as superior and others as subordinate." See *White by Law*, 31. See also Dana L. Cloud's chapter on the questions surrounding Eleanor Roosevelt's sexuality: "The First Lady's Privates," 23–44.

68. In the British tradition, the political position overpowered the individual. The U.S. office of the presidency and the role of first lady likewise exuded an institutional memory that dictated expected performances. See William Roscoe Thayer, "Biography in the Nineteenth Century: I," *The North American Review* 211 (May 1920): 634.

69. See S. J. Parry-Giles and Blair, "The Rise of the Rhetorical First Lady," 565–599; and Roberts II, *Rating the First Ladies*, ix.

70. Tickner, *Gendering World Politics*, 54.

71. Geoff Eley and Ronald Grigor Suny, "Introduction: From the Moment of Social History to the Work of Cultural Representation," in *Becoming National: A Reader*, ed. Geoff Eley and Ronald Grigor Suny (New York: Oxford University Press, 1996), 32.

72. See Barker-Plummer, "News and Feminism," 146.

73. Barry, *Visual Intelligence*, 292.

74. See Nehamas, *Virtues of Authenticity*, xxxii; and Plato, *The Republic*, trans. R. E. Allen (New Haven, CT: Yale University Press, 2006).

75. Aristotle, *Physiognomonica*, in *The Works of Aristotle*, vol. 6, trans. T. Loveday and E. S. Forster, ed. W. D. Ross (Oxford: Clarendon Press, 1913).

76. Taylor, *The Ethics of Authenticity*, 25–26, 28, 64.

77. Baruš, *Authentic Knowing*, 152.

78. See Ferrara, *Modernity and Authenticity*, 136; and Orvell, *The Real Thing*, xvi, xv.

79. Golomb, *In Search of Authenticity*, 7.

80. Ferrara, *Reflective Authenticity*, 16. See also Forbes, "Rousseau, Ethnicity, and Difference," 228.

81. Heidegger, *Being and Time*, 300–305.

82. Carman, *Heidegger's Analytic*, 268.

83. Berman, *The Politics of Authenticity*, 216; and Rousseau, *Politics and the Arts*.

84. Berman, *The Politics of Authenticity*, xv, xix (emphasis in original); and Gitlin, *The Whole World is Watching*, 293.

85. Rossinow, *The Politics of Authenticity*, 4.

86. Yuval-Davis, *Gender & Nation*, 45.

87. Jean Pickering and Suzanne Kehde, eds., "Introduction," in *Narratives of Nostalgia, Gender, and Nationalism* (New York: New York University Press, 1997), 3.

88. Sigelman, "There You Go Again," 407–10.

89. Mitchell, *Picture Theory*, 423.

90. Meyrowitz, *No Sense of Place*.

91. I first defined notions of "political authenticity" in "Political Authenticity, Television News, and Hillary Rodham Clinton," 211–227. See also S. J. Parry-Giles, "John F. Kerry," 99–125.

92. Morse, "The Television News Personality and Credibility," 55.

93. Baudrillard, *Simulacra and Simulation*, 1.

94. In one random search for articles about authenticity and politics in LexisNexis on June 13, 2007, 135 entries appeared.

95. Thurow, "Dimensions of Presidential Character," 15–29.

96. S. J. Parry-Giles and Parry-Giles, "Meta-Imaging," 28–45; and S. J. Parry-Giles and Parry-Giles, *Constructing Clinton*.

97. Hart, *The Sound of Leadership*, 138.

98. Hardt, "Authenticity, Communication, and Critical Theory," 49–69.

99. I take an intersectionality perspective within this book, which assumes, according to Maxine Baca Zinn and Bonnie Thornton Dill, that "women and men throughout the social order experience different forms of privilege and subordination, depending on their race, class, gender, and sexuality." See Zinn and Dill, "Theorizing Difference," 327. See also Lisa Burns's discussion of "the 'ideals of American womanhood'" as a force of tradition in the newspaper coverage of first ladies (*First Ladies*, 8); and K. V. Anderson's discussion of "The First Lady," 17–30.

100. Gopal Balakrishnan, ed., "The National Imagination," in *Mapping the Nation* (London: Verso, 1996), 206; Mosse, *Nationalism and Sexuality*, 18; Ida Blom, "Gender and Nation in International Comparison," in Blom, Hagemann, and Hall, eds., *Gendered Nations*, 8.

101. Kersh, *Dreams of a More Perfect Union*, 26, 44, 94, 118.

102. Anne McClintock, "'No Longer in a Future Heaven': Gender, Race and Nationalism," in McClintock, Mufti, and Shohat, eds., *Dangerous Liaisons*, 91.

103. Yuval-Davis, *Gender & Nation*, 92; and Mayer, *Gender Ironies*, 1–2, 6.

104. McClintock, "'No Longer in a Future Heaven,'" 91.

105. Mostov, "Sexing the Nation/Desexing the Body," 91.

106. Hannah Arendt reminds us that the discernment between the public political sphere and private domestic space has roots in antiquity. See Arendt, *The Human Condition*, 32.

107. Smith-Rosenberg, "Political Camp," 275.

108. Kerber, *Women of the Republic*.

109. Kerber, *No Constitutional Rights to be Ladies*, 146. For more on the history of women, politics, and U.S. citizenship, see the following Ph.D. dissertation: Lindsay Hayes, "Congressional Widowhood and Gubernatorial Surrogacy: A Rhetorical History of Women's Distinct Paths to Public Office" (Department of Communication, University of Maryland, 2013).

110. Theodore Roosevelt, ed., "The Strenuous Life," in *The Strenuous Life: Essays and Addresses* (New York: The Century Company, 1901), 4, 16. For an examination of presidential contributions to gender dynamics, see V. B. Beasley, *You the People*; and Dorsey, *We are All Americans*.

111. Zaeske, "The 'Promiscuous Audience' Controversy," 191–207.

112. Ryan, "Gender and Public Access," 259–88.

113. Matthews, *The Rise of Public Woman*, 4–8.

114. Johnson, *Gender and Rhetorical Space*, 48, 53, 64.

115. Cameron, *On Language and Sexual Politics*, 104–5.

116. Falk, *Women for President*, 31.

117. See Al-Malki, Kaufer, Ishizaki, and Dreher, *Arab Women in Arab News*, 244–52; and Alexander and Hawkesworth, eds., *War and Terror*.

118. Lazar, ed., "Politicizing Gender in Discourse," 12–13.

119. As Mary Vavrus rightly reminds us, most of what we know about politics, including the broadcasting of political debates, speeches, or advertisements, is relayed via "mediated forms." See Vavrus, "Working the Senate," 213–35.

120. Goffman, *Frame Analysis*.

121. Entman and Herbst, "Reframing Public Opinion," 203; and Entman, "Framing," 51–58.

122. Pippa Norris, Montague Kern, and Marion Just, eds., "Framing Terrorism," in *Framing Terrorism: The News Media, the Government, and the Public* (New York: Routledge, 2003), 10–11.

123. Gitlin, *The Whole World is Watching*, 49.

124. Stuart Hall, "The Work of Representation," in Hall, Evans, and Nixon, eds., *Representation*, 17 (emphasis in original). Hall also believes in "pluralized" conceptions of "cultural codes" that allow for a "multiplicity of readings" and thus a multiplicity of meanings. Hall parts company with postmodernists and is particularly critical of

both Baudrillard and Foucault. He argues that "Postmodernism attempts to close off the past by saying that history is finished, therefore you needn't go back to it. There is only one present, and all you can do is be with it, immersed in it." Hall seems perpetually in search of such multiplicity of "meanings," past and present. See Grossberg, ed., "On Postmodernism and Articulation," 49–50.

125. Jamieson and Waldman, *The Press Effect*, 168.

126. See Meyrowitz, *No Sense of Place*, 268–304.

127. S. J. Parry-Giles and Parry-Giles, *Constructing Clinton*.

128. Jamieson and Waldman, *The Press Effect*, 136.

129. Zelizer, *Remembering to Forget*, 5.

130. Jamieson and Waldman, *The Press Effect*, xv. See also Kelley, *The Rhetoric of First Lady Hillary Rodham Clinton*, 27.

131. Allan, "(En)gendering the Truth Politics of News Discourse," 129, 133–34. Falk also discusses the news media's propensity to "mark gender." See Falk, *Women for President*, 91–96.

132. See Falk, "Gender Bias and Maintenance," 219–31; and Falk, *Women for President*, 177.

133. Vavrus, *Postfeminist News*, 151, 155.

134. Arthurs and Grimshaw, eds., "Introduction," 13. See also Sloop, *Disciplining Gender*, 22.

135. Foucault, *Discipline and Punish*, 215–16.

136. Arthurs and Grimshaw, eds., "Introduction," 10, 15.

137. Brown, "Feminism and Cultural Politics," 255.

138. John Angus Campbell demonstrates how texts can be extracted from their original context and relocated in a different time and place. See "Between the Fragment and the Icon," 346–76.

139. Except where designated, the citations from the news sources originated from the actual broadcasts themselves. While I took great care in transcribing the visual and verbal dimensions of the news broadcasts, I also take responsibility should there be any errors in transcription. During Hillary Clinton's presidential bid, I also accessed television news coverage from LexisNexis.

140. Jones, Nast, and Roberts, eds., *Thresholds in Feminist Geography*, xxxiii. Jones, Nast, and Roberts argue that "disciplinary practices" help control "persons in space." Karrin Vasby Anderson makes the claim that references to Hillary Clinton as a "bitch" functioned as a "contemporary rhetoric of containment disciplining women of power." See "'Rhymes with Rich,'" 600.

141. Betty Houchin Winfield shows the struggle over Clinton's image between the White House handlers and the news media. See "The Making of an Image," 241–53.

142. For more on the role of whiteness and Hillary Clinton, see Dickinson and Anderson, "Fallen," 271–96.

143. Hillary Clinton reports that she visited all fifty states in the United States and seventy-eight countries during her time as first lady and when Bill Clinton campaigned for political office. See *Living History*, x.

144. Winfield further discusses the news media's struggle to cover Hillary Clinton when they were more accustomed to covering traditional first ladies. See "The Making of an Image," 243. Regina G. Lawrence and Melody Rose offer a clear sense of the stereotypical coverage of Clinton during the 2008 campaign. See *Hillary Clinton's Race for the White House*.

Chapter 1. Hillary Clinton as Campaign Surrogate

1. "I'm In," Hillary for President, www.hillaryclinton.com/video/2.aspx (accessed January 3, 2008).

2. Fox News, *The O'Reilly Factor*, June 5, 2007, 2, online at LexisNexis Academic, June 26, 2007.

3. MSNBC News, *Tucker*, January 22, 2007, 1, online at LexisNexis Academic, June 26, 2007.

4. CBS News, *60 Minutes*, January 26, 1992.

5. *CBS Evening News*, March 16, 1992.

6. MSNBC News, *Tucker*, January 29, 2007, 2, online at LexisNexis Academic, June 26, 2007.

7. MSNBC News, *Hardball*, June 1, 2007, 1, online at LexisNexis Academic, June 26, 2007.

8. CNN News, *Paula Zahn Now*, March 6, 2007, 8, 12, online at LexisNexis Academic, June 26, 2007.

9. *CBS Evening News*, May 12, 1992.

10. CNN News, *The Situation Room*, June 18, 2007, 7, online at LexisNexis Academic, June 26, 2007.

11. MSNBC News, *The Chris Matthews Show*, March 11, 2007, 8, online at LexisNexis Academic, June 26, 2007.

12. MSNBC News, *Tucker*, January 22, 2007, 3.

13. See MSNBC News, *Hardball*, June 11, 2007, 3, 18–20, online at LexisNexis Academic, June 26, 2007; and Fox News, *The O'Reilly Factor*, June 5, 2007, 3.

14. For a more in-depth discussion involving the stereotyping of political women in the news, see Falk, *Women for President*, 53–82; and Carlin and Winfrey, "Have You Come a Long Way, Baby?" 326–43.

15. For more on the debate over sound bites in television news, see Stephens, *The Rise of the Image*, 143–47.

16. Julie Drew, William Lyons, and Lance Svehla argue that "sound bite sabotage" represents an act of "distortion and bias." See *Sound-Bite Saboteurs*, 4–8.

17. CBS News, *60 Minutes*, January 26, 1992.

18. *ABC World News Tonight*, November 3, 1992.

19. CBS News, *60 Minutes*, February 1, 1998. Kroft made this statement when *60 Minutes* rebroadcasted the 1992 episode with newly released out-takes after allegations surfaced that Bill Clinton had engaged in an extramarital affair with Monica Lewinsky.

20. Clinton, *Living History*, 108–9.

21. *CBS Evening News*, March 16, 1992.

22. *NBC Nightly News*, March 16, 1992.

23. *NBC Nightly News*, March 16, 1992.

24. *NBC Nightly News*, April 7, 1992.

25. Clinton, *Living History*, 110.

26. Entman and Rojecki, *The Black Image*, 49. For further insight into the fusion of morality judgments and character assessments, see S. J. Parry-Giles and Kaufer, "Lincoln Reminiscences," 199–234.

27. Fiske, *Media Matters*, 30–31.

28. Kaufer and Butler, *Rhetoric and the Arts of Design*, 139–40.

29. *NBC Nightly News*, March 16, 1992. ABC shows a clip that suggests the quotation originated in an ABC *Primetime Live* episode. See *ABC World News Tonight*, July 14, 1992.

30. ABC News, *Nightline*, March 26, 1992.

31. *NBC Nightly News*, April 7, 1992.

32. *NBC Nightly News*, March 21, 1992.

33. *NBC Nightly News*, April 7, 1992.

34. *NBC Nightly News*, March 16, 1992.

35. *ABC World News Tonight*, July 14, 1992.

36. *CBS Evening News*, September 9, 1992.

37. K. Campbell, "The Rhetorical Presidency," 180.

38. *ABC World News Tonight*, August 12, 1992.

39. *ABC World News Tonight*, August 18, 1992.

40. *CBS Evening News*, August 18, 1992.

41. *ABC World News Tonight*, August 19, 1992.

42. Lisa M. Burns talks about the news media's use of such shorthand phrases. See *First Ladies*, 7–11.

43. *CBS Evening News*, May 12, 1992.

44. *CBS Evening News*, September 9, 1992. See also "The Hillary Factor: Is She Helping or Hurting Her Husband?" *Time*, September 14, 1992.

45. *NBC Nightly News*, November 19, 1992.

46. *CBS Evening News*, May 12, 1992.

47. CNN News, *Capital Gang*, August 15, 1992.

48. Burns, *First Ladies*, 7–11.

49. Scheufele, "Frames, Schemata, and News Reporting," 67.

50. Gitlin, *The Whole World is Watching*, 98.

51. Jamieson and Waldman, *The Press Effect*, xiii.

52. *NBC Nightly News*, April 7, 1992.

53. *ABC World News Tonight*, November 13, 1992.

54. *CBS Evening News*, September 25, 1992.

55. For more on the news coverage during the Year of the Woman, see Vavrus, *Postfeminist News*, 75–104.

56. *NBC Nightly News*, July 14, 1992.

57. *NBC Nightly News*, August 7, 1992.

58. *CBS Evening News*, September 9, 1992.

59. *CBS Evening News*, May 12, 1992.

60. *ABC World News Tonight*, July 14, 1992.

61. *CBS Evening News*, May 12, 1992.

62. *CBS Evening News*, September 9, 1992.

63. Douglas, *Where the Girls Are*, 223.

64. *NBC Nightly News*, March 16, 1992.

65. *NBC Nightly News*, March 21, 1992 (emphasis added).

66. *CBS Evening News*, March 27, 1992.

67. *NBC Nightly News*, March 21, 1992.

68. *NBC Nightly News*, April 7, 1992.

69. *NBC Nightly News*, July 8, 1992.

70. For a discussion of some of the changes that Hillary Clinton made during the 1992 presidential campaign, see Troy, *Affairs of State*, 352–54.

71. *NBC Nightly News*, August 7, 1992.

72. *CBS Evening News*, September 9, 1992.

73. *ABC World News Tonight*, November 13, 1992.

74. Lakoff, *The Language War*, 19.

75. See *CBS Evening News*, September 9, 1992; *CBS Evening News*, December 15, 1992; and *ABC World News Tonight*, November 13, 1992.

76. See ABC News, *Nightline*, November 19, 1992; and *ABC World News Tonight*, July 14, 1992. CBS featured a statement from an editorial writer that compared Barbara Bush to "Mrs. Cleaver." See *CBS Evening News*, May 12, 1992.

77. For a more in-depth discussion of news coverage, Hillary Clinton, and the public-private divide, see Kaufer, Parry-Giles, and Klebanov, "The 'Image Bite,'" 336–56.

78. Kaufer, Parry-Giles, and Beigman Klebanov, "The 'Image Bite,'" 336–56.

79. Butler, *Bodies That Matter*, 2.

80. Gal, "A Semiotics of the Public/Private Distinction," 77–95.

81. Fiske, *Television Culture*, 93.

82. Lazar, ed., "Performing State Fatherhood," 140.

83. See *CBS Evening News*, October 8, 1996; and *NBC Nightly News*, October 21, 1996.

84. *CBS Evening News*, August 1, 1996.

85. ABC News, "Two Women," *Nightline*, October 18, 1996.

86. *NBC Nightly News*, October 21, 1996.

87. *CBS Evening News*, February 17, 1996.

88. *CBS Evening News*, October 8, 1996.

89. *NBC Nightly News*, August 27, 1996.

90. *NBC Nightly News*, October 22, 1996.

91. CNN News, "They Don't Bake Cookies Anymore," *Democracy in America*, October 13, 1996.

92. CNN News, "They Don't Bake Cookies Anymore," *Democracy in America*, October 13, 1996.

93. CNN News, "Inside Politics," November 3, 1995.

94. *CBS Evening News*, August 27, 1996.

95. *ABC World News Tonight*, August 28, 1996.

96. *CBS Evening News*, August 26, 1996.

97. *CBS Evening News*, February 17, 1996.

98. ABC News, "Two Women," *Nightline*, October 18, 1996.

99. ABC News, "Two Women," *Nightline*, October 18, 1996.

100. Walsh, *Gender and Discourse*, 34.

101. Walsh, *Gender and Discourse*, 2.

102. ABC News, *Nightline*, April 17, 1996.

103. See CNN News, "They Don't Bake Cookies Anymore," *Democracy in America*, October 13, 1996; and *NBC Nightly News*, October 21, 1996.

104. See CNN News, "They Don't Bake Cookies Anymore," *Democracy in America*, October 13, 1996.

105. *NBC Nightly News*, August 15, 1996.

106. *NBC Nightly News*, August 27, 1996.

107. K. Campbell, "The Discursive Performance of Femininity," 6.

108. Kitch, *The Girl on the Magazine Cover*.

109. ABC News, "Two Women," *Nightline*, October 18, 1996.

110. CNN News, *Morning News*, October 11, 1996.

111. CNN News, "They Don't Bake Cookies Anymore," *Democracy in America*, October 13, 1996.

112. Barker-Plummer, "News and Feminism," 193.

113. D'Emilio and Freedman, *Intimate Matters*, 316.

114. *NBC Nightly News*, October 22, 1996.

115. ABC News, *Nightline*, April 17, 1996.

116. *CBS Evening News*, August 26, 1996.

117. *NBC Nightly News*, August 26, 1996.

118. Vavrus, *Postfeminist News*, 27.

119. See CNN News, "They Don't Bake Cookies Anymore," *Democracy in America*, October 13, 1996.

120. ABC News, *Nightline*, April 17, 1996.

121. ABC News, "Two Women," *Nightline*, October 18, 1996.

122. CNN News, "They Don't Bake Cookies Anymore," *Democracy in America*, October 13, 1996.

123. *NBC Nightly News*, October 22, 1996.

124. Sloop, *Disciplining Gender*, 12.

125. Kaufer and Butler, *Designing Interactive Worlds*, 56.

126. Fischer, *Made in America*, 203.

127. Casper, *Constructing American Lives*, 6.

128. *ABC World News Tonight*, November 13, 1992.

Chapter 2. Hillary Clinton as Legislative Activist and Legal Defendant

1. NBC News, *Today*, August 14, 2007.

2. *CBS Evening News*, September 17, 2007.

3. ABC News, *Good Morning America*, September 17, 2007.

4. See ABC News, *Good Morning America*, October 19, 2007; ABC News, *This Week*, September 23, 2007; and *ABC World News Tonight*, September 17, 2007.

5. *CBS Evening News*, September 27, 2007.

6. ABC News, *Good Morning America*, September 17, 2007.

7. Fox News, *Hannity & Colmes*, June 27, 2007.

8. *CBS Evening News*, September 17, 2007.

9. CNBC, *Kudlow and Company*, May 29, 2007.

10. ABC News, *Nightline*, January 22, 2007.

11. NBC News, *Today*, August 14, 2007.

12. Fox News, *Hannity & Colmes*, June 27, 2007.

13. NBC News, *Today*, January 22, 2007.

14. ABC News, *Nightline*, January 22, 2007.

15. *ABC World News Sunday*, September 16, 2007.

16. ABC News, *Good Morning America*, May 28, 2007.

17. *CBS Evening News*, January 25, 1993.

18. Goldman, "Political Virtue," 49.

19. See Dawes, *The Language of War*.

20. Edelman, *Constructing the Political Spectacle*, 67–68.

21. Edelman, *Political Language*, 3.

22. Dawes, *The Language of War*, 18–19.

23. *CBS Evening News*, January 25, 1993.

24. *NBC Nightly News*, January 25, 1993.

25. *CBS Evening News*, January 25, 1993.

26. *ABC World News Tonight*, January 22, 1993.

27. Gill Troy and John Pope both talk of how Betty Ford used the concept of "pillow talk" when trying to downplay the influence she contributed to her presidential husband's decision making. See Troy, *Mr. and Mrs. President*, 223, 232, and 256; and Pope, "Elizabeth Ann (Betty) Bloomer Ford," 371.

28. *NBC Nightly News*, February 8, 1993.

29. *NBC Nightly News*, February 9, 1993.

30. ABC News, *Nightline*, March 11, 1993.

31. *NBC Nightly News*, March 9, 1993.

32. *NBC Nightly News*, October 26, 1993.

33. *NBC Nightly News*, September 21, 1993.

34. *ABC World News Tonight*, September 28, 1993.

35. *ABC World News Tonight*, January 22, 1993.

36. *NBC Nightly News*, January 11, 1993.

37. *ABC World News Tonight*, January 22, 1993.

38. *CBS Evening News*, January 25, 1993.

39. *NBC Nightly News*, January 24, 1993.

40. *CBS Evening News*, February 4, 1993.

41. *ABC World News Tonight*, February 16, 1993.

42. *NBC Nightly News*, April 30, 1993.

43. *NBC Nightly News*, February 8, 1993.

44. *NBC Nightly News*, September 28, 1993.

45. *CBS Evening News*, February 4, 1993.

46. ABC News, *Nightline*, March 11, 1993.

47. *NBC Nightly News*, February 8, 1993.

48. *NBC Nightly News*, January 27, 1993.

49. *CBS Evening News*, February 15, 1993.

50. See, for example, *CBS Evening News*, March 30, 1994.

51. *NBC Nightly News*, February 27, 1993.

52. *NBC Nightly News*, February 16, 1993.

53. *ABC World News Tonight*, February 16, 1993.

54. *NBC Nightly News*, February 8, 1993. Gangel made the following reference to Hillary Clinton's honeymoon with Congress: "But while she gets high marks now her honeymoon with Congress won't last forever." The first one hundred days of presidential office is typically referred to as a "honeymoon." Yet, when the person in power is a woman shown interacting only with men, the connotations of the honeymoon take on more enhanced sexualized sentiment.

55. *CBS Evening News*, February 4, 1993.

56. Fiske, *Media Matters*, 217.

57. Foucault, *Discipline and Punish*, 177.

58. *NBC Nightly News*, February 27, 1993.

59. *CBS Evening News*, February 4, 1993.

60. *ABC World News Tonight*, March 4, 1993.

61. *NBC Nightly News*, March 10, 1993.

62. *ABC World News Tonight*, June 23, 1993; and *NBC Nightly News*, July 25, 1994.

63. Katherine Ellison, *Imelda: Steel Butterfly of the Philippines* (New York: McGraw Hill, 1988).

64. ABC News, *Nightline*, March 11, 1993.

65. *NBC Nightly News*, March 10, 1993.

66. ABC News, *Nightline*, March 11, 1993.

67. Rose, *Feminism and Geography*, 146.

68. Ross and Sreberny-Mohammadi, "Playing House," 104.

69. *NBC Nightly News*, February 8, 1993.

70. For more on the history of the Clinton administration's health care reform efforts, see Aaron, *The Problem that Won't Go Away*.

71. See Colonel Don G. Gaylor, *From Barnstorming to Bush Pilot* (Bloomington: IUniverse, 2010), 5; and Larry Sabato and Howard R. Ernst, *Encyclopedia of American Political Parties and Elections* (New York: Facts on File, 2007), 23.

72. *CBS Evening News*, February 11, 1993.

73. *ABC World News Tonight*, April 8, 1994.

74. *NBC Nightly News*, February 11, 1993.

75. *CBS Evening News*, February 22, 1993.

76. For more on Hillary Clinton and health care, see McKinney, Davis, and Delbert, "The First—and Last—Woman Standing," 125–47.

77. *CBS Evening News*, April 5, 1994.

78. *CBS Evening News*, July 27, 1994.

79. *CBS Evening News*, April 5, 1994.

80. *NBC Nightly News*, March 9, 1993.

81. *NBC Nightly News*, April 30, 1993; and *NBC Nightly News*, September 21, 1993.

82. Lakoff, *The Language War*, 48.

83. *NBC Nightly News*, February 24, 1994.

84. *NBC Nightly News*, July 22, 1994; and *NBC Nightly News*, August 10, 1994.

85. *NBC Nightly News*, February 24, 1994.

86. *CBS Evening News*, May 4, 1994.

87. *NBC Nightly News*, March 19, 1994.

88. *ABC World News Tonight*, July 28, 1994.

89. *ABC World News Tonight*, June 23, 1994.

90. *NBC Nightly News*, March 23, 1994.

91. *CBS Evening News*, March 23, 1994.

92. *NBC Nightly News*, June 14, 1994.

93. *ABC World News Tonight*, August 2, 1994.

94. *NBC Nightly News*, August 3, 1994.

95. *NBC Nightly News*, July 22, 1994.

96. *NBC Nightly News*, August 10, 1994.

97. *NBC Nightly News*, July 22, 1994.

98. Dawes, *The Language of War*, 185.

99. *ABC World News Tonight*, April 5, 1994.

100. *CBS Evening News*, July 22, 1994.

101. *CBS Evening News*, September 15, 1994.

102. *ABC World News Tonight*, February 11, 1993.

103. *CBS Evening News*, February 4, 1994.

104. *NBC Nightly News*, February 11, 1993.

105. *ABC World News Tonight*, September 28, 1993.

106. *ABC World News Tonight*, February 16, 1994.

107. *ABC World News Tonight*, August 10, 1994.

108. *CBS Evening News*, September 29, 1993.

109. *CBS Evening News*, September 22, 1995.

110. *NBC Nightly News*, August 3, 1994.

111. *CBS Evening News*, August 8, 1995.

112. For further details on Whitewater, see Branch, *The Clinton Tapes*. See also the "Time Line" of Whitewater provided by the *Washington Post*, www.washingtonpost.com/wp-srv/politics/special/whitewater/timeline.htm (accessed July 27, 2011).

113. See, for example, Schwartz, "The Character of Washington," 213–14.

114. *CBS Evening News*, March 7, 1994.

115. *CBS Evening News*, March 4, 1994.

116. *NBC Nightly News*, March 15, 1994.

117. *CBS Evening News*, December 21, 1993.

118. *CBS Evening News*, March 7, 1994.

119. *NBC Nightly News*, April 23, 1994.

120. Conway, *Private Interests*, 27–28.

121. For a further discussion of phrenology, see George Combe, *Elements of Phrenology*, 3rd ed. (London: John Anderson, Jun. Edinburgh, 1928); L. Perry Curtis Jr., *Apes and Angels: The Irishman in Victorian Caricature* (Washington, DC: Smithsonian Institution Press, 1971); and Lukasik, *Discerning Characters*, 187. According to Lukasik, phrenology represented "an extension of physiognomy in the sense of reading moral qualities from the head." Phrenology involved more scientific "measurement" techniques. See also Finnegan, "Recognizing Lincoln," 31–58.

122. Hartley, *Physiognomy*, 3, 6, 102. See Aristotle, *Physiognomonica*, in *The Works of Aristotle*, vol. 4, trans. and ed. W. D. Ross (Oxford: Clarendon Press, 1913), I, 805, 1.

123. Hartley, *Physiognomy*, 33.

124. Twigg, "The Performative Dimension of Surveillance," 322.

125. For more on such decontextualization practices, see Messaris, "'Visual Manipulation,'" 181–95; and Messaris, *Visual Literacy*.

126. *CBS Evening News*, March 13, 1994.

127. As representative examples, see *NBC Nightly News*, January 10, 1994; *NBC Nightly News*, January 15, 1994; *CBS Evening News*, March 4, 1994; and *CBS Evening News*, March 29, 1994.

128. *CBS Evening News*, March 4, 1994.

129. See Condit, "Hegemony in a Mass-mediated Society," 205–30.

130. *ABC World News Tonight*, December 19, 1995.

131. *ABC World News Tonight*, December 19, 1995.

132. See Williams, *Confounding Images*, 11.

133. ABC News, *Nightline*, December 19, 1995.

134. CNN News, *CNN World View*, May 17, 1997.

135. ABC News, *Nightline*, April 26, 1994.

136. *ABC World News Tonight*, March 23, 1994.

137. *CBS Evening News*, March 30, 1994.

138. *NBC Nightly News*, January 10, 1994.

139. *CBS Evening News*, April 22, 1994.

140. ABC News, *Nightline*, January 19, 1996.

141. *ABC World News Tonight*, April 22, 1994.

142. *ABC World News Tonight*, April 25, 1998.

143. See *ABC World News Tonight*, May 17, 1997; and *CBS Evening News*, October 26, 1997.

144. *NBC Nightly News*, January 10, 1994.

145. *NBC Nightly News*, March 7, 1994.

146. *NBC Nightly News*, January 9, 1996. See also William Safire, "Blizzard of Lies," *The New York Times*, January 8, 1996, 27.

147. *CBS Evening News*, March 30, 1994.

148. *CBS Evening News*, January 11, 1996.

149. *CBS Evening News*, March 4, 1994.

150. *ABC World News Tonight*, March 12, 1994.

151. *ABC World News Tonight*, January 10, 1996.

152. *CBS Evening News*, January 14, 1997.

153. *NBC Nightly News*, January 10, 1994.

154. *NBC Nightly News*, September 20, 2000.

155. ABC News, *Nightline*, August 24, 1998.

156. ABC News, *Nightline*, January 19, 1996.

157. *CBS Evening News*, August 29, 1994.

158. Dawes, *The Language of War*, 17. Dawes draws on the work of Catharine Mac-Kinnon. See MacKinnon, *Only Words*, 105–9.

159. Stefan Dudink, Karen Hagemann, and John Tosh make the point that "hegemony denotes both the unequal social relations which empower certain groups of men, and the model of masculinity—often unconscious—which legitimises those relations." They argue further that "the role of the mass media in taking up and reinforcing dominant expressions of masculinity is clearly central to the maintenance of hegemonic masculinity in modern societies." See Dudink, Hagemann, and Tosh, eds., *Masculinities in Politics and War*, 44.

160. Clinton, *Living History*, 246.

161. See Lakoff, *The Language War*, 186. Karrin Vasby Anderson makes a similar point with the use of the word *bitch* functioning as a rhetoric of "containment." See "'Rhymes with Rich,'" 600.

162. Dawes, *The Language of War*, 18. Dawes is drawing on the work of Bourdieu, *Language and the Symbolic Power*, and Butler, *Excitable Speech*.

163. Butler, *Excitable Speech*, 5. See also Austin, *How to Do Things with Words*.

164. *CBS Evening News*, September 15, 1994.

165. *CBS Evening News*, November 29, 1994.

166. *ABC World News Tonight*, December 5, 1994.

167. *CBS Evening News*, March 30, 1994.

168. *CBS Evening News*, November 29, 1994.

169. MSNBC, *Hardball*, May 25, 2007.

170. See Alasdair MacIntyre who argues that "for the virtues; whether classical or Christian, presuppose a 'teleological view of human nature,' that is, a 'view of man

as having an essence which defines his true end.'" See *After Virtue*, 52–53, 65. See also Walhout, "The Liberal Saint," 176.

171. *NBC Nightly News*, January 22, 2007.

172. Butler, *Excitable Speech*, 16, 27, 39.

Chapter 3. Hillary Clinton as International Emissary and Scorned Wife

1. Fox News, *The O'Reilly Factor*, May 31, 2007.

2. MSNBC News, *Hardball*, May 25, 2007. See also Bernstein, *A Woman in Charge*.

3. MSNBC News, *Hardball*, May 25, 2007.

4. See Smith, *For Love of Politics*.

5. Fox News, *The Big Story with John Gibson*, November 1, 2007.

6. See Bill Clinton, Map Room speech, August 17, 1998, CNN—All Politics, www.cnn.com/ALLPOLITICS/1998/08/17/speech/transcript.html (accessed August 18, 2011).

7. CBS News, *The Early Show*, October 23, 2007.

8. MSNBC News, *The Chris Matthews Show*, October 28, 2007.

9. Fox News, *The Big Story with John Gibson*, November 1, 2007.

10. ABC News, *Good Morning America*, October 25, 2007.

11. MSNBC News, *The Chris Matthews Show*, October 28, 2007.

12. For additional information on the Clinton impeachment process, see Dershowitz, *America on Trial*; and Gormley, *The Death of American Virtue*.

13. For a discussion of some of the changes that Hillary Clinton made in her first lady comportment in the aftermath of the health care debate, see Troy, *Affairs of State*, 366–71, 378–79.

14. Grabe and Bucy, *Image Bite Politics*.

15. *NBC Nightly News*, January 10, 1995.

16. Roosevelt, *My Day*.

17. *ABC World News Tonight*, July 23, 1995.

18. *CBS Evening News*, October 26, 1997.

19. *ABC World News Tonight*, April 17, 1997.

20. *CBS Evening News*, April 17, 1997.

21. *NBC Nightly News*, May 16, 1995.

22. *CBS Evening News*, March 27, 1995.

23. *ABC World News Tonight*, March 17, 1997.

24. *ABC World News Tonight*, March 18, 1997.

25. Even as recently as the 1970s, women's issues were often *not* construed as political issues. During a 1975 *60 Minutes* interview, Betty Ford was defending her decision to support the Equal Rights Amendment. When asked about a first lady being so outspoken, Ford responded: "What I've spoken out on were issues pertaining to women. I'm not getting into the political issues." "The First Lady—Betty Ford," *60 Minutes*, August 10, 1975, Gerald R. Ford Presidential Library, East Lansing, Michigan. See also S. J. Parry-Giles and Blair, "The Rise of the Rhetorical First Lady," 565–99.

26. CNN News, *CNN World View*, April 10, 1997.

27. CNN News, *CNN World View*, November 17, 1997.

28. CNN also would resort to the same tactics of speaking over video images of Clinton's international trips. See CNN News, *CNN World View*, October 16, 1995.

29. *ABC World News Tonight*, March 21, 1999.

30. *NBC Nightly News*, August 26, 1995.

31. *CBS Evening News*, August 20, 1995.

32. *CBS Evening News*, August 23, 1995.

33. *CBS Evening News*, August 26, 1995.

34. *NBC Nightly News*, September 4, 1995.

35. *CBS Evening News*, September 4, 1995.

36. *NBC Nightly News*, September 3, 1995.

37. *CBS Evening News*, September 4, 1995.

38. *NBC Nightly News*, September 4, 1995.

39. *NBC Nightly News*, September 4, 1995.

40. *CBS Evening News*, September 5, 1995.

41. *ABC World News Tonight*, September 5, 1995.

42. For a discussion of the double binds that political women, particularly Hillary Clinton, face, see Jamieson, *Beyond the Double Bind*.

43. Bill Clinton, "Response to the Lewinsky Allegations," January 26, 1998, The Miller Center of Public Affairs, University of Virginia, millercenter.org/president/speeches/detail/3930 (accessed August 31, 2011).

44. NBC News, *Today*, January 27, 1998.

45. See Posner, *An Affair of State*, 9.

46. NBC News, *Today*, January 27, 1998.

47. *CBS Evening News*, January 27, 1998.

48. *NBC Nightly News*, January 27, 1998.

49. CNN News, *CNN World View*, January 28, 1998.

50. See *CBS Evening News*, January 30, 1998; and CBS News, *60 Minutes*, February 1, 1998.

51. *NBC Nightly News*, August 14, 1998.

52. CNN News, *Larry King Live*, August 17, 1998.

53. ABC News, *Nightline*, August 24, 1998.

54. *CBS Evening News*, September 29, 1998.

55. For more on the competing portrayals of Hillary Clinton's agency, see Kaufer, Parry-Giles, and Klebanov, "The 'Image Bite,'" 336–56.

56. *ABC World News Tonight*, August 17, 1998.

57. *NBC Nightly News*, August 17, 1998.

58. CNN News, "Investigating the President," August 17, 1998.

59. CNN News, *Larry King Live*, August 17, 1998.

60. ABC News, *Nightline*, August 24, 1998.

61. Michael Shortland, "Skin Deep: Barthes, Lavater and the Legible Body," *Economy and Society* 14 (1985): 295.

62. In covering the memorial ceremony at Andrews Air Force Base on August 14, 1998, NBC did not take these images out of context. From that point forward, NBC used the memorial service images without mentioning their original context. See *NBC Nightly News*, August 14, 1998.

63. To review additional essays that touch on this image, see S. J. Parry-Giles, "Mediating Hillary Rodham Clinton," 205–26; S. J. Parry-Giles, "Political Authenticity," 211–27; and Kaufer, Parry-Giles, and Klebanov, "The 'Image Bite,'" 336–56. To view the originating footage from C-Span, see "Ceremony for Embassy Bombing Victims," C-Span, August 13, 1998, Purdue Research Foundation, www.c-spanvideo.org/program/109911–1 (accessed September 1, 2011).

64. *NBC Nightly News*, August 17, 1998.

65. NBC News, *Dateline*, September 12, 1998.

66. See Rivers, *Face Value*, 80–83; and Stocker, *Physiognomy*.

67. *NBC Nightly News*, August 17, 1998.

68. NBC News, *Time & Again*, September 19, 1998.

69. To see how these images were used over the span of eighteen months, see Kaufer, Parry-Giles, and Klebanov, "The 'Image Bite,'" 336–56.

70. ABC News, *Nightline*, March 3, 1999.

71. CNN News, *CNN World View*, August 2, 1999.

72. CNN News, *CNN Today*, August 17, 1998.

73. CNN News, *CNN Today*, August 17, 1998.

74. MSNBC News, "Investigating the President," August 24, 1998.

75. The 1992 campaign represented the moment when Dan Quayle offered his critique of a fictionalized television character named Murphy Brown, who opted to have a baby without marrying the baby's father. See Fiske, *Media Matters*.

76. ABC News, *Nightline*, August 24, 1998.

77. ABC News, *Nightline*, August 24, 1998.

78. *NBC Nightly News*, December 14, 1998.

79. *NBC Nightly News*, September 11, 1998.

80. *NBC Nightly News*, September 11, 1998.

81. *NBC Nightly News*, December 14, 1998.

82. *CBS Evening News*, September 10, 1998.

83. *NBC Nightly News*, September 11, 1998.

84. NBC News, *Dateline*, September 12, 1998.

85. CBS News, *Inside Washington*, September 12, 1998.

86. Mostov, "Sexing the Nation/Desexing the Body," 91.

87. ABC News, *Nightline*, August 24, 1998.

88. Melissa Deem offered an insightful discussion about the coverage of the Clinton-Lewinsky scandal and the portrayal of feminism. Because Hillary Clinton was portrayed as exuding immense levels of power, the "shoring up of traditional masculinity" was undermined. Deem also argued that feminism was "disciplined" given how Bill Clinton's actions were more normalized. See Deem, "Scandal," 86, 88.

89. R. W. Connell talks of how patriarchy reasserts itself in modified ways. The reconfiguration process of hegemonic masculinity, nevertheless, still preserves the "dominant position of men and the subordination of women" even when patriarchy is "eroded." See: *Masculinities*, 77.

90. *ABC World News Tonight*, January 24, 1998.

91. CNN News, "Investigating the President," August 17, 1998.

92. CNN News, *Larry King Live*, August 17, 1998.

93. NBC News, *Dateline*, September 12, 1998.

94. ABC News, *Nightline*, March 3, 1999.

95. MSNBC News, "The Female Factor," September 10, 1998.

96. See, for example, *CBS Evening News*, February 11, 1998; ABC News, *Nightline*, August 24, 1998; and MSNBC News, *Time & Again*, September 19, 1998.

97. *NBC Nightly News*, September 21, 1998.

98. CNN News, *Larry King Live*, August 17, 1998.

99. ABC News, *Nightline*, March 3, 1999.

100. *NBC Nightly News*, September 21, 1998.

101. Yuval-Davis, *Gender & Nation*, 37.

102. NBC News, "The President and the People," *Dateline*, September 12, 1998. When the government shut down, interns and other volunteers filled in for regular employees until the government reopened.

103. NBC News, "The President and the People," *Dateline*, September 12, 1998.

104. CNN, *Larry King Live*, August 17, 1998.

105. NBC News, "The President and the People," *Dateline*, September 12, 1998.

106. NBC News, "The President and the People," *Dateline*, September 12, 1998.

107. *NBC Nightly News*, September 11, 1998.

108. *NBC Nightly News*, September 11, 1998.

109. ABC News, *Nightline*, March 3, 1999.

110. NBC News, "The President and the People," *Dateline*, September 12, 1998.

111. NBC News, "The President and the People," *Dateline*, September 12, 1998.

112. *ABC World News Tonight*, August 1, 1999.

113. *ABC World News Tonight*, August 1, 1999. See also *ABC World News Tonight*, August 2, 1999.

114. *CBS Evening News*, August 1, 1999.

115. CNN News, August 1, 1999.

116. *NBC Nightly News*, August 1, 1999.

117. *CBS Evening News*, August 2, 1999.

118. *ABC World News Tonight*, August 2, 1999.

119. *NBC Nightly News*, August 2, 1999.

120. Samuels, *Romances of the Republic, 15*.

121. Damian Whitworth, "Oral History: The Monica Lewinsky Scandal Ten Years On," *London Sunday Times*, January 15, 2008, women.timesonline.co.uk/tol/life_and_style/women/relationships/article3185449.ece (accessed September 19, 2011).

122. Amal Al-Malki, David Kaufer, Suguru Ishizaki, and Kira Dreher make the case that news coverage can "freeze" images of women over time. See *Arab Women in Arab News*, 363.

123. MSNBC News, *Time & Again*, September 19, 1998.

124. *CBS Evening News*, January 20, 1999.

125. *CBS Evening News*, January 20, 1999.

126. Ronald Bishop talks about journalists as makeshift psychologists. See *Taking on the Pledge of Allegiance*, 75.

127. *NBC Nightly News*, January 22, 1999.

128. *CBS Evening News*, January 20, 1999.

129. ABC News, *Nightline*, August 24, 1998.

130. ABC News, *Nightline*, January 11, 2000.

131. MSNBC News, *Race for the White House with David Gregory*, March 26, 2008.

132. MSNBC News, *Hardball*, March 26, 2008.

Chapter 4. Hillary Clinton as Political Candidate

1. CNN News, *Reliable Sources*, May 25, 2008.

2. CNN News, *Late Edition with Wolf Blitzer*, June 8, 2008.

3. See CNN News, *CNN Election Center*, April 3, 2008; Fox News, *Fox Special Report with Brit Hume*, May 27, 2008; and CNN News, *Reliable Sources*, May 25, 2008.

4. CNN News, *CNN Election Center*, September 10, 2008.

5. CNN News, *Reliable Sources*, May 25, 2008.

6. MSNBC News, *Tucker*, November 2, 2007.

7. CNN News, *This Week in Politics*, September 7, 2008.

8. Fox News, *Fox Special Report with Brit Hume*, May 27, 2008.

9. The language used in the broadcast was that Hillary Clinton reminded men of "their nagging wives." See CNN News, *Reliable Sources*, May 25, 2008.

10. Fowler, *Language in the News*, 1. See also Bell, *The Language of News Media*, 7.

11. NBC News, *Meet the Press*, May 25, 2008.

12. NBC News, *Meet the Press*, May 25, 2008. For more on the coverage of Bill Clinton during Hillary Clinton's 2008 presidential campaign, see Khan and Blair, "Writing Bill Clinton," 56–71.

13. Fox News, *Hannity & Colmes*, April 1, 2008.

14. NBC News, *Meet the Press*, January 3, 1999.

15. *ABC World News Tonight*, February 15, 1999.

16. *ABC World News Tonight*, February 14, 1999.

17. *ABC World News Tonight*, February 14, 1999.

18. *NBC Nightly News*, July 3, 1999.

19. NBC News, *Time & Again*, January 27, 2000.

20. *ABC World News Tonight*, February 5, 2000.

21. *CBS Evening News*, February 16, 1999.

22. *NBC Nightly News*, April 17, 1999.

23. *NBC Nightly News*, March 3, 1999.

24. ABC News, *Nightline*, February 17, 1999.

25. ABC News, *Nightline*, June 23, 1999.

26. *NBC Nightly News*, February 15, 1999.

27. ABC News, *Nightline*, February 17, 1999.

28. *ABC World News Tonight*, March 3, 1999.

29. ABC News, *Nightline*, February 17, 1999.

30. *ABC World News Tonight*, July 7, 1999.

31. *CBS Evening News*, March 22, 1999.

32. *NBC Nightly News*, March 3, 1999. For more on the sexist coverage of Clinton, see Samek, "Political Skin," 426–30.

33. *CBS Evening News*, February 16, 1999.

34. ABC News, *Nightline*, June 23, 1999.

35. The election process as a whole is often featured as a courting ritual. See S. J. Parry-Giles, "Constituting Presidentiality and U.S. Citizenship," 139–79.

36. *ABC World News Tonight*, February 16, 1999.

37. ABC News, *Nightline*, June 23, 1999.

38. *ABC World News Tonight*, February 16, 1999.

39. *CBS Evening News*, June 3, 1999.

40. Fox News, *Fox News Sunday*, November 28, 1999.

41. *CBS Evening News*, February 16, 1999.

42. *NBC Nightly News*, August 14, 2000.

43. For more on carpetbagging, see Hume and Gough, *Blacks, Carpetbaggers, and Scalawags*.

44. *NBC Nightly News*, May 20, 1999.

45. *CBS Evening News*, July 7, 1999.

46. *CBS Evening News*, July 11, 1999.

47. CNN News, *CNN World View*, February 21, 1999.

48. NBC News, *Hardball*, April 10, 2000.

49. *NBC Nightly News*, November 23, 1999.

50. McDowell, *Gender, Identity, and Place*, 4, 100, 214.

51. Charles R. Warner, *The Team America Loves to Hate: Why Baseball Fans Despise the New York Yankees* (New York: Praeger, 2008).

52. NBC News, *Today*, June 10, 1999.

53. *ABC World News Tonight*, June 10, 1999.

54. *NBC Nightly News*, July 3, 1999.

55. *ABC World News Tonight*, February 5, 2000.

56. CNN News, *Inside Politics*, October 20, 2000.

57. *NBC Nightly News*, July 6, 1999.

58. MSNBC, *Hotwire*, July 6, 1999.

59. ABC News, *Nightline*, September 13, 1999.

60. Burstyn, *The Rites of Men*, 3, 13, 61.

61. Excerpts of Giuliani's statements were shown on CNN and NBC News. See CNN News, *CNN World View*, November 13, 1999; and *NBC Nightly News*, November 13, 1999.

62. CNN News, *CNN World View*, November 13, 1999.

63. *NBC Nightly News*, November 13, 1999.

64. *CBS Evening News*, November 22, 1999.

65. *NBC Nightly News*, November 23, 1999.

66. *ABC World News Tonight*, November 23, 1999.

67. *ABC World News Tonight*, November 23, 1999.

68. *NBC Nightly News*, November 13, 1999.

69. *CBS Evening News*, November 23, 1999.

70. CNN News, *CNN World View*, November 13, 1999.

71. CNN News, *CNN World View*, July 29, 2000.

72. *NBC Nightly News*, February 12, 2000.

73. *CBS Evening News*, April 6, 2000.

74. *NBC Nightly News*, April 7, 2000.

75. *NBC Nightly News*, May 17, 2000.

76. *ABC World News Tonight*, November 23, 1999.

77. *NBC Nightly News*, May 17, 2000.

78. CNN News, February 6, 2000.

79. *NBC Nightly News*, May 17, 2000.

80. MSNBC News, *Hardball*, June 7, 2000.

81. MSNBC News, *Feedback*, April 11, 2000.

82. *NBC Nightly News*, June 22, 2000.

83. *ABC World News Tonight*, October 8, 2000.

84. *NBC Nightly News*, July 7, 1999.

85. *ABC World News Tonight*, December 15, 2000.

86. *ABC World News Tonight*, August 14, 2000.

87. MSNBC News, *Hardball*, April 20, 2000.

88. Schwartz, "The Character of Washington," 217.

89. MSNBC News, *The Mitchell Report*, October 27, 2000.

90. P. D. Marshall, *Celebrity and Power*, xi.

91. These linguistic frames were used in the following newscasts in order of appearance in the chapter: *CBS Evening News*, March 3, 1999; *CBS Evening News*, May 20, 2000; *CBS Evening News*, December 9, 2000; and *NBC Nightly News*, May 17, 2000.

92. *ABC World News Tonight*, March 3, 1999.

93. NBC News, *Today*, May 17, 2000.

94. ABC News, *This Week*, May 21, 2000.

95. See MSNBC News, *The Mitchell Report*, September 13, 2000; CNBC News, *Upfront Tonight*, May 16, 2000; and CNN News, *Larry King Live*, August 25, 2000.

96. *CBS Evening News*, December 9, 1999.

97. *NBC Nightly News*, January 5, 2000.

98. NBC News, *Today*, May 11, 2000.

99. CNN News, *Inside Politics*, August 29, 2000.

100. *CBS Evening News*, August 14, 2000.

101. CNN News, *Inside Politics*, August 10, 2000.

102. ABC News, *Nightline*, June 23, 1999.

103. *ABC World News Tonight*, October 8, 2000.

104. MSNBC News, *The Mitchell Report*, September 13, 2000.

105. NBC News, *Meet the Press*, May 28, 2000.

106. MSNBC News, *The Mitchell Report*, May 28, 2000.

107. CNN News, *Inside Politics*, July 7, 2000.

108. CNN News, *Inside Politics*, June 23, 2000.

109. CNN News, *Inside Politics*, July 5, 2000.

110. CNN News, *Inside Politics*, September 12, 2000.

111. NBC News, *Today*, May 20, 2000.

112. *CBS Evening News*, May 20, 2000.

113. CBS News, *The Early Show*, June 28, 2000.

114. CNN News, *The Spin Room*, January 3, 2001.

115. ABC News, *Nightline*, February 17, 1999.

116. *CBS Evening News*, July 27, 1999.

117. *CBS Evening News*, May 20, 2000.

118. ABC News, *This Week*, September 17, 2000.

119. *CBS Evening News*, July 27, 1999.

120. *CBS Evening News*, March 3, 1999.

121. ABC News, *This Week*, September 17, 2000.

122. Fox News, *Fox News Sunday*, May 28, 2000.

123. ABC News, *Nightline*, February 17, 1999.

124. *NBC Nightly News*, February 15, 1999.

125. CNN News, *Inside Politics*, September 12, 2000.

126. ABC News, *Nightline*, February 17, 1999.

127. *NBC Nightly News*, September 10, 2000.

128. *NBC Nightly News*, May 19, 2000.

129. *CBS Evening News*, May 26, 1999.

130. *ABC World News Tonight*, March 5, 2000.

131. ABC News, *Nightline*, February 17, 1999.

132. ABC News, *Nightline*, February 17, 1999.

133. Other scholars make similar arguments that women are held responsible for the violence directed toward them because they trespassed into spaces where they did not belong or they engaged in provocative behavior that invited such violence. See Tonn, Endress, and Diamond, "Hunting and Heritage on Trial," 165–81; and Meyers, "African American Women and Violence," 95–118.

134. ABC News, *Nightline*, June 23, 1999.

135. For more on the news coverage of the rape against women during this war, see A. Jones, *Gender Inclusive*; Kaufman and Williams, *Women, the State, and War*; and MacKinnon, "Rape, Genocide, and Women's Human Rights."

136. Helms, "'Politics is a Whore,'" 252–53. See also Al-Malki, Kaufer, Ishizaki, and Dreher, *Arab Women in Arab News*, 276–304.

137. MSNBC News, *Hardball*, April 10, 2000. See also William A. Wellman, dir., *The Public Enemy* (Burbank, CA: Warner Brothers, 1931).

138. See "New York Senatorial Campaign Debate," C-Span Video Library, September 13, 2000, C-Span, www.c-spanvideo.org/program/159214–1 (accessed October 18, 2011).

139. *CBS Evening News*, September 14, 2000.

140. ABC News, *This Week*, September 17, 2000.

141. *CBS Evening News*, January 19, 2000. Cornelia Ilie makes the point that Clinton was often "held accountable for other people's actions" during the 2008 presidential campaign. See Ilie, "The Gender Divide," 146.

142. See *CBS Evening News*, May 20, 2000. See also Tina Turner, *I, Tina: My Life Story* (New York: HarperCollins, 2010).

143. NBC News, *Today*, September 14, 2000.

144. *NBC Nightly News*, October 8, 2000.

145. Willis C. Newman and Esmeralda Newman, *Domestic Violence: Causes and Cures and Anger Management* (Tacoma, WA: Newman International, 2008), 9.

146. Burke, *A Grammar of Motives*, 407.

147. Fox News, *Hannity & Colmes*, February 25, 2008. Karrin Vasby Anderson portrays the same Fox broadcast as evidence of the ways in which the U.S. news media engaged in a rhetoric of "pornification" in its coverage of Hillary Clinton during the 2008 presidential campaign. See "'Rhymes with Blunt,'" 327–68.

148. See, for example, Matt Lauer of NBC's *Today* show asking if Democratic Party leaders were giving Clinton a "gentle push" to get out of the primary contest. Terry Moran of ABC's *Nightline* suggested that there was "a lot of pushing from party leaders" to encourage Clinton out of the race as the primaries came to a close. See NBC News, *Today*, June 5, 2008; and ABC News, *Nightline*, June 4, 2008.

149. MSNBC News, *The Mitchell Report*, May 28, 2000.

150. NBC News, *Today*, October 28, 2000.

151. Caroli, *First Ladies*, 318.

152. *ABC World News Tonight*, November 8, 2000.

153. *NBC Nightly News*, November 8, 2000.

154. *NBC Nightly News*, November 8, 2000.

155. *CBS Evening News*, December 9, 2000.

156. *ABC World News Tonight*, December 6, 2000.

157. CNN News, *The Point—Greta Van Susteren*, January 3, 2001.

158. *ABC World News Tonight*, December 6, 2000.

Conclusion

1. Fox News, *The Beltway Boys*, May 17, 2008. For more on the rhetoric surrounding Hillary Clinton's exit from the 2008 presidential campaign, see Lawrence and Rose, "Bringing Out the Hook," 870–83.

226 • *Notes to Conclusion*

2. CNN News, *Showbiz Tonight*, June 6, 2008.

3. Joe Klein, "The State of Hillary: A Mixed Record on the Job," *Time*, November 5, 2009, www.time.com/time/magazine/article/0,9171,1935090,00.html (accessed November 10, 2011).

4. B. Anderson, *Imagined Communities*, 6.

5. For more on character and authenticity, see Fischer, *Made in America*; Nehamas, *Virtues of Authenticity*; Pottle, "The Adequacy as Biography," 156; and Trees, *The Founding Fathers*.

6. Casper, *Constructing American Lives*, 87.

7. Clinton, *Living History*, 140.

8. Maria Elizabeth Grabe and Erik Page Bucy talk about the authenticity struggles John Kerry experienced. See *Image Bite Politics*, 131. For a discussion of Mitt Romney's authenticity issues, see Ceaser, Busch, and Pitney, *Epic Journey*, 63.

9. Joel Achenbach, "The Authentic Mitt Romney," *Washington Post*, February 28, 2012, www.washingtonpost.com/blogs/achenblog/post/the-authentic-mitt-romney/2012/02/28/gIQAj5D1fR_blog.html (accessed January 20, 2013).

10. See John B. Alley, in *Reminiscences of Abraham Lincoln by Distinguished Men of His Time,* ed. Allen Thorndike Rice (New York: Haskell House Publishers, 1971), 576.

11. Amber Day offers an interesting discussion of whether the use of "irony, parody, or poking fun" actually promotes cynicism or enhances political engagement. She also discusses the relationship between irony and authenticity. See *Satire and Dissent*, 28, 178–85.

12. See the following for more information on the memorial service image that NBC used across multiple news stories: Kaufer, Parry-Giles, and Klebanov, "The 'Image Bite,'" 336–56.

13. Claudette Guzan Artwick argues that "purposefully misleading the audience" through altering the "image's meaning . . . must not be tolerated." Yet, the notion of what it means to purposefully mislead is likely open to debate across newsrooms. See *Reporting and Producing for Digital Media*, 27.

14. Messaris and Abraham, "The Role of Images," 220.

15. Michael Powell, "Hillary Clinton, the New Ideal: They're Crazy About Her in New York—But What Are We to Make of Her?" *Washington Post*, March 25, 1999, C1.

16. Most physiognomists believed that the inner self functioned as the site of the most authentic self, with the soul serving as the location of the true self. See Hartley, *Physiognomy and the Meaning of Expression*, 33.

17. David Rothkopf, "It's 3 a.m. Do You Know Where Hillary Clinton Is?" *Washington Post*, August 23, 2009, B1.

18. Zelizer, *Covering the Body*, 9.

19. CNN, *Larry King Live*, January 3, 2001.

20. Comedy Central, "The Snuke," *South Park*, March 28, 2007, Southparkstudios .com, www.southparkstudios.com/guide/episodes/s11e04-the-snuke (accessed November 11, 2011).

21. *The Kalb Report*, George Washington Global Media Institute, National Press Club, Joan Shorenstein Center on the Press, Politics and Public Policy, Harvard University's Kennedy School, C-Span Television, November 7, 2011, www.c-span.org/Events/C-SPAN -Event/10737425304/ (accessed November 9, 2011).

22. See, for example, Susan B. Carbon, director, Office on Violence Against Women, "The Increased Importance of the Violence Against Women Act in Times of Economic Crisis," Department of Justice, Statement before the Committee on the Judiciary, U.S. Senate, 2010, www.ovw.usdoj.gov/docs/statement-impt-economic-crisis.pdf (accessed August 26, 2012); and Jeanne Ward and Mendy Marsh, "Brief Paper—Symposium on Sexual Violence in Conflict and Beyond," *Sexual Violence Against Women and Girls in War and Its Aftermath: Realities, Responses, and Required Resources*, United Nations Population Fund, 2006, www.unfpa.org/emergencies/symposium06/docs/finalbrusselsbriefingpaper .pdf (accessed August 26, 2012).

23. Meyers, *News Coverage of Violence against Women*, 14.

24. Vavrus, *Postfeminist News*, 168.

25. Rachel Weiner, "Hillary Clinton's Popularity Reaches Near-Record High," *Washington Post*, March 31, 2011, www.washingtonpost.com/blogs/the-fix/post/hillary -clintons-popularity-reaches-near-record-high/2011/03/31/AFJWTXAC_blog.html (accessed November 12, 2011).

26. CNN, *Anderson Cooper 360 Degrees*, January 25, 2013.

27. Regina G. Lawrence and Melody Rose argue that part of the "negative tone" of Clinton's news coverage stemmed from the "media's constant search for a riveting story," especially during the 2008 campaign, "and from a long-running cycle of press antipathy toward Hillary Clinton, and Clinton antipathy toward the press." See *Hillary Clinton's Race for the White House*, 202.

28. Burns, *First Ladies*, 10.

29. See Burns for a discussion of news media shortcuts (*First Ladies*, 7–11).

30. CNBC News, *Early Today*, July 25, 2001.

31. CNN News, *Saturday Morning News*, September 8, 2001. Bush's congressional testimony had to be rescheduled because the September 11, 2001, terrorist attacks occurred on the same morning as her trip to Capitol Hill.

32. CNN News, *Late Edition with Wolf Blitzer*, May 19, 2002.

33. MSNBC News, *The Chris Matthews Show*, December 12, 2004.

34. *NBC Nightly News*, September 30, 2007. For a story covering Obama's statement in Wisconsin, see "Michelle Obama: 'For the First Time in My Adult Lifetime, I'm Really Proud of My Country,'" ABCNews.com, February 18, 2008, abcnews.go.com/ blogs/politics/2008/02/michelle-obama-1–2/ (accessed September 2, 2012).

35. Fox News, *The O'Reilly Factor*, February 19, 2008.

36. CNN News, *Glenn Beck*, June 11, 2008.

37. CNN News, *Glenn Beck*, June 11, 2008.

38. ABC News, *Good Morning America*, June 15, 2008.

39. CNN News, *Anderson Cooper 360 Degrees*, June 17, 2008.

40. "The Administration: First Lady Michelle Obama," *The White House: President Barack Obama*, www.whitehouse.gov/administration/first-lady-michelle-obama (accessed November 14, 2011). See also Jodi Kantor, "Michelle Obama and the Evolution of a First Lady," *The New York Times*, January 6, 2012, www.nytimes.com/2012/01/07/us/politics/michelle-obamas-evolution-as-first-lady.html?pagewanted=1&nl=todays headlines&emc=tha23 (accessed January 10, 2012); and Kantor, *The Obamas*.

41. "Michelle Obama Popularity Falls," *Washington Examiner*, August 12, 2010, washington examiner.com/blogs/beltway-confidential/michelle-obama-popularity-falls (accessed November 14, 2011). There have been moments when she became a subject of controversy because she took high-priced vacations that some alleged showed a lack of sensitivity to the economic exigencies facing the nation.

42. Jodi Kantor, "Change Comes: After 4 Years, Friends See Shifts in the Obamas," *The New York Times*, January 20, 2013, www.nytimes.com/2013/01/20/us/politics/after-4-years-friends-see-shifts-in-obamas.html?pagewanted=1&_r=0&nl=todays headlines&emc=edit_th_20130120 (accessed January 20, 2013).

43. Jeffrey M. Jones, "Michelle Obama Remains Popular in U.S," *Gallup Politics*, May 30, 2012, www.gallup.com/poll/154952/michelle-obama-remains-popular.aspx (accessed January 25, 2013).

44. See Chamallas, "The Backlash against Feminist Legal Theory," 69–70; and Chunn, Boyd, and Lessard, eds., "Feminism, Law, and Social Change," 6.

45. Gal, "A Semiotics of the Public/Private Distinction," 85.

46. Gal, "A Semiotics of the Public/Private Distinction," 85.

47. For more information on matters of equality in the newsroom, see Liza Gross, "Invisible in the Media," *Empowering Women: Progress or Not, UN Chronicle* 47 (2010): 27–30.

48. Erika Falk maintains that during the 2008 presidential campaign, Clinton "was treated better than the women who preceded her" in vying for the presidency in the following three ways: (1) she received nearly as much coverage as her Democratic primary rival—Barack Obama; (2) her positions on the issues received roughly the same amount of attention as the positions espoused by Obama; and (3) she and Obama received equalized attention in terms of their "physical descriptions." See *Women for President*, 176.

49. Richard Stengel, "On the Road with Hillary Clinton," *Time*, November 7, 2011, 4.

50. "Libya," *Time*, November 7, 2011, 28–33.

51. Lisa Miller, "Hillary Clinton Finally Has Permission to be a Bitch," *NYMAG.COM*, January 24, 2013, nymag.com/thecut/2013/01/hillary-finally-has-permission-to-be -a-bitch.html (accessed January 25, 2013) (emphasis in original).

52. For more on references to Clinton as a "bitch," see K. V. Anderson, "'Rhymes with Rich,'" 599–623.

53. Vivian, *Public Forgetting*, 50.

54. To read a more recent recounting of the struggle for U.S. women's suffrage, see Stillion Southard, *Militant Citizenship*. For an assessment that examines the battle over women's suffrage more globally, see Corrigan, "Cuban Feminism," 131–54.

Bibliography

Aaron, Henry J. *The Problem That Won't Go Away: Reforming U.S. Health Financing*. Washington, DC: Brookings Institution, 1996.

Al-Malki, Amal, David Kaufer, Suguru Ishizaki, and Kira Dreher. *Arab Women in Arab News: Old Stereotypes and New Media*. Doha, Qatar: Bloomsbury, 2012.

Alexander, Karen, and Mary E. Hawkesworth, eds. *War and Terror: Feminist Perspectives*. Chicago: University of Chicago Press, 2008.

Allan, Stuart. "(En)gendering the Truth Politics of News Discourse." In *News, Gender and Power*, edited by Cynthia Carter, Gill Branston, and Stuart Allan, 121–37. London: Routledge, 1998.

Allgor, Catherine. *Parlor Politics: In Which the Ladies of Washington Help Build a City and a Government*. Charlottesville: University Press of Virginia, 2000.

Anderson, Benedict. *Imagined Communities: Reflections on the Origin and Spread of Nationalism*. London: Verso, 1991.

Anderson, Karrin Vasby. "'Rhymes with Rich': 'Bitch' as a Tool of Containment in Contemporary Politics." *Rhetoric & Public Affairs* 2 (1999): 599–623.

———. "From Spouses to Candidates: Hillary Rodham Clinton, Elizabeth Dole, and the Gendered Office of U.S. President." *Rhetoric & Public Affairs* 5 (2002): 105–32.

———. "The First Lady: A Site of 'American Womanhood.'" In *Inventing a Voice: The Rhetoric of American First Ladies of the Twentieth Century*, edited by Molly Meijer Wertheimer. Lanham, MD: Rowman & Littlefield, 2004.

———. "'Rhymes with Blunt': Pornification and U.S. Political Culture." *Rhetoric & Public Affairs* 14 (2011): 327–68.

Anderson, Karrin Vasby, and Kristina Horn Sheeler. *Governing Codes: Gender, Metaphor, and Political Identity*. Lanham, MD: Lexington Books, 2005.

Arendt, Hannah. *The Human Condition*. Chicago: University of Chicago Press, 1958.

Armstrong, Pat. "Restructuring Public and Private: Women's Paid and Unpaid Work." In *Challenging the Public/Private Divide: Feminism, Law, and Public Policy*, edited by Susan B. Boyd, 37–61. Toronto: University of Toronto Press, 1997.

Arthurs, Jane, and Jean Grimshaw, eds. "Introduction." In *Women's Bodies: Discipline and Transgression*, 1–15. London: Cassell, 1999.

Artwick, Claudette Guzan. *Reporting and Producing for Digital Media*. Oxford: Blackwell Publishing, 2004.

Austin, J. L. *How to Do Things with Words*. New York: Oxford University Press, 1965.

Balakrishnan, Gopal, ed. *Mapping the Nation*. London: Verso, 1996.

Barker-Plummer, Bernadette. "News and Feminism: A Historic Dialog." *Journalism and Communication Monographs* 12 (2010): 145–203.

Barry, Ann Marie Seward. *Visual Intelligence: Perception, Image, and Manipulation in Visual Communication*. Albany: State University of New York Press, 1997.

Baruš, Imants. *Authentic Knowing: The Convergence of Science and Spiritual Aspiration*. West Lafayette, IN: Purdue University Press, 1996.

Baudrillard, Jean. *Simulacra and Simulation*. Trans. S. F. Glaser. Ann Arbor: University of Michigan Press, 1994.

Beasley, Maurine, ed. *The White House Press Conferences of Eleanor Roosevelt*. New York: Garland Publishing, 1983.

Beasley, Vanessa B. *You the People: American National Identity in Presidential Rhetoric*. College Station: Texas A&M University Press, 2004.

Bell, Allan. *The Language of News Media*. Oxford: Blackwell, 1991.

Berman, Marshall. *The Politics of Authenticity: Radical Individualism and the Emergence of Modern Society*. New York: Atheneum, 1970.

Bernstein, Carl. *A Woman in Charge: The Life of Hillary Rodham Clinton*. New York: Alfred A. Knopf, 2007.

Beynon, John. *Masculinities and Culture*. Buckingham, UK: Open University Press, 2002.

Bishop, Ronald. *Taking on the Pledge of Allegiance: The News Media and Michael Newdow's Constitutional Challenge*. Albany: State University of New York Press, 2007.

Blair, Diane M. "No Ordinary Time: Eleanor Roosevelt's Address to the 1940 Democratic National Convention." *Rhetoric & Public Affairs* 4 (2001): 203–44.

———. "'We Go Ahead Together or We Go Down Together': The Civil Rights Rhetoric of Eleanor Roosevelt." In *Civil Rights Rhetoric and the American Presidency*, edited by James Arnt Aune and Enrique D. Rigsby, 62–82. College Station: Texas A&M University Press, 2005.

Blom, Ida, Karen Hagemann, and Catherine Hall, eds. *Gendered Nations: Nationalisms and Gender Order in the Long Nineteenth Century*. New York: Oxford University Press, 2000.

Boorstin, Daniel J. *The Image: A Guide to Pseudo-Events in America*. New York: Random House, 1961/1987.

Bourdieu, Pierre. *Language and the Symbolic Power*. Trans. Gino Raymond and Matthew Adamson. Cambridge, MA: Harvard University Press, 1991.

Boys-Stones, George. "Physiognomy and Ancient Psychological Theory." In *Seeing the Face, Seeing the Soul: Poleman's Physiognomy from Classical Antiquity to Medieval Islam*, edited by Simon Swain, 19–124. Oxford: Oxford University Press, 2007.

Braden, Maria. *Women Politicians and the Media*. Lexington: University Press of Kentucky, 1996.

Branch, Taylor. *The Clinton Tapes: Wrestling History with the President*. New York: London, 2009.

Brown, Mary Ellen. "Feminism and Cultural Politics: Television Audiences and Hillary Rodham Clinton." *Political Communication* 14 (1997): 255–70.

Bruner, M. Lane. *Strategies of Remembrance: The Rhetorical Dimensions of National Identity Construction*. Columbia: University of South Carolina Press, 2002.

Buchanan, Bay. *The Extreme Makeover of Hillary (Rodham) Clinton*. Washington, DC: Regnery Publishing, Inc., 2007.

Burke, Kenneth. *A Grammar of Motives*. Berkeley: University of California Press, 1945.

Burns, Lisa M. "Ellen Axson Wilson: A Rhetorical Reassessment of a Forgotten First Lady." In *Inventing a Voice: The Rhetoric of American First Ladies of the Twentieth Century*, edited by Molly Meijer Wertheimer, 79–101. Lanham, MD: Rowman & Littlefield, 2004.

———. *First Ladies and the Fourth Estate: Press Framing of Presidential Wives*. DeKalb: Northern Illinois University Press, 2008.

Burstyn, Varda. *The Rites of Men: Manhood, Politics, and the Culture of Sport*. Toronto: University of Toronto Press, 2000.

Butler, Judith. *Bodies That Matter: On the Discursive Limits of Sex*. New York: Routledge, 1993.

———. *Excitable Speech*. New York: Routledge, 1997.

Bystrom, Dianne G., Mary Christine Banwart, Lynda Lee Kaid, and Terry A. Robertson. *Gender and Candidate Communication: VideoStyle, WebStyle, and NewsStyle*. New York: Routledge, 2004.

Cameron, Deborah. *On Language and Sexual Politics*. London: Palgrave, 2006.

Campbell, John Angus. "Between the Fragment and the Icon: Prospect for a Rhetorical House of the Middle Way." *Western Journal of Communication* 54 (1990): 346–76.

Campbell, Karlyn Kohrs. "The Rhetorical Presidency: A Two-Person Career." In *Beyond the Rhetorical Presidency*, edited by Martin J. Medhurst, 179–95. College Station: Texas A&M University Press, 1996.

———. "The Discursive Performance of Femininity: Hating Hillary." *Rhetoric & Public Affairs* 1 (1998): 1–19.

Cardoso, Gustavo. *The Media in the Network Society: Browsing, News, Filters and Citizenship*. Lisbon, Portugal: Centre for Research and Studies in Sociology, 2006.

Carlin, Diana B., and Kelly L. Winfrey. "Have You Come a Long Way, Baby? Hillary Clinton, Sarah Palin, and Sexism in 2008 Campaign Coverage." *Communication Studies* 60 (2009): 326–43.

Carman, Taylor. *Heidegger's Analytic: Interpretation, Discourse, and Authenticity in "Being and Time."* Cambridge: Cambridge University Press, 2003.

Caroli, Betty Boyd. *First Ladies: From Martha Washington to Michelle Obama*. Oxford: Oxford University Press, 2010.

Carter, Cynthia, Gill Branston, and Stuart Allan, eds. *News, Gender and Power*. London: Routledge, 1998.

Casper, Scott E. *Constructing American Lives: Biography and Culture in Nineteenth-Century America*. Chapel Hill: University of North Carolina Press, 1999.

Ceaser, James W., Andrew E. Busch, and John J. Pitney Jr. *Epic Journey: The 2008 Elections and American Politics*. Lanham, MD: Rowman & Littlefield Publishers, 2009.

Chamallas, Martha. "The Backlash against Feminist Legal Theory." In *Theorizing Backlash: Philosophical Reflections on the Resistance to Feminism*, edited by Anita M. Superson and Ann E. Cudd, 67–87. Lanham, MD: Rowman & Littlefield Publishers, 2002.

Chunn, Dorothy E., Susan B. Boyd, and Hester Lessard, eds. "Feminism, Law, and Social Change: An Overview." In *Reaction and Resistance: Feminism, Law, and Social Change*, 1–28. Vancouver: University of British Columbia Press, 2007.

Clark, Allan C. *Life and Letters of Dolly Madison*. Washington, DC: Press of W. F. Roberts Company, 1914.

Clinton, Hillary Rodham. *Living History*. New York: Simon & Schuster, 2003.

Cloud, Dana L. "The First Lady's Privates: Queering Eleanor Roosevelt for Public Address Studies." In *Queering Public Address: Sexualities in American Historical Discourse*, edited by Charles E. Morris III, 23–44. Columbia: University of South Carolina Press, 2007.

Condit, Celeste Michelle. "Hegemony in a Mass-mediated Society: Concordance about Reproductive Technologies." *Critical Studies in Mass Communication* 11 (1994): 205–30.

Connell, R. W. *Masculinities*. Berkeley: University of California Press, 1995.

Conway, Alison. *Private Interests: Women, Portraiture, and the Visual Culture of the English Novel, 1709–1791*. Toronto: University of Toronto Press, 2001.

Corrigan, Lisa M. "Cuban Feminism: From Suffrage to Exile, 1898–2003." *Advances in the History of Rhetoric* 8 (2006): 131–54.

Crouse, Timothy. *The Boys on the Bus*. New York: Ballantine Books, 1972.

Dawes, James. *The Language of War: Literature and Culture in the U.S. from the Civil War through World War II*. Cambridge, MA: Harvard University Press, 2002.

Day, Amber. *Satire and Dissent: Interventions in Contemporary Political Debate*. Bloomington: Indiana University Press, 2011.

Deem, Melissa. "Scandal, Heteronormative Culture, and the Disciplining of Feminism." *Critical Studies in Mass Communication* 16 (1999): 86–93.

D'Emilio, John, and Estelle B. Freedman. *Intimate Matters: A History of Sexuality in America*, 2nd ed. Chicago: University of Chicago Press, 1997.

Denton, Robert E., Jr., ed. *Studies of Identity in the 2008 Presidential Campaign*. Lanham, MD: Rowman & Littlefield Publishers, 2010.

DePauw, Linda Grant, Conover Hunt-Jones, and Miriam Schneir. *Remember the Ladies: Women in America, 1750–1815*. New York: Viking Press, 1976.

Dershowitz, Alan M. *America on Trial: Inside the Legal Battles That Transformed Our Nation.* New York: Warner Books, 2004.

Dickinson, Greg, and Karris Vasby Anderson. "Fallen: O.J. Simpson, Hillary Rodham Clinton, and the Re-Centering of White Patriarchy." *Communication and Critical/Cultural Studies* 3 (2004): 271–96.

Domosh, Mona, and Joni Seager. *Putting Women in Place: Feminist Geographers Make Sense of the World.* New York: Guilford Press, 2001.

Dorsey, Leroy G. *We are All Americans Pure and Simple: Theodore Roosevelt and the Myth of Americanism.* Tuscaloosa: University of Alabama Press, 2007.

Douglas, Susan J. *Where the Girls Are: Growing Up Female with the Mass Media.* New York: Three Rivers Press, 1994/1995.

Dow, Bonnie J. *Prime-Time Feminism: Television, Media Culture, and the Women's Movement since 1970.* Philadelphia: University of Pennsylvania Press, 1996.

Drew, Julie, William Lyons, and Lance Svehla. *Sound-Bite Saboteurs: Public Discourse, Education, and the State of Democratic Deliberation.* Albany: State University of New York Press, 2010.

Dudink, Stefan, Karen Hagemann, and John Tosh, eds. *Masculinities in Politics and War: Gendering Modern History.* Manchester: Manchester University Press, 2004.

Eberly, Don E., ed. "The Quest for America's Character." In *The Content of America's Character: Recovering Civic Virtue,* 3–24. Lanham, MD: Madison Books, 1995.

Edelman, Murray. *Political Language: Words That Succeed and Policies That Fail.* Orlando: Academic Press, Inc., 1977.

———. *Constructing the Political Spectacle.* Chicago: University of Chicago Press, 1988.

Eley, Geoff, and Ronald Grigor Suny, eds. *Becoming National: A Reader.* New York: Oxford University Press, 1996.

Enloe, Cynthia. *The Morning After: Sexual Politics at the End of the Cold War.* Berkeley: University of California Press, 1993.

Entman, Robert M. "Framing: Toward Clarification of a Fractured Paradigm." *Journal of Communication* 43 (1993): 51–58.

Entman, Robert M., and Susan Herbst. "Reframing Public Opinion as We Have Known It." In *Mediated Politics: Communication in the Future of Democracy,* edited by W. Lance Bennett and Robert M. Entman, 203–25. Cambridge: Cambridge University Press, 2001.

Entman, Robert M., and Andrew Rojecki. *The Black Image in the White Mind: Media and Race in America.* Chicago: University of Chicago Press, 2000.

Etzioni, Amitai. *The Active Society: A Theory of Social and Political Processes.* New York: The Free Press, 1968.

Faderman, Lillian. *Odd Girls and Twilight Lovers: A History of Lesbian Life in Twentieth-Century America.* New York: Columbia University Press, 1991.

Falk, Erika. "Gender Bias and Maintenance: The Press Coverage of Senator Hillary Clinton's Announcement to Seek the White House." In *Gender and Political Communication in America: Rhetoric, Representation, and Display,* edited by Janis L. Edwards, 219–31. Lanham, MD: Lexington Books, 2009.

——. *Women for President: Media Bias in Nine Campaigns*. 2nd ed. Urbana: University of Illinois Press, 2010.

Faludi, Susan. *Backlash: The Undeclared War against American Women*. New York: Anchor Books, 1991.

Ferrara, Alessandro. *Modernity and Authenticity: A Study of the Social and Ethical Thought of Jean-Jacques Rousseau*. Albany: State University of New York Press, 1993.

——. *Reflective Authenticity: Rethinking the Project of Modernity*. London: Routledge, 1998.

Finnegan, Cara A. "Recognizing Lincoln: Image Vernaculars in Nineteenth-Century Visual Culture." *Rhetoric & Public Affairs* 9 (2005): 31–58.

Fischer, Claude S. *Made in America: A Social History of American Culture and Character*. Chicago: University of Chicago Press, 2010.

Fiske, John. *Television Culture*. London: Methuen, 1987.

——. *Media Matters: Everyday Culture and Political Change*. Minneapolis: University of Minnesota Press, 1996.

Flinn, Susan K. *Speaking of Hillary: A Reader's Guide to the Most Controversial Woman in America*. Ashland, OR: White Cloud Press, 2000.

Forbes, H. D. "Rousseau, Ethnicity, and Difference." In *The Legacy of Rousseau*, edited by Clifford Orwin and Nathan Tarcov, 220–45. Chicago: University of Chicago Press, 1997.

Foucault, Michel. *Discipline and Punish: The Birth of the Prison*. Trans. Alan Sheridan. New York: Vintage Books, 1975/1977.

Fowler, Roger. *Language in the News: Discourse and Ideology in the Press*. London: Routledge, 1991.

Furman, Bess. *Washington Byline: The Personal History of a Newspaperwoman*. New York: Alfred A. Knopf, 1949.

——. *White House Profile: A Social History of the White House, Its Occupants and Its Festivities*. Indianapolis: Bobbs-Merrill, 1951.

Gal, Susan. "A Semiotics of the Public/Private Distinction." *differences* 13 (2002): 77–95.

Gerth, Jeff, and Don Van Natta Jr. *Her Way: The Hopes and Ambitions of Hillary Rodham Clinton*. New York: Little, Brown and Company, 2007.

Giesberg, Judith Ann. *Civil War Sisterhood: The U.S. Sanitary Commission and Women's Politics in Transition*. Boston: Northeastern University Press, 2000.

Gilbert, Melissa R. "Identity, Space, and Politics: A Critique of the Poverty Debates." In *Thresholds in Feminist Geography: Difference, Methodology, Representation*, edited by John Paul Jones III, Heidi J. Nast, and Susan M. Roberts, 29–45. Lanham, MD: Rowman & Littlefield Publishers, 1997.

Ginzberg, Lori D. *Women and the Work of Benevolence: Morality, Politics, and Class in the Nineteenth-Century United States*. New Haven, CT: Yale University Press, 1990.

Gitlin, Todd. *The Whole World is Watching: Mass Media in the Making and Unmaking of the New Left*. Berkeley: University of California Press, 1980.

Goffman, Erving. *Frame Analysis: An Essay on the Organization of Experience*. New York: Harper & Row, 1974.

Goldman, Perry M. "Political Virtue in the Age of Jackson." *Political Science Quarterly* 87 (1972): 46–62.

Golomb, Jacob. *In Search of Authenticity: From Kierkegaard to Camus*. London: Routledge, 1995.

Gorham, Eric B. *National Service, Citizenship, and Political Education*. Albany: State University of New York Press, 1992.

Gormley, Ken. *The Death of American Virtue: Clinton vs. Starr*. New York: Crown Publishers, 2010.

Gould, Lewis L., ed. "Hillary Rodham Clinton (1947-), First Lady: 1993- ." In *American First Ladies: Their Lives and Their Legacy*, 632–48. New York: Garland, 1996.

Grabe, Maria Elizabeth, and Erik Page Bucy. *Image Bite Politics: News and the Visual Framing of Elections*. New York: Oxford University Press, 2009.

Green, Constance McLaughlin. *Washington: A History of the Capital, 1800–1950*. Princeton, NJ: Princeton University Press, 1962.

Greenberg, David. *Nixon's Shadow: The History of an Image*. New York: W. W. Norton, 2003.

Grossberg, Lawrence, ed. "On Postmodernism and Articulation: An Interview with Stuart Hall." *Journal of Communication Inquiry* 10 (1986): 45–60.

Gutgold, Nichola D. *Almost Madam President: Why Hillary Clinton "Won" in 2008*. Lanham, MD: Lexington Books, 2009.

Gutin, Myra G. *The President's Partner: The First Lady in the Twentieth Century*. New York: Praeger/Greenwood, 1989.

Hall, Stuart. *Representation: Cultural Representations and Signifying Practices*. London: Sage, 1997/2003.

Halley, Patrick S. *On the Road with Hillary: A Behind-the-Scenes Look at the Journey from Arkansas to the U.S. Senate*. New York: Viking, 2002.

Hallin, Daniel C. *We Keep America on Top of the World: Television Journalism and the Public Sphere*. London: Routledge, 1994.

Hardesty, Nancy. *Women Called to Witness: Evangelical Feminism in the Nineteenth Century*. 2nd ed. Knoxville: University of Tennessee Press, 1999.

Hardt, Hanno. "Authenticity, Communication, and Critical Theory." *Critical Studies in Mass Communication* 10 (1993): 49–69.

Harpaz, Beth J. *The Girls in the Van: A Reporter's Diary of the Campaign Trail*. New York: Thomas Dunne Books, 2001.

Hart, Roderick P. *The Sound of Leadership: Presidential Communication in the Modern Age*. Chicago: University of Chicago Press, 1987.

Hart, Roderick P., Sharon E. Jarvis, William P. Jennings, and Deborah Smith-Howell. *Political Keywords: Using Language That Uses Us*. New York: Oxford University Press, 2005.

Hartley, Lucy. *Physiognomy and the Meaning of Expression in Nineteenth-Century Culture*. Cambridge: Cambridge University Press, 2001.

Hayes, Lindsay. "Congressional Widowhood and Gubernatorial Surrogacy: A Rhetorical History of Women's Distinct Paths to Public Office." PhD diss. Department of Communication, University of Maryland, 2013.

Heidegger, Martin. *Being and Time*. Trans. Joan Stambaugh. Albany: State University of New York Press, 1953/1996.

Helms, Elissa. "'Politics is a Whore': Women, Morality and Victimhood in Post-War Bosnia-Herzegovina." In *The New Bosnian Mosaic: Identities, Memories and Moral Claims in a Post-War Society*, edited by Xavier Bougarel, Elissa Helms, and Gerlachlus Duijzings, 235–72. Burlington, VT: Ashgate Publishing, 2007.

Holloway, Laura C. *The Ladies of the White House*. New York: U.S. Publishing Co., 1870.

hooks, bell. *Feminism is for Everybody: Passionate Politics*. London: Pluto Press, 2000.

Hume, Richard L., and Jerry B. Gough. *Blacks, Carpetbaggers, and Scalawags: The Constitutional Conventions of Radical Reconstruction*. Baton Rouge: Louisiana State University Press, 2008.

Ilie, Cornelia. "The Gender Divide in Election Campaign Interviews: Questioning Barack Obama and Calling into Question Hillary Clinton." *Redescriptions: Yearbook of Political Thought, Conceptual History and Feminist Theory* 15 (2011): 125–46.

Ingraham, Laura. *The Hillary Trap: Looking for Power in all the Wrong Places*. San Francisco: Encounter Books, 2000.

Jamieson, Kathleen Hall. *Beyond the Double Bind: Women and Leadership*. Oxford: Oxford University Press, 1995.

Jamieson, Kathleen Hall, and Paul Waldman. *The Press Effect: Politicians, Journalists, and the Stories That Shape the Political World*. New York: Oxford University Press, 2003.

Johnson, Nan. *Gender and Rhetorical Space in American Life, 1866–1910*. Carbondale: Southern Illinois University Press, 2002.

Jones, Adam. *Gender Inclusive: Essays on Violence, Men and Feminist International Relations*. New York: Routledge, 2009.

Jones, John Paul, III, Heidi J. Nast, and Susan M. Roberts, eds. *Thresholds in Feminist Geography: Difference, Methodology, Representation*. Lanham, MD: Rowman & Littlefield Publishers, 1997.

Kantor, Jodi. *The Obamas*. New York: Little, Brown & Company, 2012.

Kaufer, David S., and Brian S. Butler. *Rhetoric and the Arts of Design*. Mahwah, NJ: Lawrence Erlbaum Associates, 1996.

———. *Designing Interactive Worlds with Words: Principles of Writing as Representational Composition*. Mahwah, NJ: Lawrence Erlbaum Associates, Publishers, 2000.

Kaufer, David S., Shawn J. Parry-Giles, and Beata Beigman Klebanov. "The 'Image Bite,' Political Language, and the Public/Private Divide: NBC News Coverage of Hillary Clinton from Scorned Wife to Senate Candidate." *Journal of Language and Politics* 11 (2012): 336–56.

Kaufman, Joyce P., and Kristen P. Williams. *Women, the State, and War: A Comparative Perspective on Citizenship and Nationalism*. Lanham, MD: Lexington Books, 2007.

Kelley, Colleen Elizabeth. *The Rhetoric of First Lady Hillary Rodham Clinton: Crisis Management Discourse*. Westport, CT: Praeger, 2001.

Kerber, Linda K. *Women of the Republic: Intellect & Ideology in Revolutionary America*. Chapel Hill: University of North Carolina Press, 1980.

————. *No Constitutional Rights to be Ladies: Women and the Obligations of Citizenship*. New York: Hill and Wang, 1998.

Kersh, Rogan. *Dreams of a More Perfect Union*. Ithaca, NY: Cornell University Press, 2001.

Khan, Kherstin, and Diane M. Blair. "Writing Bill Clinton: Mediated Discourses on Hegemonic Masculinity and the 2008 Presidential Primary." *Women's Studies in Communication* 36 (2013): 56–71.

Kitch, Carolyn. *The Girl on the Magazine Cover: The Origins of Visual Stereotypes in American Mass Media*. Chapel Hill: University of North Carolina Press, 2001.

Lakoff, Robin Tolmach. *The Language War*. Berkeley: University of California Press, 2000.

Landes, Joan B. "Further Thoughts on the Public/Private Distinction." *Journal of Women's History* 15 (2003): 28–39.

Lash, Joseph P. *Eleanor and Franklin*. New York: W. W. Norton & Company, 1971.

Lawrence, Regina G., and Melody Rose. *Hillary Clinton's Race for the White House: Gender Politics and the Media on the Campaign Trail*. Boulder, CO: Lynne Rienner Publishers, 2010.

————. "Bringing Out the Hook: Exit Talk in Media Coverage of Hillary Clinton and Past Presidential Campaigns." *Political Research Quarterly* 64 (2011): 870–83.

Laws, Glenda. "Women's Life Courses, Spatial Mobility, and State Policies." In *Thresholds in Feminist Geography: Difference, Methodology, Representation*, edited by John Paul Jones III, Heidi J. Nast, and Susan M. Roberts, 47–64. Lanham, MD: Rowman & Littlefield Publishers, 1997.

Lazar, Michelle M., ed. "Performing State Fatherhood: The Remaking of Hegemony." In *Feminist Critical Discourse Analysis: Gender, Power and Ideology in Discourse*, 139–63. New York: Palgrave Macmillan, 2005.

————. "Politicizing Gender in Discourse: Feminist Critical Discourse Analysis as Political Perspective and Praxis." In *Feminist Critical Discourse Analysis: Gender, Power and Ideology in Discourse*, 1–28. New York: Palgrave Macmillan, 2005.

Limbacher, Carl. *Hillary's Scheme: Inside the Next Clinton's Ruthless Agenda to Take the White House*. New York: Crown Forum, 2003.

López, Ian F. Haney. *White by Law: The Legal Construction of Race*. New York: New York University Press, 1996.

Lukasik, Christopher J. *Discerning Characters: The Culture of Appearance in Early America*. Philadelphia: University of Pennsylvania Press, 2011.

MacIntyre, Alasdair. *After Virtue: A Study in Moral Theory*. 2nd ed. Notre Dame, IN: University of Notre Dame Press, 1981/1984.

MacKinnon, Catharine A. *Only Words*. Cambridge, MA: Harvard University Press, 1993.

————. "Rape, Genocide, and Women's Human Rights." In *Mass Rape: The War against Women in Bosnia-Herzegovina*, edited by Alexandra Stiglmayer and translated by Marion Faber, 183–96. Lincoln: University of Nebraska Press, 1994.

Marshall, P. David. *Celebrity and Power: Fame in Contemporary Culture*. Minneapolis: University of Minnesota Press, 1997.

Marshall, Susan E. *Splintered Sisterhood: Gender and Class in the Campaign against Woman Suffrage*. Madison: University of Wisconsin Press, 1997.

Marx, Anthony W. *Making Race and Nation: A Comparison of South Africa, the United States, and Brazil*. Cambridge: Cambridge University Press, 1998.

Matthews, Glenna. *The Rise of Public Woman: Woman's Power and Woman's Place in the United States, 1630–1970*. New York: Oxford University Press, 1992.

May, Elaine Tyler. *Homeward Bound: American Families in the Cold War Era*. New York: Basic Books, 1996.

Mayer, Tamar, ed. *Gender Ironies of Nationalism: Sexing the Nation*. London: Routledge, 2000.

McClintock, Anne, Aamir Mufti, and Ella Shohat, eds. *Dangerous Liaisons: Gender, Nation, & Postcolonial Perspectives*. Minneapolis: University of Minnesota Press, 1997.

McDowell, Linda. "Spatializing Feminism: Geographic Perspectives." In *Body Space: Destabilizing Geographies of Gender and Sexuality*, edited by Nancy Duncan, 28–44. Routledge: London, 1996.

———. *Gender, Identity, and Place: Understanding Feminist Geographies*. Minneapolis: University of Minnesota Press, 1999.

McKinney, Mitchell S., and Mary C. Banwart, eds. *Communication in the 2008 U.S. Election: Digital Natives Elect a President*. New York: Peter Lang Publishing, 2010.

McKinney, Mitchell S., Corey B. Davis, and Jeffery Delbert. "The First—and Last—Woman Standing: Hillary Rodham Clinton's Presidential Primary Debate Performance." In *Cracked but Not Shattered: Hillary Rodham Clinton's Unsuccessful Campaign for the Presidency*, edited by Theodore F. Sheckels, 125–47. Lanham, MD: Rowman & Littlefield Publishers, 2009.

Means, Marianne. *The Woman in the White House: The Lives, Times, and Influence of Twelve Notable First Ladies*. New York: Random House, 1962.

Messaris, Paul. *Visual Literacy: Images, Mind, and Reality.* Boulder, CO: Westview, 1994.

———. "'Visual Manipulation': Visual Means of Affecting Responses to Images." *Communication* 13 (1994): 181–95.

Messaris, Paul, and Linus Abraham. "The Role of Images in Framing News Stories." In *Framing Public Life: Perspectives on Media and Our Understanding of the Social World*, edited by Stephen D. Reese, Oscar H. Gandy Jr., and August E. Grant, 215–26. Mahwah, NJ: Lawrence Erlbaum Associates, 2003.

Meyers, Marian. *News Coverage of Violence against Women: Engendering Blame*. Newbury Park, CA: Sage, 1997.

———. "African American Women and Violence: Gender, Race, and Class in the News." *Critical Studies in Media Communication* 21 (2004): 95–118.

Meyrowitz, Joshua. *No Sense of Place: The Impact of Electronic Media on Social Behavior*. New York: Oxford University Press, 1985.

Mitchell, W. J. T. *Picture Theory: Essays on Verbal and Visual Representation*. Chicago: University of Chicago Press, 1994.

Morrison, Susan, ed. *Thirty Ways of Looking at Hillary: Reflections by Women Writers*. New York: HarperCollins Publishers, 2008.

Morse, Margaret. "The Television News Personality and Credibility: Reflections on the News in Transition." In *Studies in Entertainment: Critical Approaches to Mass Culture*, edited by Tania Modleski, 55–79. Bloomington: Indiana University Press, 1986.

Mosse, George L. *Nationalism and Sexuality: Respectability and Abnormal Sexuality in Modern Europe*. New York: Howard Fertig, 1985.

Mostov, Julie. "Sexing the Nation/Desexing the Body: Politics of National Identity in the Former Yugoslavia." In *Gender Ironies of Nationalism: Sexing the Nation*, edited by Tamar Mayer, 89–110. London: Routledge, 2000.

Nehamas, Alexander. *Virtues of Authenticity: Essays on Plato and Socrates*. Princeton, NJ: Princeton University Press, 1999.

Nelson, Anson, and Fanny Nelson, *Memorials of Sarah Childress Polk: Wife of the Eleventh President of the United States*. New York: Anson D. F. Randolph and Company, 1892.

Nelson, John S., and G. R. Boynton. *Video Rhetorics: Televised Advertising in American Politics*. Urbana: University of Illinois Press, 1997.

Norris, Pippa, Montague Kern, and Marion Just, eds. *Framing Terrorism: The News Media, the Government, and the Public*. New York: Routledge, 2003.

Offen, Karen. "Defining Feminism: A Comparative Historical Approach." *Signs* 14 (1988): 119–57.

Orvell, Miles. *The Real Thing: Imitation and Authenticity in American Culture, 1880–1940*. Chapel Hill: University of North Carolina Press, 1989.

Palczewski, Catherine H. "The Male Madonna and the Feminine Uncle Sam: Visual Argument, Icons, and Ideographs in 1909 Anti-Woman Suffrage Postcards." *Quarterly Journal of Speech* 91 (2005): 365–94.

Parry-Giles, Shawn J. "Mediating Hillary Rodham Clinton: Television News Practices and Image-Making in the Postmodern Age." *Critical Studies in Media Communication* 17 (2000): 205–26.

——. "Political Authenticity, Television News, and Hillary Rodham Clinton." In *Politics, Discourse and American Society: New Agendas*, edited by Roderick P. Hart and Bartholomew H. Sparrow, 211–27. Lanham, MD: Rowman & Littlefield Publishers, 2001.

——. "John F. Kerry: Speech before the U.S. Senate Committee on Foreign Relations" (1971). *Voices of Democracy* [on-line journal] 2 (2007): 99–125, voicesofdemocracy.umd.edu/.

——. "Constituting Presidentiality and U.S. Citizenship in Campaign 2004: Nascar Dads, Security Moms, and Single Women Voters." In *Rhetoric and Democracy: Pedagogical and Political Practices*, edited by David Timmerman and Todd McDorman, 139–79. East Lansing: Michigan State University Press, 2008.

Parry-Giles, Shawn J., and Diane M. Blair. "The Rise of the Rhetorical First Lady: Politics, Gender Ideology, and Women's Voice, 1789–2002." *Rhetoric & Public Affairs* 5 (2002): 565–99.

Parry-Giles, Shawn J., and David S. Kaufer. "Lincoln Reminiscences and Nineteenth-Century Portraiture: The Private Virtues of Presidential Character." *Rhetoric & Public Affairs* 15 (2012): 199–234.

Parry-Giles, Shawn J., and Trevor Parry-Giles. "Meta-Imaging, *The War Room*, and the Hyperreality of U.S. Politics." *Journal of Communication* 49 (1999): 28–45.

———. *Constructing Clinton: Hyperreality and Presidential Image-Making in Postmodern Politics*. New York: Peter Lang Publishing, 2002.

Parry-Giles, Trevor, and Shawn J. Parry-Giles. *The Prime-Time Presidency: The West Wing and U.S. Nationalism*. Urbana: University of Illinois Press, 2006.

Pickering, Jean, and Suzanne Kehde. *Narratives of Nostalgia, Gender, and Nationalism*. New York: New York University Press, 1997.

Pope, John Pope. "Elizabeth Ann (Betty) Bloomer Ford." In *American First Ladies: Their Lives and Their Legacy*, 2nd ed., edited by Lewis L Gould, 363–76. New York: Routledge, 2001.

Posner, Richard A. *An Affair of State: The Investigation, Impeachment, and Trial of President Clinton*. Cambridge, MA: Harvard University Press, 1999.

Pottle, Frederick A. "The Adequacy as Biography of Boswell's *Life of Johnson*." In *Boswell's Life of Johnson: New Questions, New Answers*, edited by John A. Vance, 147–60. Athens: University of Georgia Press, 1985.

Radcliffe, Donnie. *Hillary Rodham Clinton: A First Lady for Our Time*. New York: Warner Books, 1993.

Rivers, Christopher. *Face Value: Physiognomical Thought and the Legible Body in Marivaux, Lavater, Balzac, Gautier, and Zola*. Madison: University of Wisconsin Press, 1994.

Roberts, John B., II. *Rating the First Ladies: The Women Who Influenced the Presidency*. New York: Citadel Press Books, 2003.

Roosevelt, Eleanor. *My Day: The Best of Eleanor Roosevelt's Acclaimed Newspaper Columns, 1936–1962*. Ed. David Emblidge. Boston: Da Capo Press, 2001.

Rose, Gillian. *Feminism and Geography: The Limits of Geographical Knowledge*. Minneapolis: University of Minnesota Press, 1993.

Ross, Karen, and Annabelle Sreberny-Mohammadi. "Playing House—Gender, Politics and the News Media in Britain." *Media, Culture & Society* 19 (1997): 101–9.

Rossinow, Doug. *The Politics of Authenticity: Liberalism, Christianity, and the New Left in America*. New York: Columbia University Press, 1998.

Rousseau, Jean-Jacques. *Politics and the Arts*. Trans. Allan Bloom. Glencoe, IL: The Free Press, 1960.

Ryan, Mary P. "Gender and Public Access: Women's Politics in Nineteenth-Century America." In *Habermas and the Public Sphere*, edited by Craig Calhoun, 259–88. Cambridge, MA: MIT Press, 1992.

Samek, Alyssa A. "Political Skin: (Un)Covering the Presidential Candidates." *Feminist Media Studies* 8 (2008): 426–30.

Samuels, Shirley. *Romances of the Republic: Women, the Family, and Violence in the Literature of the Early American Nation*. New York: Oxford University Press, 1996.

Scheufele, Bertram. "Frames, Schemata, and News Reporting." *Communications* 32 (2006): 65–83.

Schwartz, Barry. "The Character of Washington: A Study in Republican Culture." *American Quarterly* 38 (1986): 202–22.

Scott, Anne Firor. *Making the Invisible Woman Visible.* Urbana: University of Illinois Press, 1984.

Sheckels, Theodore F., ed. *Cracked But Not Shattered: Hillary Rodham Clinton's Unsuccessful Campaign for the Presidency.* Lanham, MD: Lexington Books, 2009.

Sigelman, Lee. "There You Go Again: The Media and the Debasement of American Politics." *Communication Monographs* 59 (1992): 407–10.

Sims, Anastatia. *The Power of Femininity in the New South: Women's Organizations and Politics in North Carolina, 1880–1930.* Columbia: University of South Carolina Press, 1997.

Sloop, John M. *Disciplining Gender: Rhetorics of Sex Identity in Contemporary U.S. Culture.* Amherst: University of Massachusetts Press, 2004.

Smith, Sally Bedell. *For Love of Politics: Bill and Hillary Clinton: The White House Years.* New York: Random House, 2007.

Smith-Rosenberg, Carroll. "Political Camp or the Ambiguous Engendering of the American Republic." In *Gendered Nations: Nationalisms and Gender Order in the Long Nineteenth Century*, edited by Ida Blom, Karen Hagemann, and Catherine Hall, 271–92. Oxford: Berg, 2000.

Starr, Paul. *The Creation of the Media: Political Origins of Modern Communications.* New York: Basic Books, 2004.

Stephens, Mitchell. *The Rise of the Image, the Fall of the Word.* New York: Oxford University Press, 1998.

Stillion Southard, Belinda A. *Militant Citizenship: Rhetorical Strategies of the National Women's Party, 1913–1920.* College Station: Texas A&M University Press, 2011.

Stocker, Richard Dimsdale. *Physiognomy: Ancient and Modern or Phreno-Metoposcopy.* London: Simpkin, Marshall, Hamilton, Kent and Co., 1900.

Taylor, Charles. *The Ethics of Authenticity.* Cambridge, MA: Harvard University Press, 1992.

Theriot, Nancy M. *Mothers and Daughters in Nineteenth Century America: The Biosocial Construction of Femininity.* Lexington: University of Kentucky Press, 1996.

Thurow, Glen E. "Dimensions of Presidential Character." In *Beyond the Rhetorical Presidency*, edited by Martin J. Medhurst, 15–29. College Station: Texas A&M University Press, 1996.

Tickner, J. Ann. *Gendering World Politics: Issues and Approaches in the Post–Cold War Era.* New York: Columbia University Press, 2001.

Tomasky, Michael. *Hillary's Turn: Inside Her Improbable, Victorious Senate Campaign.* New York: The Free Press, 2001.

Tonn, Mari Boor, Valerie A. Endress, and John N. Diamond. "Hunting and Heritage on Trial: A Dramatistic Debate over Tragedy, Tradition, and Territory." *Quarterly Journal of Speech* 79 (1993): 165–81.

Trachtenberg, Alan. *Lincoln's Smile and Other Enigmas*. New York: Hill and Wang, 2007.

Traister, Rebecca. *Big Girls Don't Cry: The Election That Changed Everything for American Women*. New York: The Free Press, 2010.

Trees, Andrew S. *The Founding Fathers and the Politics of Character*. Princeton, NJ: Princeton University Press, 2004.

Trilling, Lionel. *Sincerity and Authenticity*. Cambridge, MA: Harvard University Press, 1971.

Troy, Gil. *Mr. and Mrs. President: From the Trumans to the Clintons*. 2nd ed. Lawrence: University Press of Kansas, 2000.

——. *Hillary Rodham Clinton: Polarizing First Lady*. Lawrence: University Press of Kansas, 2006.

——. *Affairs of State: The Rise and Rejection of the Presidential Couple since World War II*. New York: The Free Press, 2007.

Twigg, Reginald. "The Performative Dimension of Surveillance: Jacob Riis' *How the Other Half Lives*." *Text and Performance Quarterly* 12 (1992): 305–28.

Vavrus, Mary Douglas. "Working the Senate from the Outside In: The Mediated Construction of a Feminist Political Campaign." *Critical Studies in Mass Communication* 15 (1998): 213–35.

——. *Postfeminist News: Political Women in Media Culture*. Albany: State University of New York Press, 2002.

Vivian, Bradford. *Public Forgetting: The Rhetoric and Politics of Beginning Again*. University Park: Pennsylvania State University Press, 2010.

Waldstreicher, David. *In the Midst of Perpetual Fetes: The Making of American Nationalism, 1776–1820*. Chapel Hill: University of North Carolina Press, 1997.

Walhout, M. D. "The Liberal Saint: American Liberalism and the Problem of Character." In *There before Us: Religion, Literature, and Culture from Emerson to Wendell Berry*, edited by Roger Lundin, 172–93. Grand Rapids, MI: William B. Eerdmans Publishing Company, 2007.

Walsh, Clare. *Gender and Discourse: Language and Power in Politics, the Church and Organisations*. Harlow, England: Pearson Education, 2001.

Ward, Harry M. *The War for Independence and the Transformation of American Society*. London: UCL Press, 1999.

Warner, Judith. *Hillary Clinton: The Inside Story*. New York: A Signet Book, 1993/1999.

Watson, Robert P. *The Presidents' Wives: Reassessing the Office of First Lady*. Boulder, CO: Lynne Rienner Publishers, 2000.

Welter, Barbara. "The Cult of True Womanhood: 1820–1860." *American Quarterly* 18 (1966): 151–74.

Werbner, Pnina. "Political Motherhood and the Feminisation of Citizenship: Women's Activisms and the Transformation of the Public Sphere." In *Women, Citizenship, and Difference*, edited by Nira Yuval-Davis and Pnina Webner, 221–45. London: Zed Books, 1999.

Wertheimer, Molly Meijer, ed. *Inventing a Voice: The Rhetoric of American First Ladies of the Twentieth Century*. Lanham, MD: Rowman & Littlefield, 2004.

West, Guida, and Rhoda Lois Blumberg, eds. "Reconstructing Social Protest from a Feminist Perspective." In *Women and Social Protest*, 3–35. New York: Oxford University Press, 1990.

Williams, Susan S. *Confounding Images: Photography and Portraiture in Antebellum American Fiction*. Philadelphia: University of Pennsylvania Press, 1997.

Winfield, Betty Houchin. "Introductory Note." *Political Communication* 14 (1997): 221–24.

———. "The Making of an Image: Hillary Rodham Clinton and American Journalists." *Political Communication* 14 (1997): 241–53.

Witt, Linda, Karen M. Paget, and Glenna Matthews. *Running as a Woman: Gender and Power in American Politics*. New York: The Free Press, 1995.

Yarbrough, Jean M. *American Virtues: Thomas Jefferson on the Character of a Free People*. Lawrence: University Press of Kansas, 1998.

Yuval-Davis, Nira. *Gender & Nation*. London: Sage, 1997.

Zaeske, Susan. "The 'Promiscuous Audience' Controversy and the Emergence of the Early Woman's Rights Movement." *Quarterly Journal of Speech* 81 (1995): 191–207.

Zelizer, Barbie. *Covering the Body: The Kennedy Assassination, the Media, and the Shaping of Collective Memory*. Chicago: University of Chicago Press, 1992.

———. *Remembering to Forget: Holocaust Memory through the Camera's Eye*. Chicago: University of Chicago Press, 1998.

Zinn, Maxine Baca, and Bonnie Thornton Dill. "Theorizing Difference from Multiracial Feminism." *Feminist Studies* 22 (1996): 321–31.

Index

SHAWN J. PARRY-GILES is a professor of communication and director of the Center for Political Communication and Civic Leadership at the University of Maryland and the coauthor of *The Prime-Time Presidency: The West Wing and U.S. Nationalism.*

The University of Illinois Press
is a founding member of the
Association of American University Presses.

Composed in 10.5/13 Marat Pro
with Trade Gothic LT display
by Lisa Connery
at the University of Illinois Press
Manufactured by Thomson-Shore, Inc.

University of Illinois Press
1325 South Oak Street
Champaign, IL 61820-6903
www.press.uillinois.edu